The Scenic Resources of the

Tennessee
Valley

The Scenic Resources of the

Tennessee Valley

A Descriptive and Pictorial Inventory

Prepared by the

TENNESSEE VALLEY AUTHORITY

Department of Regional Planning Studies

KNOXVILLE, TENNESSEE

THE material contained in this report
was obtained from surveys undertaken during
1934–37 by the Tennessee Valley Authority,
Department of Regional Planning Studies.*
Supplemental information was obtained
through the cooperation of the following
agencies:

TENNESSEE STATE PLANNING COMMISSION

KENTUCKY STATE PLANNING BOARD

VIRGINIA STATE PLANNING BOARD

NORTH CAROLINA STATE PLANNING BOARD

SOUTH CAROLINA STATE PLANNING BOARD

ALABAMA STATE PLANNING BOARD

UNITED STATES FOREST SERVICE

NATIONAL PARK SERVICE

WPA FEDERAL WRITERS' PROJECTS

AGRICULTURAL EXTENSION SERVICE

* Prepared under the direction of Earle S. Draper, Director, with the
following staff members participating: Tracy B. Augur, Herbert E.
Hudson, Malcolm H. Dill, Robert M. Howes, David A. Johnston, and
H. Jay Wallace.

*

Price $1.00 a copy
Tennessee Valley Authority
Knoxville, Tennessee

*

U. S. GOVERNMENT PRINTING OFFICE · WASHINGTON ·1938

16618

Foreword

SCENERY, like art, is a thing which cannot be classified, tagged, and set apart from all human and other physical contacts and relationships. Scenic resources are living, dynamic, highly subject to the influences of man and all the elements. For that reason, before beginning the actual inventory of those material features which combine to make up what we call scenery, it is wise to paint in broad strokes a general background picture of the Tennessee Valley, including the river system, the main variations in elevation of the earth's surface, the characteristics of the region's rocks and soils, the forms of vegetation that are found, the differing climatic conditions that obtain in various parts of the Valley, and finally, the types of people who have more or less modified the original scenery of the area.

THE TENNESSEE RIVER SYSTEM

From the steep mountain slopes of western North Carolina and Virginia flow the French Broad and Holston Rivers, uniting at Knoxville to form the Tennessee. From this confluence, the river follows a generally southwestward course through east Tennessee, accumulating waters from the Little Tennessee, Clinch, Hiwassee, and lesser tributaries. Just west of Chattanooga, it cuts its way through Walden Ridge, an isolated portion of the high Cumberland Plateau and, appropriating the valley of the Sequatchie River, resumes its southwestward course. At Guntersville, Ala., the Tennessee swings northwest across Alabama to the northeast corner of Mississippi, and into Tennessee. It then turns north and crosses Tennessee and Kentucky to join the Ohio River at Paducah. Together with its tributaries, the Tennessee River drains 40,600 square miles in parts of seven southeastern States.

CONTOURS

The Tennessee Valley has a range of elevation greater than that of any other major river system of the eastern United States. Forty peaks of the Blue Ridge Province, which forms the southeast rim of the Valley, attain elevations above 6,000 feet. Of these, Mount Mitchell's elevation of 6,684 feet is exceeded by none east of South Dakota's Black Hills. At Paducah, the river's mouth is but 300 feet above sea level. Between these extremes are the Cumberland Plateaus and Cumberland Mountains of northern Alabama, Tennessee, southeastern Kentucky, and western Virginia, separated from the Blue Ridge Province by the parallel folds of the ridge and valley country of east Tennessee; the rolling or level cotton land of north Alabama; the dissected Highland Rim, surrounding the Nashville Basin of central Tennessee. All these diverse types of landscape are related to the Tennessee River system in their contributions of surface water and eroded soil.

GEOLOGY

The crystalline and metamorphosed sedimentary rocks which make up the Blue Ridge Province are among the oldest on the North American continent, but limestone of a much later period characterizes the rest of the Valley. In some places, notably the Cumberlands, the limestone still retains thick overlayers of sandstone, shale, and coal. Deposits of iron, copper, phosphate, clays, and marble underlie other parts of the Valley.

VEGETATION

Early settlers found an almost unbroken forest blanket over the Tennessee Valley, ranging in composition from southern hardwoods in the lower elevations to northern conifers on the mountain peaks. Within this range grow nearly 200 species of trees. In addition, where undergrowth has not been subjected to periodic burning off, shrubs and wild flowers may be found in extraordinary variety. Dogwoods make unforgettable Aprils. Rhododendron, laurel, azaleas, and other members of the heath family form mass displays of color on the mountains and plateaus during the spring and early summer. Equally colorful autumn blazes with sumac, sourwood, sweet and sour gum, dogwood, oak, and maple. Luxuriant forests, together with the almost ever-present haze, soften mountain contours and cloak them with mystery. Only a few thousand acres of virgin forest remain today, in isolated coves and on remote mountain slopes. A broad public forestry program, however, seeks to restore vigorous forests on the estimated 13 million acres of the Valley which are considered too steep for cultivation or otherwise best suited to various forest uses.

CLIMATE

Extremes of altitude contribute to the Tennessee Valley a climatic range equal to that of the United States between the Great Lakes and the Gulf of Mexico. Contrary to the prevalent idea that summers in the South are uncomfortably warm, resorts in the highlands have maximum summer temperatures comparable to those of resorts in New England, Wisconsin, and Minnesota. Even in the Valley lowlands, summer nights average 10° to 20° below daytime readings; and in the highlands, thermometers drop from 15° to 25° below the day's maximum. Temperatures of long springs and autumns are delightfully moderate.

The Valley has a heavy annual rainfall—an average of 52 inches; but it may vary 20 inches from year to year and as much as 40 inches from place to place. Asheville and Highlands, N. C., for instance, are but 50 miles apart—yet the annual rainfall at Asheville is 40 inches; at Highlands, 82 inches. Heavy rainfall encourages lush growth of vegetation, and assures atmospheric freshness and relative freedom from dust during the summer months, when much of the United States experiences drought or meager rainfall.

THE PEOPLE

The physiography of the Tennessee Valley has naturally shaped the history of its inhabitants: prescribing the modes of Indian life, and directing, through its infrequent mountain gaps, the tides of white migration. Cherokee Indians lived in the valleys, hunting in adjacent mountains and finding refuge there in time of war. Archeological remains, now being explored, may prove to be among the richest in the United States. The lowlands formed the routes of white settlement, chiefly by English and Scotch-Irish. Before the Civil War, they supported along traveled routes, in the Nashville Basin, and at Muscle Shoals, an opulent agrarian civilization.

Following the overcrowding of lowland areas by an agricultural population—a movement began which continues today—families ventured over the mountain walls to discover rich, hidden valleys guarded by high gaps and long ridges. Later immigrants took up increasingly isolated homesteads. Cornfields became steeper, trees were felled, erosion set in, rich topsoil ran down to the rivers; isolation resulted in the preservation of an indigenous craft culture, with its own language, music, arts, and distinctive architecture. But also came poverty, illiteracy, suspicion of the outside world, and lack of normal social contacts. The resources of an agrarian people were gradually but inexorably dissipated.

INDUSTRY

Agriculture continues to form the principal land use in lowland areas of the Tennessee Valley and the chief source of income for three-fourths of its 2¼ million inhabitants. Cotton forms the principal cash crop in the west valley; tobacco, in the east. Increased industrialization in cities and small towns reveals a significant trend throughout the Valley. Too frequently industries have been attracted by a surplus of labor, a rural population accustomed to low incomes. Some, however, are founded squarely on the resource base: Mining and processing of coal, iron, zinc, copper, phosphate, bauxite, and limestone; quarrying of marble; lumbering of fine hardwoods, manufacturing of wood extracts and pulp from softer species; canning, refining, and packing of agricultural products. The visitor will see these plants, mines, and quarries in and near towns, and along the highways.

The sale of handcraft products offers another means of supplementing income derived from agriculture. Preserved by isolation and poverty, hand methods of furniture making, wood carving, dyeing, spinning, weaving, metal working, pottery making are still practiced in rural homes throughout the Tennessee Valley. These products have an artistic appeal not to be found in factory-made products and have become known to a widening group of people throughout the country. In competition with factory-made goods and sold under adverse marketing conditions, they offer only a small return; but freed from such competition and given an adequate market, they promise a definite means of raising income levels. A growing number of craft centers in towns and along highways now offer authentic native craft products for sale to tourists.

An additional resource of the Tennessee Valley has lately been recognized by inhabitants and visitors alike. Particularly in the southern highlands, centered about the eastern half of the Valley, the scenic endowment is coming to be regarded as the basis for a potentially great recreational industry. With this recognition necessarily goes acknowledgment that the resources, both natural and human, must not be destroyed by short-sighted exploitation. State and Federal authorities are administering large acreages of public park and forest land; other land must be added to the public domain. These reservations attract visitors in increasing numbers and for longer stays. Scattered towns become resort centers, dispensing to visitors services and local products. Gradually new income accrues to an area where poverty has been all too general. Recognition of the southern highlands as one of the Nation's great recreational regions is imminent.

THE SCENIC INVENTORY

The area covered by this inventory includes the 40,600 square miles drained by the Tennessee River, and adjacent land in the seven Valley States and South Carolina, totaling approximately 65,000 square miles, an area slightly larger than New England.

In order to facilitate study of the scenic resources of the region, it has proved desirable to divide the Valley into six sections, each one composing a chapter of this inventory. The text for each section is accompanied by a map on which areas are outlined and features located. Maps are provided with a system of coordinates, and the coordinate of each feature is given in the text. [For example: Montgomery Bell Park, G–5.] Description of tracts not yet established as recreational areas, and features within such areas are captioned in the text by a special heading summarizing pertinent data concerning location, size, type, and characteristics. These headings also serve to differentiate proposed and potential recreational areas from those now existing. Suggestions for appropriate design and use of each proposed and potential area are carried in these headings.

APPENDIX

The various types of recreational areas—intensive-use area, developed scenic area, wilderness area, etc.—are defined in the appendix, Nonurban Outdoor Recreation. This appendix is an analysis of the functions, forms, and types of recreational areas, and is intended to clarify designation of various types of areas according to their appropriate use.

Corrections

WHILE this volume has been in process of publication, changes have occurred in the name or status of the following areas:

1. BUFFALO SPRINGS FISH AND GAME PRESERVE (III, E–3), page 113, is now known as the BUFFALO SPRINGS GAME FARM, managed by the Tennessee Department of Conservation.

2. CARYVILLE LAKE (III, C–2), page 131, has been renamed COVE LAKE. It gives its name to an 850-acre State park now being developed cooperatively through the ECW program by the TVA, the Tennessee Department of Conservation, and the National Park Service. This development represents a modification of proposals for CARYVILLE LAKE AND GAME REFUGE, described on page 131.

3. GRUNDY LAKES (IV, D–4), page 160, have been renamed HEADDON LAKES GAME PRESERVE.

4. LEWIS STATE FOREST, Lewis County, Tennessee, has recently become a part of the public forest domain administered by the Forestry Division of the Tennessee Department of Conservation. It includes 1,257 acres of the MAURY STATE FOREST PURCHASE UNIT (V, E–2), page 190, proposed for purchase under the Fulmer Act.

5. CROSS CREEK STATE FOREST (IV, C–5), page 161, is now known as the MARION-FRANKLIN STATE FOREST, administered by the Forestry Division of the Tennessee Department of Conservation. It has been expanded to include 7,500 acres in Marion and Franklin Counties.

6. NATHAN BEDFORD FORREST MEMORIAL STATE PARK (VI, E–5), page 203, is now known as NATHAN BEDFORD FORREST MEMORIAL PARK and is more appropriately classified as a State monument. It is under the jurisdiction of a special park commission.

7. NORRIS LAKE FOREST (III, D–2), page 115, technically ceased to exist on July 1, 1937, when its management was transferred from the Forestry Division of TVA to the Department of Reservoir Property Management. It is now referred to as the NORRIS RESERVOIR AREA.

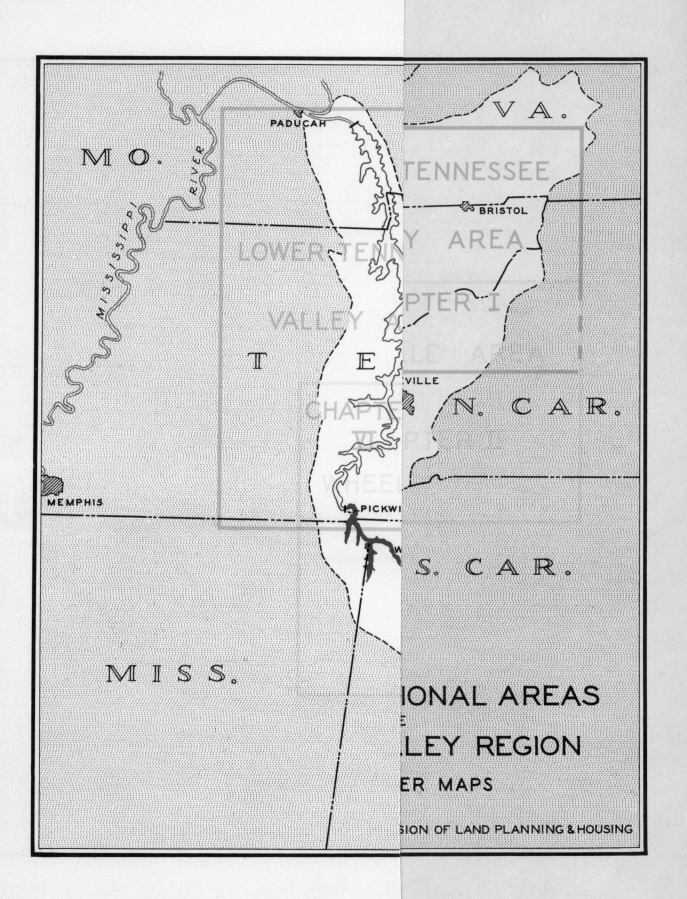

Contents

Introduction

As A PART of the act of Congress creating the Tennessee Valley Authority, the Authority was empowered to conduct studies and make plans for Federal and State activities looking to the proper use, conservation, and development of the natural resources of the Tennessee River drainage basin, and the adjacent territory. The region formed by the drainage basin of the Tennessee River has a natural endowment of great variety and richness, but among its many assets, none, perhaps, is more distinctive or potentially more valuable than the scenic quality of its mountains, streams, and forests. Scenery is as real and important a natural resource of the Tennessee Valley as are its soils, minerals, timber, or water power.

To secure a measure of the extent, quality, and value of this resource, the Tennessee Valley Authority, through its Department of Regional Planning Studies has compiled what is here termed a "Scenic Inventory"—a collection, from many sources, of descriptive material, maps, and photographs of the outstanding scenic features of the region. Much of this material was collected through field studies and research conducted during 1935 and 1936 by members of the Department's staff, with the helpful cooperation of other Departments of the Authority. The remainder has been compiled from materials generously contributed by numerous individuals, private organizations, and public agencies. The results of this collection, in somewhat condensed form, are herewith published for the benefit of those who are interested in the scenery and potential recreational opportunities of the Tennessee Valley region.

The inventory has furnished information of direct value to two phases of the Tennessee Valley Authority activity. It is the first step in the analysis of the scenic resources of the region and in the evolution of plans for their use and conservation in accordance with section 22 of the act. The scenic attractions of the area invite enjoyment by the 2¼ million people living there, by the approximately 80 million within 1 day's travel distance, and, in fact, by tourists and vacationists from all parts of the United States. The supplying of necessary services to those enjoying the recreational advantages of the region is potentially an industry of the first magnitude. From both the social and economic standpoints, the wise conservation, development, and use of the scenic attractions of the Tennessee Valley is a matter of vital concern to the region, and to the Nation of which it is a part.

The Authority has another substantial interest in and responsibility for the development of recreational resources in the Tennessee Valley. The river development program of the Authority is creating a series of inland lakes along the Tennessee River and its major tributaries. In a region devoid of natural lakes, these have distant recreational significance in addition to their primary purposes of navigation, power, and flood control. Along these lakes the Authority has acquired, and is continuing to acquire, large areas of land. Although purchased for reasons of reservoir construction and control, these lands, by virtue of their location and character, constitute an important public domain of great scenic and recreational interest. As trustee of this domain, the Tennessee Valley Authority is under obligation to put the lands within its jurisdiction to their best and most appropriate use. The scenic inventory has been of great assistance in determining the recreational use and development for which they may be suited.

As its name implies, the inventory is a compilation, a catalog of scenic features in and around the Tennessee Valley which should be fitted into the regional recreation pattern. Described here are such attractions as public park and forest areas, and individual features such as mountain peaks, fishing streams, waterfalls, caves, bluffs, gorges: areas and landmarks now used or potentially usable for recreation in its broadest aspect. It is hoped that all features of recreational significance have been included, but no claim is made that the information here presented is either complete or wholly exact in detail. Additions are being made continually, and further suggestions from the readers of this volume will be welcomed. To the many agencies and individuals who have contributed to its preparation, grateful acknowledgment is made for invaluable assistance in locating and describing points of interest, for the loan of valuable photographs and records, and for the constructive criticism and review which has helped to eliminate error and prevent omission.

The Upper Tennessee Valley Area

GENERAL DESCRIPTION OF THE AREA

THE Upper Tennessee Valley Area includes that portion of Tennessee north and east of Newport; southeastern Kentucky; southwestern Virginia; and North Carolina generally north and west of Blowing Rock. The Great Appalachian Valley cuts diagonally across the section from northeast to southwest, between the mountains of the Blue Ridge Province in the southeast and the Cumberland Mountains in the northwest.

Within this area the Great Valley is sufficiently broad to include the systems of four major rivers, the Powell, the Clinch, the Holston, and the French Broad-Nolichucky—all flowing in a generally southwest direction. Paralleling the courses of these rivers is a series of valley ridges, the most prominent of which is knifelike Clinch Mountain. Others of almost equal prominence include Bays Mountain, Walker Mountain, Powell Mountain, Stone Mountain, and Wallen Ridge. Numerous other lesser ridges and knobby areas interrupt the valley floor.

In the Great Valley is concentrated the bulk of the population of the section. Four cities, Bristol, Elizabethton, Kingsport, and Johnson City, have industrial importance; five, Greeneville and Morristown, in Tennessee, and Abingdon, Marion, and Saltville, in Virginia, are primarily agricultural and trading centers; three, in Virginia, Appalachia, Big Stone Gap, and Norton, are mining centers. Roan Mountain, Tenn., and several towns in North Carolina, in the Blue Ridge Province, have significance as vacation and resort centers.

The Blue Ridge Province is one of rugged mountains, for the most part forested. Along the edge of the Great Valley these mountains take the form of ridges parallel to its general topographic lines; such ridges include the Cherokee, Buffalo, Stone, Gap Creek Holston, Iron, and Doe Mountains. Mountains of the interior do not display pronounced directional lines but align themselves at varying angles. The Bald Mountains culminate in Flattop, with an elevation of 4,954 feet; Unaka Mountain, 5,258 feet in elevation, is the highest peak in a range of the same name; majestic Roan Mountain, 6,313 feet above sea level, caps the Iron Mountains; Whitetop, 5,520 feet in elevation, lies close to Mount Rogers, 5,719 feet, the highest mountain in Virginia; Grandfather, on the Blue Ridge in North Carolina, reaches an elevation of 5,964 feet. Much of the province is included within national forest boundaries. The management program of the United States Forest Service is working with steady progress toward restoration of healthy stream and cover conditions, with an accompanying increase in scenic values, fish and game. As a result of this program, the North Carolina portion of the province has become an outstanding recreational province for eastern United States.

The highest elevations of the Cumberland Mountains obtain within this section where they culminate in Big Black, 4,100 feet in elevation, and High Knob, elevation 4,188 feet. On the south the Cumberlands extend out into the Great Valley to join Wallen Ridge and Powell Mountain. On the north they merge into

1

the Appalachian plateaus of West Virginia and Kentucky. For many years their steep, escarpment-like walls and narrow valleys formed an almost insurmountable barrier to the settlement of the "Great Meadow" to the west. Pioneer civilization pushed past them and beyond by way of Cumberland Gap. The potential wealth of the coal fields which underlie the mountains could not, however, remain long untouched. Within the past half-century roads and railroads have gradually opened up the country for settlement by a large mining population. Recently, the Jefferson National Forest has taken over many thousands of acres in the area.

Recreational land problems in the Upper Tennessee Valley are not as serious as in other sections of the Valley. In some portions, mining operations have impaired scenic values, and in two localities forest exploitation has, perhaps, permanently removed the possibility of forest recreation. This section, along with others, lacks water bodies suitable for recreational use. It cannot look to the TVA program of reservoir construction to remedy this deficiency in the near future.

From a recreational point of view, two portions suffer most from present mining operations: Mitchell and Yancey Counties in North Carolina and Wise County in Virginia. The clay, mica, and feldspar mines of the former area have left large piles of waste and slag which somewhat mar the landscape; more serious, however, is the pollution of streams by clay and other fine mineral particles in suspension. One waterfall, on Crabtree Creek, west of Little Switzerland, has been spoiled by mining operations which dump great amounts of slag over its crest.

The coal mining operations of southwestern Virginia leave scars on the landscape, which, because of their location next to motor roads and other travelways, assume to the visitor in the area a significance much greater than their actual importance. Great piles of slate, clinkers, and obsolete machinery litter the roadside. Seepage of chemicals from these waste piles and mine entrances into nearby streams pollutes the water and kills large numbers of fish.

The presence of extensive manganese deposits in Unicoi and Carter Counties in Tennessee, although largely undeveloped at the present time, may in the future present an obstacle to recreational development if the increasing demands for this valuable mineral lead to exploitation of deposits in this area. Such exploitation would be conducted entirely by surface operations and have particular significance on the

recreational developments in the Unaka Division of the Cherokee National Forest.

Two areas, the Konnarock Basin in Washington County, Va., and the slopes of Unaka Mountain in Unicoi County, Tenn., evidence severe forest exploitation. In both cases burning followed the lumberman to destroy scenic effects. These areas, however, are exceptional for, although the greater portion of the section has been cut over and forest fires still present a serious problem, the forest cover as a whole has a thrifty appearance.

A paucity of water bodies suitable for recreation characterizes the Upper Tennessee Valley, which lacks the power reservoirs of western North Carolina and north Georgia. Although a program of dam construction by the TVA would help materially in this respect, the section will have to look to some other source for immediate provision because that portion of the TVA program is far in the future. For this reason, it has been impossible to study in detail the effect of the TVA program on the Holston and French Broad Rivers on the scenic and recreational endowment of the section. It would seem, however, that the majority of reservoirs constructed would have an adequate protection of forest stands already in existence and that malaria control should not present a serious problem.

The Upper Tennessee Valley affords several interesting comparisons with other sections treated in the Scenic Inventory. Compared with recreational development in the Asheville and Knoxville sections, little has taken place in the Upper Tennessee Valley. Although one-fourth of the area is included within the boundaries of national forests, development of the scenic features of these forests has been to a considerable extent neglected by the Forest Service and most of the features have been comparatively little known even in their own locality.

As a whole, the region does not have the spectacular scenic quality which characterizes both the Asheville and the Knoxville areas. No mountain masses can compare with the Black Mountains or the Smokies. For this reason, the recreational developments of the type found in western North Carolina have scarcely filtrated beyond the State line, and other portions have not received the attention which has been paid to areas further south.

On the other hand, the Upper Tennessee Valley possesses a great variety of individual features, many of which are outstanding examples of various types of scenic features. Superlative examples include Roan and the Grandfather Mountains, the Doe River

Gorge, Twisting Falls, Dutch Creek Falls, the Natural Tunnel of Virginia, Bishops Cave, and the Great Falls Bluffs of the Holston.

Although no major cities lie more than 25 miles from potential wilderness recreation in a national forest, none has an outing area available within that distance. The single State park, Hungry Mother, in Smyth County, Va., serves only a limited population because of its location with respect to main highways and population centers. For this reason, several areas such as Steele Creek, Worlie Cave, Ebbing Springs, and Fall Mills, though not spectacularly scenic, have been noted in this inventory as being adapted to development as outing areas.

A number of valley ridges have been selected as potential forest land, not only as a matter of scenic protection but because peculiar conditions, such as tendency to erode, infertile soil, and depleted forest growth, seem to render them a public responsibility. Their optimum destiny is inclusion in some form of public forest domain, which probably would be managed by State governments.

Lofty peaks guard this sun-bathed cove, the valley of Roane Creek, in Cherokee National Forest.

3

Paint Rock Bluffs, on the Tennessee-North Carolina State line, have long been a landmark to travelers through the French Broad Gorge.

EXISTING REGIONAL RECREATION AREAS

CHEROKEE NATIONAL FOREST
[F-3, D-4]

THE Cherokee National Forest runs in a northeast-southwest direction through Tennessee, with its easterly margin slightly overlapping the North Carolina border. The Great Smoky Mountains National Park separates the forest into two divisions, the Cherokee Division southwest of the park, and the Unaka Division northeast. Only the latter division falls within the area described in this chapter, the Cherokee being described in chapter III, the Knoxville area. It includes 744,427 acres in Cocke, Greene, Washington, Unicoi, Carter, Johnson, and Sullivan Counties. "Unaka" is the Cherokee Indian word for "white." The name was applied to the Unaka Mountains, apparently, because of the white haze which gathers about their summits. In addition to the Unaka Mountains, from which the division took its name, Unaka Forest includes the Holston, Iron, Stone, and Bald Mountains.

These mountains, for the most part, form ranges or ridges which parallel the major axis of the forest. Together with other lesser ranges and isolated peaks, they make up the bulk of the forest, for the western boundary of the forest follows closely the base of various ranges and includes little or no valley land. The area is drained by the Holston, Doe, Nolichucky, and Watauga Rivers and their tributary streams. The original forest stand of pines, oaks, hemlocks, and yellow poplar has been almost entirely cut; in some cases, notably the east slope of Unaka Mountain, cutting and subsequent burning has been so destructive as to impair permanently future forest growth.

The creation of the Unaka National Forest, now part of the Unaka Division, followed soon after the enactment of the Weeks Law in 1911. Since its establishment, the forest has seen comparatively little recreational development; that which exists today is largely the result of private enterprise. Several private resort developments are scattered through the forest, and recently the Forest Service has established camp grounds at several places.

Paint Rock Bluffs
[C-5]

Paint Rock Bluffs, downstream from the town of Hot Springs, N. C., on the French Broad River, stand on both sides of Paint Rock Creek where that stream flows into the river. The bluff on the east side of the creek is about 120 feet high and the one on the opposite side rises somewhat higher. In places the exposed rock faces, which are very rough and highly stratified, are a light buff or a yellow color, hence the name "Paint Rock." The attractive 6-mile drive to Paint Rock Bluffs from Hot Springs follows the river bank closely.

The drive along Paint Rock Creek valley is also attractive, but the stream's two waterfalls, located about 2 miles apart and both about 30 feet high, are somewhat spoiled because the road passes so close to them.

Beauty Spot
[E-4]

A section of Unaka Mountain between North Carolina and Tennessee, on the boundaries of Unicoi and Mitchell Counties, has locally been given the name of Beauty Spot. Either naturally bald or cleared in the past, and 4,500 feet in elevation, it extends for a mile along the State line. The place is unspoiled and thoroughly charming, an intimate spot which affords breathless views in all directions. The entire area is carpeted with a thick turf; great quantities of spring flowers, such as violets, bluets, wild strawberry, and may-apple give color in the springtime. Superb specimens of hawthorn, dogwood, and other shrubs are grouped in almost park-like composition. Large maples and beeches of luxuriant growth contrast with the picturesque boles of dead chestnuts. These trees frame many vistas of the Black Mountains to the south, Roan Mountain to the east, Stone and Buffalo Mountains to the north, and the Bald Mountains to the west.

Beauty Spot—an apt name for this natural garden of hawthorns.

Beauty Spot may be reached by Forest Service truck trail from United States Highways 23 and 19 W. One mile north of Erwin, a loop road from the highway leads up Rock Creek, 6 miles to Indian Grave Gap on the State line. From the gap the road leads a mile and a half along the State line and around a shoulder of Unaka Mountain. It then descends for a distance of 14 miles down the east slope of the mountain to Limestone Cove, whence a road leads 5 miles back to United States Highways 23 and 19 W at the village of Unicoi.

The road on the east slope of Unaka Mountain has little scenic interest. Although it offers extensive distant views, the foreground is marred as the result of forest exploitation in its most extreme form. The entire slope of the mountain was clear cut and sub-sequently burned over, with consequent severe erosion, until at the present time no vestige of the original soil remains. For as far as the eye can see, the slope is strewn with a weathered jumble of rock fragments, above which a few charred stumps may still be seen. Great roots still hold the stumps in their original position and the space between the stumps and the rocks which they straddle indicates the depth of soil which has been removed from the mountain. In a few places the fire cherry, blackberry, and birch indicate the first stages of nature's reclamation of this area. The contrast between this area and the verdant loveliness of Beauty Spot is an object lesson in wise and unwise land use, a lesson which carries an explicit moral in conservation methods to anyone who may happen to visit the two places.

Fisher, Asheville

Bluff Mountain appears on the horizon above the French Broad River Valley and intervening ridges in this view from Rich Mountain.

Rich Mountain
[C-5]

The Forest Service fire tower on the summit of Rich Mountain, elevation 3,643 feet, affords commanding views in all directions, with a prospect extending across the mountains to the north and south and across the Great Valley of East Tennessee to the west. This tower may be reached by surfaced roads from United States Highways 25 and 70 and from Tennessee Highway 70. The easiest approach is from a point 4 miles east of Hot Springs on United States Highways 25 and 70. From this point it is 3 miles to the summit.

Roan Mountain
[E-4]

Roan Mountain, on the State line between North Carolina and Tennessee, ranks among eastern America's outstanding mountain heights. One of the earliest mountain peaks to receive recreational exploitation,

it has become well known to thousands of tourists from all sections of the country who come to the mountain during the rhododendron season.

Roan is a massive mountain, with two distinct peaks, Roan High Bluff, 6,287 feet, and Roan High Knob, 6,313 feet. A long spur connects it to the Iron Mountains at the north, and only Carvers Gap 5,500 feet, separates it from Grassy Ridge Bald, 6,300 feet, part of another ridge extending northeast along the State line. The north slopes of the mountain are heavily timbered with second growth trees varying, according to elevation, from cove hardwoods to spruce. On the south, while the slopes are predominantly wooded, a surprising degree of cultivation prevails at even the higher altitudes. The summit is somewhat wooded, but great patches of moss and grassland intersperse masses of rhododendron. On Roan High Bluff is the rhododendron garden, an outstanding display of the shrub in its natural setting.

Roan Mountain is noted for its rhododendron gardens more than 6,000 feet above sea level.

7

The mountain embraces dramatic and spectacular views. On High Knob a fire tower maintained by the Tennessee Forest Service commands 360-degree panoramic views across the Great Valley to the north and over succeeding lines of mountains toward other points of the compass. From the rhododendron garden views become more restricted but are ever varied in composition as one moves from one vantage point to another. While Grassy Ridge Bald is the dominating feature of all vistas to the east, the higher peaks of Grandfather may be seen above it. Flattop and Unaka Mountains dominate the views toward the west.

The mountain is accessible by a 14-mile motor toll road from the village of Roan Mountain, Tenn., and a second toll road from Bakersville, N. C. The former village is on United States Highway 19 E and the latter on North Carolina Highway 26, accessible from Spruce Pine, also on United States Highway 19 E. The toll roads are tortuously winding and steeply graded. Their solid rock bases assure permanence in spite of lack of maintenance so that it is possible, though difficult, to ascend the mountain by car. In former days these roads gave access to a hotel at the top of the mountain. This hotel, Cloudland, built in the 1880's and torn down 20 years later, was a fashionable resort during the period.

Laurel Falls
[E-3]

Laurel Falls, with the rugged gorge in which it lies, constitutes one of the most spectacular scenic features of the Cherokee National Forest. Far removed from highways, and separated from minor roads by steep ridges, the falls lies in a very wild portion of the forest. Because of its inaccessibility, it is known to only a few people. The falls is reached by hiking 2 miles up the Laurel Fork of the Doe River from Hampton, Tenn., on United States Highway 19 E. The trail follows the bed of a lumber railroad and fishermen's paths along the stream, crossing and recrossing the streambed at several points; near the falls, the gorge is so narrow that approach is nearly impossible, unless one follows the old railroad cut on the side of the gorge, 100 to 200 feet above the stream.

The course of the stream is tortuous and winding where the rock has been worn by the stream which has followed varying strata at many different angles. The gorge increases in interest as the trail nears the falls. Hardwood and pine are succeeded by hemlock and a dense growth of the Carolina rhododendron which in May colors the walls of the gorge with a brilliant pink, a color which is repeated in the blooms of the moss locust.

The first glimpse of the falls comes suddenly around a shoulder of the gorge far below. Before reaching this point, however, a minor trail leads down to the very base of the 50-foot-high falls which leaps over a series of five descending shelves, each approximately 10 feet high. The tumbling course of the falls beats the water into a foamy whiteness of unusual intensity. In contrast to this animation, a solid mass of rock looms 300 feet above and directly behind the falls.

Some distance above, is a smaller cascade of quite unusual character. Here the stream is interrupted by a diagonal ledge, over which the water plunges, resulting in a falls whose crest is some 60 feet wide across a 20-foot stream. Although only 10 to 15 feet high, the resulting waterfall has an unusual distinction lent by this peculiar formation.

Much of the charm and distinction of the place may be credited to its wildness, a quality which would be destroyed even by trails for easy access. A Forest Service truck trail, although completely isolated from the gorge by the intervening ridge of Black Mountain, gives access to the surrounding forest for fire-prevention so that trails are unnecessary for this

Shrubs of Carolina rhododendron obtain meager footholds on the steep walls of Laurel Creek Gorge.

8

purpose. Although the area has been lumbered and traces of the logging railroad still exist, nature is rapidly healing these scars, and will soon restore the area to its original condition. The hike to the falls is one which should be taken only by experienced trampers, clad in rough clothes; the trail is treacherous because of the great quantities of loose rock which are still falling from the side walls of the gorge. The ridges of Pond Mountain and Black Mountain form the natural boundaries of this wild area.

Buried in the wilds of the Cherokee National Forest, Laurel Falls, a 50-foot cascade, is reached only after a difficult and exciting hike.

Doe River Gorge
[E-3]

Not far removed from the gorge of Laurel Fork is the Doe River Gorge. Lying 2 miles south of the village of Hampton, and more spectacularly scenic than Laurel Fork Gorge it has less primitive character because of its traversal by the track of the Western North Carolina & East Tennessee Railroad, a narrow-gage line extending from Johnson City, Tenn., to Boone, N. C. Doe River Gorge is so narrow as to be inaccessible, except by this railroad. The walls rise steeply from the edge of the river, a stream considerably larger than that of Laurel Falls Creek, to a height 1,000 feet or more above the stream bed. During rainy seasons many tiny streams cascade down the walls of the gorge, but these become dry during most of the year. Although the gorge is owned by the United States Forest Service, little recreational development is suggested within it. A trip through the gorge on the railroad between Hampton and Roan Mountain, Tenn., is a locally popular tourist diversion.

Wilbur Lake
[E-3]

Wilbur Lake, storage reservoir of the East Tennessee Light & Power Co., lies in the narrow gorge of the Watauga River, 7 miles east of Elizabethton, Tenn. The lake is approximately a mile and a half long, 200 to 300 yards wide, with a shoreline between 3 and 4 miles in length. The north and east shorelines are composed of a precipitous bluff, whose rock strata are upturned to a nearly vertical position. The bluff is sparsely wooded with a second growth of pitch pine and mixed hardwood. The south and west shores, with the exception of a peninsula of 20 acres, are equally precipitous but the bluffs are not as high. Cardens Bluff is the most prominent portion of this western shore. The peninsula has been cleared and

Cultivation penetrates the smallest valley bottoms in the Doe River Gorge.

10

supports several isolated small farms, which serve as homes of the dam's operators.

Active recreational use of the lake is confined to some swimming and fishing, for which permission must be obtained from the company. Such use is limited and is not encouraged. Shortly after the dam was built, a severe cloudburst on the watershed of the Watauga brought large amounts of debris and silt into the reservoir. Its storage capacity is seriously impaired and a slight draw-down exposes large areas of mud flats. Wilbur Lake, for this reason, ranks low among other power reservoirs as a scenic feature.

Over this barrel-like ledge Elk Creek plunges 60 feet in the last of three successive drops which form Twisting Falls.

Twisting Falls
[F-3]

The Twisting Falls, also known as the Big Falls of the Elk or as Greasy Falls, are located in a narrow, constricted portion of the Elk Creek Gorge, 6 miles airline south of Butler, Johnson County, Tenn. The falls themselves lie in Carter County.

Elk Creek at this point drops a vertical distance of 200 feet in three successive major falls, separated by short series of rapids. The name "Twisting" is peculiarly apt, for the river course shifts abruptly from one direction to another. The upper falls, ap-proximately 30 feet high, is a V-shaped cleft which the river approaches from one side. Sufficient water, however, flows around the apex of the V and over the opposite side so that a continuous crest is formed around the entire distance inside of the V. The waters within this cleft flow out and down a series of rapids to the center falls, which is approximately 25 feet high. Below the center falls, the river flows back under an overhanging cliff then suddenly reverses its course and plunges over a great barrellike ledge with a height of 60 feet and a crest of 80 feet, which is divided at times of low water into two separate falls.

11

Backbone Rock, a narrow spur of Butt Mountain, is 75 feet high, 20 feet thick. The tunnel was pierced for a logging railroad.

Below this lower falls the river flows on and out into a more open portion of the gorge.

At the falls, the sides of the gorge rise sheer to a point 100 feet or more above the stream. These cliffs are broken by intervening gullies and crevices forming great isolated chimneys between them. Such rock formations allow spirited rock climbing, but conspire to prevent close access to the falls. However, they lend an interest to the vicinity of the falls which would otherwise be lacking in an area so thoroughly cut over. No large trees remain among the scrubby second-growth timber studded with such weed shrubs and vines as the blackberry, the devil's walkingstick, and smilax. A few rhododendron shrubs remain close to the water's edge in the immediate vicinity of the falls.

The best approach to Twisting Falls, from Butler by way of a county road to Elk Mills, crosses and recrosses the Elk River at frequent intervals, and gains interest thereby. The falls may first be seen from this road at a point 10½ miles south of the bridge at Butler. The county road then continues for 1 mile up the gorge to a point from which the Forest Service has recently built a truck trail on up Elk Creek. The nearest access to the falls leads from a point one-half mile beyond the start of the truck trail, from which it is necessary to plunge almost headlong through briars and brambles down the steep wall of the gorge.

Backbone Rock
[G-2]

A narrow spur of Butt Mountain, known as Backbone Rock, in the northeast corner of Johnson County, Tenn., is a vertically faced ridge some 75 feet high and but 20 feet thick. A small tunnel has been pierced through the rock to allow passage of a logging railroad whose bed now serves as a Forest Service truck trail. The unusual formation has attracted considerable local interest which is recognized by a camp and picnic grounds developed below the rock. From this center, trails lead to the top of the rock, to a pool in the nearby Beaver Dam Creek, and to a small waterfall in the vicinity.

JEFFERSON NATIONAL FOREST
[D-1, G-1, G-2]

The Jefferson National Forest, newest national forest within the Tennessee Valley Basin, lies for the most part in southwestern Virginia on the folded ridges of the Great Appalachian Valley. The forest was created by executive order on April 21, 1936, and includes territory formerly included in the Mountain Lake Purchase Unit, the Clinch Purchase Unit, and portions of the George Washington and the old Unaka National Forests. It consists of two divisions: the Unaka, including portions of Washington, Smyth, and Grayson Counties; and the Mountain Lake, lying inside and along the western border of the State. Approximately 1,000,000 acres, or slightly more than half the gross acreage of the Jefferson National Forest, lie within the Tennessee Valley.

The Unaka Division, bounded by the Iron Mountains on the southeast and Holston Mountain on the northwest, includes the upper watersheds of the Holston South Fork and the New River. A peak of the Iron Mountains, Mount Rogers, attains an elevation of 5,719 feet, the highest in Virginia; Whitetop Mountain in the same ridge a few miles east, has an elevation only slightly lower. Between the two mountain ridges is the Konnarock Basin, a rolling, irregular valley, drained by Big Laurel Creek.

The early explorers found forest resources in great abundance and exceptional variety. The hardwood forest of the Southern Appalachians merged with the northern types and resulted in a forest of oaks in many varieties, poplar, pine, hemlock, and spruce. Although many of the same species persist, the stands are depleted and the natural associations are disturbed. The Konnarock Basin in particular has suffered severly from misuse of its forest lands and misdirected agricultural efforts. At the present time, several square miles present a picture only slightly less desolate than that presented by the Ducktown Basin in southeast Tennessee. The original stand, a superb example of the climax forest, was clear cut and the area subsequently burned and heavily pastured. The present appearance of the valley is a combination of badly eroded pasture land, dotted with scarred stumps, a few acres of stunted second growth, and very poor agricultural land. Many years will pass before this basin attains any recreational significance, although recreation may provide an additional inducement for the needed restoration of a new forest cover.

Within the Upper Tennessee Valley area, the Mountain Lake Division includes portions of Tazewell, Russell, Smyth, Washington, Wise, Scott, and Lee Counties. Lying within the watershed of the Clinch, Powell, Holston, James, and New Rivers, its topography consists for the most part of parallel ridges and streams following the long axis of the area. The west portion, north of the Clinch River, is

13

a more mountainous territory, one in which the ridges of the great valley merge with the Appalachian Plateaus. Elevations within the division range from 1,800 to 4,550 feet, and the slopes are generally steep with frequent outcroppings of sandstone.

The severe folding to which the area has been subjected creates a complex geology for the division. The sedimentary rock which forms the underlying structure has faulted and broken in many places until the edges of many strata, varying from limestone, sandstone, and conglomerate to coal measures, are exposed. A variety of soils results from the breakdown of these various rocks. On the slopes and summits of the ridges, particularly Clinch Mountain, the soil derives from shale and sandstone, and its poor quality supports largely submarginal farms and a slow growth of timber. Limited areas along the base of Clinch Mountain and in the valley of the Clinch River, underlain with deposits of decomposed limestone and overlain with a derivative soil, when cleared support rich bluegrass pastures which are the basis for a prosperous agriculture based on fattening of beef cattle. The sandstone and conglomerate layers which are associated with the coal fields north of the Clinch River once supported vast forests of mountain hardwoods mixed with hemlock and pine. The railroads and highways which opened the coal fields have given access to many areas that would have been otherwise impenetrable and have contributed to clearing all but the most inaccessible stands. Remaining forest lands of second growth are now held, not so much for their timber as for the valuable deposits of underlying coal.

The unstable economic conditions of this coal section has led to the clearing of too-steep land for small

From Stickleys Gap, on United States Highway 58, Clinch Mountain, 150 miles long, levels the horizon.

farms. Once cleared this land is easily eroded and contributes its burden of silt to the Tennessee River. There are 64,000 acres in these marginal farms, according to the forest supervisor. Although some mechanical methods of erosion control will be necessary, restoration of a healthy forest stand might well be the principal method of erosion control.

In general, the Mountain Lake Division, within the Upper Tennessee Valley, will not have the recreational appeal to be found in other forests of the Tennessee Valley. It should, however, provide valuable recreational opportunities for a considerable mining population and for such cities as Bristol, Kingsport, and numerous smaller places to which it is readily accessible. For much of the mining population, however, the forest provides hunting and fishing on a subsistence rather than a recreational basis. Until the need for subsistence hunting and fishing is removed there can be little hope of developing it for sport.

Whitetop Mountain
[G–2]

Whitetop, a majestic peak of gently rolling contour, lies on the Smyth-Grayson County line in southwest Virginia, and adjoins the southern boundary of the Unaka Division of the Jefferson National Forest. It reaches an elevation of 5,520 feet, 200 feet lower than the nearby Mount Rogers. Its crest is heavy with a virgin stand of black spruce, its saddle a natural bald of 2,300 acres. The slopes are heavily wooded with beech, birch, maple, and other northern hardwoods.

Although the dense spruce on the summit cuts off any distant surveys, the bald portion of the mountain commands views in all directions. To the south and west the view extends across the agricultural lands in Horse Creek Valley, to the wooded slopes of Pond Mountain. At the north, views over the Konnarock Basin are cut off by Iron Mountain. Toward the east the rocky peak of Mount Rogers rises above Elk Garden Ridge. The bald portion of the mountain is covered with a rich tufted turf, with a scattered pattern of gnarled and twisted oaks in natural groupings. These tree groups frame varying glimpses of the valleys below.

The wooded north and east slopes of the mountain are available for hiking and nature studies. The bald portion of the mountain is operated as a commercial recreational feature and a competitive folk festival is held on the mountain annually during August. A toll road leads across the property, and an admission charge must be paid if one is to obtain views from the mountain. The shortest approach to Whitetop from main highways may be made from Damascus, Va., through the Konnarock Basin. This road, 21 miles in length, is varied as to quality and scenic interest. The first 2½ miles lead through a narrow gorge paralleled on the opposite side of the stream by a railroad. The road is extremely narrow, but offers intimate vistas of the stream unimpaired by the nearby presence of the railroad. Two attractive but small cascades lie close to the road. The middle section of the road traverses the unattractive Konnarock Basin. The road up the mountain slope from the village of Konnarock is a rock-base gravel-surfaced road of two lanes. Its grade and alignment are excellent and afford many vantage points from which one may obtain views over the surrounding countryside.

Gnarled veterans stand guard on windswept Whitetop Mountain, in Jefferson National Forest.

Majestic Whitetop Mountain, 5,520 feet high, dominates burned and cut-over acres of the Konnarock Basin.

Mount Rogers
[G–2]

Mount Rogers, the highest mountain in Virginia, attains an elevation of 5,719 feet. It rises sharply above Elk Garden Ridge, 5 miles east of Whitetop Mountain on the Smyth and Grayson County lines. A rocky prominence, bare of vegetation, the mountain has the appearance of a northern peak which reaches above the timber line. Black spruce and its associated species grow on the mountain at the general elevation of Elk Garden Ridge. Above this point, lichens, mosses, and ericaceous shrubs form a partial cover. From the top of the mountain, one may obtain a panoramic view in all directions. The easiest access to Mount Rogers is by means of a 4-mile hike along Elk Garden Ridge from the gap of the same name, 1 mile east of Whitetop.

Brumley Mountain
[F-1]

Brumley Mountain, immediately east of Little Moccasin Gap, on the Russell-Washington County line, is the widest portion of Clinch Mountain. Its south slope rises steeply 2,000 feet above its immediate base; the crest of the slope is capped by a broken escarpment of varying height. The top of the mountain forms a broad plateau, some 5,000 acres in extent, sloping gently toward the north. Brumley Creek, a small cascading stream, with numerous small waterfalls, drains that portion of the mountain containing the narrow Brumley Creek valley. Here the side walls rise steeply to the general level of the plateau, and offer several opportunities for developing small recreational lakes.

The top of Brumley Mountain was logged only recently and is now covered, for the most part, with small second growth of mixed pine and hardwoods. The highest point on the mountain, 4,223 feet in elevation, has been cleared for several years and is known locally as the Clover Fields. This point embraces panoramic views in all directions over ridges and valleys of the Holston and Clinch River basins.

Brumley Mountain offers a large, comparatively level area with the climatic advantage inherent in

Herrick Brown, Greeneville

Mount Rogers, highest mountain of Virginia.

points at this altitude. It is conveniently located with respect to population centers in southwest Virginia; its nearness to population suggests recreational use for summer camps and cottages. The top of the mountain at present is difficult of approach, but an old logging railroad grade might be utilized for an access road. This grade approaches the top of the mountain through the valley of Brumley Creek.

High Knob
[D-1]

High Knob, a natural bald 4,188 feet in elevation, 5 miles south of Norton, Wise County, commands extensive views in all directions. To the north, the outlook extends across the valley of the North Fork of the Powell River into West Virginia; at the west, on the Kentucky line, lies Black Mountain, 4,100 feet high; toward the south and southwest the view over valleys and ridges extends to Clinch Mountain.

Several leads, some bald and others wooded with cedar and hardwood, reach out from the bald summit. Preliminary recreational plans of the Forest Service call for the intensive-use development of the cove between two of these leads. These plans include an 8-acre lake which may be used for swimming and fishing, a forest camp for under-privileged people, trails, and game management.

Virginia Highway 73 from Norton passes over a shoulder of High Knob, making the mountain accessible to the motorist.

APPALACHIAN TRAIL
[B-5, G-2]

The Appalachian Trail, a wilderness footpath leading along the crest of the Appalachian Mountains from Mount Katahdin in Maine to Mount Oglethorpe in Georgia, passes through the Upper Tennessee Valley. The trail is sponsored by the Appalachian Trail Conference, an association made up of various local hiking groups along its route. Individual members maintain this trail for the most part, although the work has been taken over within several public reservations by the CCC.

The trail enters the area from the northeast on Iron Mountain in Smyth County, Va. It passes along the ridge of Iron Mountain to Damascus, where it crosses to Holston Mountain and follows its crest to a point 8 miles northeast of Elizabethton, Tenn. This stretch of the trail offers magnificent views over the valley floor which extend, on clear days, as far as Knoxville. Dropping off the ridge of Holston, the trail crosses

Stony Creek, the Watauga River, and the Doe River at comparatively low elevations. It leaves the Doe River at Hampton, Tenn., passes up the valley of Simerly Creek to Limestone Cove and then up the east slope of Unaka Mountain to the North Carolina-Tennessee State line. From Stony Creek to Unaka Mountain the trail follows secondary roads or main highways through an area which is generally lacking in interest. The trail avoids such outstanding features as Roan Mountain, the Doe River Gorge, and Laurel Falls, any or all of which might be included in a route which would avoid the north slope of Unaka Mountain.

From Unaka Mountain the trail follows the State line along the Unaka and Bald Mountains between Unicoi County, Tenn., and Madison County, N. C., following the State line as far as Rich Mountain, where it descends to cross the French Broad River at Hot Springs, N. C. After crossing the river, it ascends immediately to Bluff Mountain on the State line, which it follows in a southerly direction past Max Patch Mountain toward the Smokies. The route of the trail southwest of Unaka Mountain lies at a high elevation, ranging up to 5,500 feet, thus opening up a territory of interest chiefly to the hiker.

Thompsons, Knoxville

Highest peak of the Bald Mountains, Cold Springs Mountain, a grassy bald of 4,889-foot elevation, carries the Appalachian Trail along a portion of the Tennessee-North Carolina line.

HUNGRY MOTHER STATE PARK
[G-1]

Hungry Mother State Park is one of six recently acquired by the Commonwealth of Virginia and developed by the Emergency Conservation Work program. Located 3 miles north of Marion in Smyth County on partially paved Virginia Highway 88, it is designed to serve as an outing park for southwestern Virginia.

The park embraces 3,000 acres of ridge and knob land in the watersheds of Walker and Hungry Mother Creeks. A large earth-fill dam has been constructed by CCC labor on Hungry Mother Creek to create a lake of some 150 acres. It is hoped eventually to increase the size of the park to 10,000 acres in order to control the entire watershed of Hungry Mother Creek above the dam. A point on Walker Mountain, 3,735 feet in elevation, is the highest point in the park. This and Marleys Top, 3,290 feet high, offer excellent vantage points from which to view the adjacent countryside. Most of the land within the park is wooded with a mixed second growth, although there is some cleared land along the lake shore.

A park drive skirts part of the shore to give access to a bathing beach, playfields, camping area, and picnic grounds. Beyond these, on a wooded hillside, a group of vacation cabins surrounds a guest lodge with three bedrooms, central hall, and dining room. From the lake, paths and trails lead through woodland to Marleys Top and Walker Mountain. That portion of the park on the side of Walker Mountain is designated as a game sanctuary.

Marleys Top in Hungry Mother State Park invites the hiker to its 3,290-foot summit.

NATURAL TUNNEL OF VIRGINIA
[C-2]

The Natural Tunnel, located in Scott County, in southwestern Virginia, is a feature of unique interest. The earliest explorers discovered it and brought back to the settlements reports of its wonder. Through the years its fame grew apace, enlivening the tales of travelers and attracting many sightseers to the spot. The number of visitors remained comparatively small, however, until development of the coal fields in the eighties and nineties brought railroads and highways.

This tunnel-like cave lies in the midst of country not remarkably scenic. An early statement has it that, "The variety of the forest-growths constitute the most striking peculiarity of this southwestern portion of Virginia"[1]—but now the timber has vanished. Carved from a small ridge of limestone rock, the tunnel has a length of some 500 to 600 feet, a width of 100 to 150 feet and varies from 30 to 80 feet in height. It follows in an S-shaped curve the course of Stock Creek, whose flow created it. The western portal opens from the foot of a sheer cliff some 300 feet high; the eastern opening penetrates the base of a huge amphitheater, 900 feet in diameter and 500 feet deep. The walls of the amphitheater are vertical and in some places overhanging. About one-third of the circumference is missing, the two terminals being abrupt and partially free-standing. A trail leading around the rim of the amphitheater, close to the edge, affords the visitor opportunity to view the precipice and the tunnel entrance from every angle and to be awed by the immensity of the spectacle.

Although in its natural state the Natural Tunnel would unquestionably have deserved preservation as a national monument, exploitation has relegated this possibility to a high improbability. It is held by a commercial development company at a high valuation. Poor highways in the vicinity have discouraged many tourists from visiting the spot, so development has been comparatively slight, but many of the details have added irreparable damage to the tunnel. Advertising matter and frail guard rails along the paths distract visitors and promote a feeling of insecurity. The abuses of commercial development, however, are mere details compared to the despoilment due to the railroad line which passes through the tunnel, completely destroying the naturalness of the place. The road was put through in 1882 when

---

[1] *Picturesque America*, a compilation by numerous artists and writers, edited by William Cullen Bryant, New York, D. Appleton & Co., 1872.

The figures in the foreground suggest the immensity of the Natural Tunnel of Virginia.   Sheer 500-foot walls form a vast amphitheater
at its southern entrance.

a smaller tunnel was artificially pierced in the outer wall of the amphitheater, the course of Stock Creek straightened, and extensive cuts and fills made in the gorge below. Since that time smoke from thousands of locomotives has blackened the walls.

A nearby cave, only partially explored, is said to be rivalled by none in its beauty. Its entrance is now blasted in pending the time when funds become available for its commercial exploitation and operation as one of the features of the Natural Tunnel.

Kelly & Green, Bristol

This Gargantuan amphitheater forms the eastern entrance to the Natural Tunnel of Virginia.

PRESSMEN'S HOME LAKE
[B–3]

A recreational lake of 22 acres has been created on a tract of land 50 acres in extent, adjoining the National Pressmen's Home, near Rogersville, Tenn. The land was donated to the state Department of Conservation, and the construction of the dam was begun in the summer of 1935 as one of the first WPA projects in Tennessee. The dam is of native stone masonry, is 400 feet long and 30 feet high. In addition to its primary use as a fish-rearing pool, the lake will be available for water sports. Although not included in the present project, a clubhouse with lockers for bathers, a bathing beach, boathouse, and picnic facilities are intended in the near future to be developed on the shore of the lake.

Pressmen's Home is reached by turning north from United States Highway 11 W, 2 miles east of Rogersville onto Tennessee Highway 70. Six miles north of this point Tennessee Highway 94 turns west from 70 and leads, after 4 miles, to Pressmen's Home.

LAKE DAVY CROCKETT
[C-4]

The Greeneville Dam of the East Tennessee Light & Power Co. on the Nolichucky River creates a reservoir some 765 acres in extent. The dam is approximately 7 miles south of Greeneville, immediately above the new bridge of relocated Tennessee Highway 70. This new highway improves a link in a potential north-south tourist route between Middlesboro and Asheville by way of Morristown and Greeneville.

The lake extends for a distance of 5 miles north and east of the dam, but it so closely follows the meanderings of the original river course that the channel distance is increased to 7 miles. The lake lies in the midst of farmland of a generally open character. However, considerable tree growth remains close to the shore and in an occasional woodlot nearby. Un-fortunately, such growth was not cleared from large portions of the basin before it was flooded. Thus, scenic values and recreational use are considerably impaired by dead trees which remain and rise above even highwater. However, approximately 300 acres of the lake just behind the dam are not thus impaired.

The power company neither invites nor discourages recreational use which is at present confined to local patronage, chiefly in the form of fishing. The lake is naturally suitable for all water sports and surrounding land would be usable for cabin sites, field sports, and other outing purposes. For this reason a State park on the north shore immediately above the dam is listed among the potential areas in this chapter. This area and other portions of the shore line are suitable for private development at the present time, subject to permission by the power company.

Six miles south of Greeneville on the Nolichucky River lies Lake Davy Crockett, a power reservoir at present without recreational development.

21

LAKEVIEW
[A-4]

Lakeview, an artificial 10-acre lake, lies 1 mile southwest of Morristown, Tenn. Built in 1921 as a commercial recreational lake with provisions for bathing and fishing, the lake is now leased to a Knoxville fishing club, available only to members. Attempts to maintain bathing facilities have been abandoned. Bathhouses once used by several hundred persons annually have fallen into unsightly decay and should be removed.

Open fields of rolling topography surround the lake, and a small grove borders a part of the shoreline. Few coves break the regularity of the nearly circular shoreline but, in these, reeds and other water plants grow in considerable proportion.

GARRETT CREEK FALLS
[F-1]

Garrett Creek Falls, near Little Moccasin Gap, northwest of Abingdon, Va., is a scenic spot already recognized as a recreational area. The falls, having a natural height of some 40 feet increased to 50 feet by an old stone dam, lie in a narrow, wooded valley beside United States Highway 19. A retaining wall has been built by highway authorities to allow parking beside the road. Steps lead from the road down to a small grass-covered shelf above the falls which is suitable for picnicking. Trails lead from the shelf to closer vantage points immediately above the falls. Additional scenic protection would be afforded the vicinity should scenic easements be acquired on the wooded hillsides either side of the highway.

Lakeview nestles in a pastoral setting 1 mile from Morristown.

POTENTIAL REGIONAL RECREATION AREAS

BEATTY CREEK NATURAL BRIDGE
[B-2]

Location: Lee County, Va., 2 miles southwest of Jonesville.
Communities served: Jonesville, 2 miles; Pennington Gap, 11 miles.
Size: 100 acres.
Type: Developed scenic area.
Characteristics: A natural bridge of limestone across Beatty Creek; small wooden ravine in midst of farm country; open forest growth of mixed hardwood and cedar.

THE natural bridge across Beatty Creek in Lee County, Va., is a natural feature of considerable interest, although small in scale. There can be no comparison between it and the more famous Natural Bridge of Virginia but it has the advantage of not being commercialized. Although a county road passes over the bridge and farm land comes to the edge of the ravine which it spans, the immediate vicinity still retains a semblance of its natural condition.

Nothing in the immediate vicinity of the bridge would indicate to the driver along the road that he was crossing a natural bridge. The bridge is just wide enough to accommodate a 20-foot roadway, and protective railings effectively disguise the fact that the bridge is not man-made. It has a span of some 30 feet and the top of the arch is some 15 feet above the stream, 10 feet below the surface of the road. The course of the stream through the bridge is somewhat curved. Water entering from the north crosses the road, turns to the east for an equal distance, and flows out again along a southerly course. Near the middle of the curve a "window", equal in size to the two portals of the bridge, allows one to see through either arch. The interior of the tunnel is well lighted so that small stalactites may be seen.

Beatty Creek, which flows under the bridge, has its source in a spring 2 miles above the bridge and flows for most of its distance through woodlands. It enters the Powell River a mile or so below the bridge. In the vicinity of the bridge the creek flows through a small ravine, wooded with sycamores, willows, and other water-loving trees. Cedars constitute the only evergreen species in the neighborhood and give the local name "The Cedars" to the area. Clearings approach close to the bridge in a half-mile strip between two large wooded areas. A small acreage would be suitable for inclusion in a recreation area.

A recreation area of 100 acres, including the bridge, a mile and a half of the stream course, a small acreage of farm land, and the balance of woodland, would serve for local use. It might be desirable to extend the boundaries one-half mile above the bridge to United States Highways 58 and 421, the Old Wilderness Trail. By so doing, the bridge would be brought to the attention of tourists passing over this route. The woodland might suitably be developed for picnicking, camping, and hiking. Clearings offer potential space for playfields for use by local citizens.

The bridge is reached by turning to the south from United States Highways 58 and 421 at the western city limits of Jonesville. The straight gravel road leads directly over the bridge 2 miles from Jonesville.

The low, vaulted ceiling of Beatty Creek Natural Bridge gives cavelike atmosphere to the scene.

EBBING SPRING
[B-3

Location: South of United States Highway 11 W, 3 miles northeast of Rogersville.
Communities served: Rogersville, 3 miles; Kingsport, 25 miles; Greeneville, 30 miles; Morristown, 30 miles.
Size: 1,800 acres.
Type: Outing area combining developed scenic and intensive-use areas.
Characteristics: Pastoral scenery; streams, ebbing spring and old mill pond and dam; open tree growth and exceptional specimen trees.

A small spring, ebbing and flowing, or "fitifying", gives its name to an area of pleasing rural character. It consists predominantly of knolls, alternately wooded and open, and watered by Big Creek and tributary streams. Mixed second growth and scrub pines compose most of the tree cover on the area, although several superb single specimens of old growth remain scattered through the open land. One grove of exceptionally large gnarled beeches covers one side of a knoll on which are situated a school and a church, both small frame structures. A large stone dam, which formerly supplied power for a grist and saw mill whose foundations and shell of superstructure still remain, has been built across Big Creek. The mill pond is considerably silted but could be dredged to form a recreational lake of some 10 acres. The spring is now nearly covered by a spring house which serves a nearby dairy.

The best entrance to the tract leads from United States Highway 11W, through a gap in the ridge, 2 miles east of Rogersville. The road, after passing through the gap, skirts a meadow which might serve for picnic grounds and a playfield, leads on past the spring and farmhouse, and joins a county road at the lake. Vacation cabins could be built on a wooded bluff overlooking the lake.

Big Spring Creek wanders through this sylvan setting near Rogersville, Tenn.

DAVY CROCKETT PARK
[C-4]

Location: On Tennessee Highway 70, 6 to 7 miles south of Greeneville. Surrounding a portion of the Davy Crockett Reservoir of the East Tennessee Light & Power Co.
Communities served: Greeneville, 7 miles; Morristown, 37 miles; Johnson City, 41 miles; Newport, 34 miles.
Size: 800 acres.
Type: Outing area for intensive use.
Characteristics: Farm land and small woodlots on shore of reservoir; views of mountains to the south.

In view of this vicinity's general lack of public facilities for water recreation, it seems that any opportunity to develop such facilities should not be neglected. Such an opportunity exists in Lake Davy Crockett, storage reservoir of the East Tennessee Light & Power Co. Approximately 800 acres of farm land surrounding the main body of the lake are of a character suitable for development as an outing park which would take advantage of water uses available on the lake. It might be feasible to work out with the power company an agreement to permit such use which would, in no way, be detrimental to the company's fundamental interests in the reservoir and would undoubtedly evoke a considerable element of good will on the part of the public.

The bulk of the land within the suggested park boundaries lies on the north side of the reservoir. This area is suitable for active park uses, playfields, bathing beach, picnicking and camp sites on land which varies from level to rolling and slopes gently to the shore of the lake. Many views of the Bald Mountains may be seen to the south. The area's open character is pleasantly broken by hedgerows and woodlots of mixed second growth, and, in contrast to the opposite side of the lake, this north shoreline is unwooded.

The predominantly wooded character of the south shore contributes much of the reservoir's scenic quality. It is essential, however, that this wooded char-acter be preserved, not only to protect scenic qualities, but to protect the reservoir against silting. Knolls with cherty soil slope steeply into the reservoir and, when cleared, erode easily and become deeply gullied. As part of a public recreation area, existing growth would be preserved and could well be augmented by additional plantations. Suitable design and control of the area would permit use of many sites for cabins and camps overlooking the reservoir.

The reservoir within a suitable park boundary has a maximum width of three-tenths of a mile and a minimum of one-tenth. It is approximately 1½ miles long. An occasional promontory allows changing vistas over the lake surface, which totals 300 acres.

The open shores of Lake Davy Crockett offer excellent opportunity for intensive-use areas.

25

GREAT FALLS BLUFFS OF THE HOLSTON
[D-3]

Location: In Sullivan County, Tenn., one-fourth mile from United
States Highway 23, 8½ miles south of Kingsport.
Communities served: Kingsport, 8½ miles; Johnson City, 11½ miles;
Bristol, 22 miles.
Size: 300 acres.
Type: Intensive-use area; natural science area.
Characteristics: River bluff towering 450 feet above rapids in
Holston River; pastoral and river views; small adjacent fields.

It often happens that an area achieves recreational
charm because civilization has passed it by. The
Great Falls Bluffs of the Holston River comprise such
an area. Rising 450 to 500 feet above the river, the
steep east face of the bluffs still retains its original vegetation. Giant beeches and sycamores form majestic
arbors for grape-vines, and shrubs in great variety,
including mock-orange, willows, alders, and vibur-
num, line the river banks and cling to footholds on
the face of the bluffs. Toward the west, the land
slopes less steeply, and supports a dense grove of
cedars. The crest of the bluffs affords views over the
river and across adjacent farm lands or for considerable distances up the river. The roar of the falls
lends an atmosphere of increased wildness to the
entire area.

In truth the falls are scarcely more than rapids,
dropping a vertical distance of 10 feet in 100 feet of
the river's course. Vertical strata across the river
bed agitate the water so vigorously that the resultant
sound is quite out of proportion to the size of the
falls. Above the falls, a quiet pool contrasts with the
churning waters of the rapids. Sand beaches allow
easy access to this pool, which is secluded from adjacent farm lands by dense hedgerows.

Because this area, although small in size, has apparently never been disturbed by man, it forms a valuable
plot of our heritage from the primeval. Not to insure
its future preservation would appear heedless indeed.
The face of the bluffs might be made part of a recreation area containing some 300 acres, a large portion of
which should be devoted to active recreation. The
existing fields are too small for profitable cultivation,
but they are suitable for playfields, camping areas, and
picnic areas. The gentle slopes on the east side of the
river might be utilized for a bathing beach located on
the shore of the large pool which is suitable for swimming and boating. A few trails could give access to
the top of the bluffs and to the extensive views, which
may be obtained from that point, of the river, nearby
fields, and distant mountains.

SALTPETRE CAVE
[E-3]

Location: East of United States Highways 23 and 19 W, 4 miles
south of Johnson City.
Communities served: Johnson City, 4 miles; Elizabethton, 8 miles.
Size: 400 acres.
Types: Outing area combining developed scenic and intensive-use
areas.

Two caves, Saltpetre and Rock House, are situated
approximately one-quarter mile apart on a tract containing numerous limestone sinks and rock outcrops
of considerable interest. The nearby Unaka Mountains rise above the area's alternating open land and
mixed second growth.

Saltpetre Cave, the larger of the two, extends for
an estimated distance of 2 miles. It was the scene
of saltpetre mining during the Civil War. Rock
House Cave contains a brook flowing into Buffalo
Creek, which borders the property. The main
entrance of the cave has a span of 100 feet and a
height varying from 25 to 40 feet. A second, much
smaller entrance lies about 500 feet away. Both
caves have interesting stalactite and stalagmite
formations.

The fact that the caves are already popular with
Johnson City people who visit them in considerable
numbers during the summer months, and that neither
cave has received commercial development, suggests
their adaptability for park purposes. Buffalo Creek
may be dammed to create a lake for swimming and
boating. In addition, the tract might be developed
for playfields, picnic grounds, hiking and bridle trails,
camping areas, and cabin sites.

WATAUGA BEACH
[E-3]

Location: Watauga River at mouth of Sinking Creek.
Communities served: Johnson City, 5 miles; Elizabethton, 4 miles.
Size: 100 acres.
Type: Outing area for intensive use.
Characteristics: Good sandy beach and interesting rock bluffs.

Watauga Beach is the best and most popular of
several beaches on the Watauga River from the standpoint of accessibility and quality of sand and water
facilities. It lies but 5 miles from Johnson City (2
miles by good stone road north from a point 3 miles
east of the city on the Glanzstoff Road, Tennessee
Highway 91) and 4 miles from Elizabethton.

The beach extends along the south shore of the river
immediately above an iron bridge. A wooded bluff
forms the opposite shore. Below the bridge where

the river curves to the north, conditions are reversed; the west bank becomes a sheer cliff, contorted, rugged, and picturesque, and with much color variation, while the eastern shore becomes a sand beach. The current at this point, however, makes the site less desirable for swimming facilities.

Bath house, diving equipment, and other swimming facilities could be provided at the beach above the bridge. Cabin sites are available on the bluff back of it. Picnic ovens, tables or benches, and a commissary might be placed on the beach below the bridge.

Most of the area, including a considerable acreage back of the cabin sites, might be bought on a sub-marginal basis. This latter acreage would be necessary for protection and access. If the tract is to retain its full value, prompt acquisition becomes important because sand at the site is being dredged in considerable quantities for commercial purposes.

Watauga Beach is the most popular of several swimming holes near Johnson City.

WORLIE CAVE
[E–3]

Location: 4 miles southeast of United States Highways 11 E an 19 W, at Bluff City.
Communities served: Bristol, 11 miles; Johnson City, 16 miles; Kingsport, 26 miles; Elizabethton, 14 miles.
Size: 2,000 acres.
Type: Outing area combining developed scenic and intensive-use areas.
Characteristics: Mountain views; pastoral scenery; three times disappearing and appearing stream; Holston South Fork; cave; varied and well dispersed tree growth; limestone sinks.

The Worlie Cave tract (or Morrill Cave), embracing 2,000 acres, displays an unusually fine example of the scenic quality of the upper Tennessee Valley. The area lies between Holston Mountain as a backdrop

and the Holston River as a foreground. Composed of open, rolling country with occasional scattered groves of evergreen and deciduous tree growth, the property contains a limestone sink 300 feet in diameter and 75 to 80 feet deep, in the side of which is the cave which gives the name to the area.

A gravel road bordering the Holston South Fork approaches the tract from Bluff City. The Holston, in this vicinity, offers several swimming sites, one or more of which might be made available to the public. Nearby fields offer opportunity for parking and play areas, and a bluff overlooking the river offers sites for vacation cabins. A creek issuing from beneath the cliff affords power for a small mill before flowing into the Holston. Beyond the cliff, the creek is glimpsed twice again before its source is lost in Worlie Cave.

Of two large caves in the south wall of the sink, the lower one forms the source of the stream. Its entrance is the more spectacular of the two, but the presence of the large stream makes exploration difficult. The dry upper cave has been penetrated for a distance of several miles.

The outstanding interest of the Worlie Cave area, however, lies not primarily in the cave itself. The general pastoral character of the surroundings derives much interest from the variations of gentle contours against the more austere Holston Mountain. An additional source of interest is the contrast of well-dispersed tree growth with open fields, which are, however, badly sheet-eroded. The highest point in the tract, 300 feet above the immediate vicinity, is a wooded eminence offering a 360-degree panorama bounded by Clinch Mountain on the north, Holston on the south and east, and the Unakas to the southwest. Nearby, the topmost branches of the sycamores at the bottom of the sink barely reach above the green of the cedars which surround it.

A point above Worlie Cave, between Johnson City and Bristol, commands this view of Holston Mountain.

STEELE CREEK
[E-2]

Location: Southwest of Bristol, adjoining city limits.
Community served: Bristol.
Size: 2,800 acres.
Type: Outing area combining developed scenic and intensive-use areas.
Characteristics: Attractive stream, with possibilities of damming to create lakes; interesting knob topography; varied tree growth.

The Steele Creek tract presents the opportunity for Bristol to acquire a much-needed park at its very doors. Although the logical entrance to the property is 4 miles west of the city on United States Highway 11 W, part of the property is bounded by the city limits. The tract has a roughly rectangular shape, 4 miles by 1½ miles, whose long axis parallels the highway.

The property as a whole is composed of steep, wooded knolls, 200 to 300 feet above adjacent territory, alternating with deep, narrow valleys. Such topography does not as a rule compose well for park purposes; no coordinating vistas nor unifying features present themselves. A feature would be created by the damming of Steele Creek to form a recreational lake. The creek, within the tract, is a stream averaging 10 feet in width and 6 to 12 inches in depth, flowing for a distance of 2 miles in a valley composed of alternating broad basins and steep-banked barriers with narrow openings. Such topography offers several opportunities for damming the stream. One basin affords the possibility of a 100-acre lake with gentle approaches suitable for beaches. Around this could be grouped the intensive features of a park: Playfields, picnic and camping grounds, lodge and cabins. A second dam might be built about a half mile below the first, creating a second and smaller lake, having a more natural and isolated environment. The remainder of the tract should be left in a natural condition with trails and shelters provided for hikers.

A tract having the relatively unspoiled character of these knobs is so unusual near an important municipality that it seems desirable to preserve them for future generations who probably will live in a much larger Bristol. Public control in the near future would protect it from undesirable residential construction and uncontrolled wood cutting which are now encroaching on the area. Most of the tract could be acquired on a submarginal basis although a limited amount of good land will also be necessary for access. In November 1936 the Bristol Chamber of Commerce commissioned the Northeast Tennessee Regional Planning Commission to make detailed studies for a lake and recreational development on Steele Creek. Thus, the first steps have been taken toward realizing the potentialities of this tract.

ABRAMS FALLS
[E-2]

Location: 10 miles northwest of Bristol, on Virginia Highway 75, 5½ miles off United States Highways 58 and 421.
Communities served: Bristol, 10 miles; Abingdon, 24 miles; Kingsport, 30 miles; Johnson City, 35 miles; Elizabethton, 30 miles.
Size: 2,700 acres.
Type: Wilderness; limited intensive-use area.
Characteristics: Two outstanding waterfalls; unspoiled scenery; excellent forest growth; interesting topography.

Abrams Creek makes an aggregate drop of over 100 feet in twice that horizontal distance to form Abrams Falls before it flows on down a gorge more than 2 miles in length. The gorge and the vicinity of the falls are of unspoiled natural character.

Abrams Falls is best approached by a pleasant circuit drive over secondary State highways. Any development plans would take over Virginia Highway 674 and convert it for use as a park drive. This road follows the narrow valley of Abrams Creek for a distance of a mile or more from Virginia Highway 75 and dead-ends several hundred feet above the falls at a point where the valley widens sufficiently to allow space for parking and picnicking. Beyond this point a few hiking trails would be ample development.

A trail along the precipitous bank approaches the falls from above. An upper falls, some 30 feet in height, is taken in a few abrupt cascades, before swirling on in rapids to the brink of the main fall where a sheer drop of 50 feet onto a jagged promontory sends up a cloud of mist which at times fills the entire basin below the fall. From this basin swift rapids take the water into the gorge below. The fall drops over sedimentary fossiliferous rock which has been worn by the stream to form the gorge whose vertical, and in many cases overhanging, sides are clothed with unspoiled native growth. Although some timber in the vicinity has been cut, it has never been clear-cut. The growth is mature, virgin in appearance, mixed evergreen (mostly hemlock) and deciduous, with a dense undergrowth of rhododendron, leucothoe and other evergreen shrubs. Above the crest of the gorge this character is not preserved, the cover being scrub and second-growth interspersed with submarginal farm land.

Any development of Abrams Falls would best retain

Abrams Falls, in an unspoiled setting, drops 50 feet onto jagged rocks.

the unspoiled character in the immediate vicinity of the falls and in the gorge. A single, inconspicuous trail might allow access to the falls and gorge.

Others should be kept above where they will give vistas over both. Roads, which have been proposed through the gorge, should be discouraged.

Kelly & Green, Bristol

Before making the 50-foot drop of Abrams Falls, the waters of Abrams Creek pitch down this 30-foot cascade.

FALL MILLS
[F-2]

Location: On South Fork Holston River, south of Abingdon, off Virginia Highway 77.

Communities served: Bristol, 20 miles; Abingdon, 8 miles.

Size: 700 acres.

Type: Outing area, combining developed scenic and intensive-use areas.

Characteristics: Pastoral scenery; interesting waterfall, cascades, spring, lagoon adjacent to Holston South Fork; historic associations with Indians.

Fall Mills is already a popular picnic ground for people of Abingdon and Bristol. It comprises pleasant rural scenery bordering the Holston River, and an attractive creek with an impressive waterfall and beautiful cascades. The area may be approached through a country lane which follows for 2 miles along the creek from the village of Green Springs to a large mill which gives the tract its name.

The falls make a single plunge of approximately 20 feet and then drop nearly twice that distance in short, swift cascades. The mill is immediately adjacent to the falls. A large, 2-story structure of good proportions, it has recreational possibilities as a lodge or small inn. A steep, rocky hillside, well wooded with deciduous growth, forms the opposite bank of the creek. The bluff on the same general level as the mill, and on the same side of the creek, offers sites for vacation cabins. Below, the land drops sharply to a river meadow of some 8 acres, associated by history and legend with the Indians as a popular camping and fishing ground in the shoaling season. A collection of Indian relics may be seen in a nearby home.

Two large springs at the base of the bluff flow through a lagoon parallel to the Holston to an ultimate confluence with the river. Across the river, wooded hills, foothills of the Holston Mountain, are included in the Jefferson National Forest.

30

The meadow as a whole might be developed as a playfield with picnicking and camping facilities near its edge along the bluff, creek, and river. The river offers swimming opportunities, and a limited amount of canoeing would be made available in the lagoon.

Fall Mills would have a valuable place in a public park program should it be acquired for use by Bristol and Abingdon residents. The land, however, is apparently of such value that only extraordinary circumstances will permit its being acquired. Meanwhile it would be desirable that the scenic quality of the property be protected through county zoning.

Kelly & Green, Bristol
Suggestive of a Gothic shrine, these formations are found in Bishops Cave, near Bristol.

This cascade at Fall Mills, near Abingdon, is the scenic focal point of a suggested recreational area.

BISHOPS CAVE
[E-2]

Location: Approximately 4 miles southeast of Bristol city limits on United States Highway 421. At north side of road immediately beyond the village of Ruthton.

Communities served: Bristol, 4 miles; Kingsport, 28 miles; Johnson City, 29 miles; Elizabethton, 24 miles.

Size: Up to 300 acres.

Type: Intensive-use area.

Characteristics: Pastoral scenery; extensive cave of limestone formation.

Bishops Cave is one of the better known caves in the vicinity of Bristol. Its small and unimpressive opening is located in the midst of farmland of only average attractiveness. A few groves of second-growth hardwoods and cedar intersperse knobby pastureland, some of which has eroded. Considerable effort would be necessary to bring to the tract any semblance of a parklike character. The cave itself extends through approximately 100 acres of land, the subterranean rights of which have been purchased by one individual. Various passages and corridors give

access to chambers, one more than 40 feet in height, on three different levels. A subterranean stream flows on the lowest level to its exit in the base of a nearby cliff. Stalactite and stalagmite formations are varied and beautiful.

CLINCH MOUNTAIN FOREST: TENNESSEE UNIT
[B-3]

Location: Extending northeastward from the intersection of Grainger, Knox, and Union Counties, Tenn., to the Virginia State line.

Size: 125,000 acres.

Type: Wilderness; outing area, (including developed scenic and intensive-use areas).

Characteristics: Long wooded ridge, supplemented by lower parallel ridges in some places, and widening out to form an enclosed cove at its southwest butt. Superb views over surrounding countryside to distant mountains.

Clinch Mountain is the longest and highest ridge in the Upper Tennessee Valley between the ranges of the Blue Ridge Province and the Cumberland Mountains. From its southwestern extremity, about 18 miles airline northeast of Knoxville, it stretches for 150 miles northeast, well into Virginia, where it terminates in its highest elevation of 4,724 feet. Within the Tennessee unit it varies from 2,000 to 2,500 feet in elevation. The actual high point in this particular area, however, is found on adjacent Short Mountain, which is over 2,700 feet high.

Several factors make it highly desirable that Clinch Mountain and adjacent ridges be included in some form of publicly owned reservation. These ridges are the sources of many streams that flow into the Clinch and Holston Rivers. Long-continued, uncontrolled logging and repeated forest fires have taken their toll of the ridges, but, at least for the present, timber cutting is definitely drawing to a close, because of the rapidly decreasing supply of merchantable material. These two factors, however, have undoubtedly had a decidedly detrimental effect on the watershed's protective role and have resulted in considerable erosion and consequent silting of the Clinch and the Holston Rivers. It is highly probable that this unwise handling of the resources will continue as long as the area is in unstable ownership. Present knowledge indicates that in the main this area represents a forest site of such low productivity that private forest exploitation is economically unsound, and the area is, therefore, evidently a public responsibility.[2]

Considered from its scenic aspect, Clinch Mountain occupies such a dominating place in the Great Valley that, if its scenic values are to be maintained, it becomes mandatory that forest fires, destructive logging, and overgrazing be prevented. Sustained forest logging under proper management, however, is permissible when properly conducted in relation to the recreational use of special areas, and would, in fact, improve the appearance of the area in general. Moreover, as the chief scenic value lies not in the mountain itself, but in the many beautiful panoramas which unfold from certain vantage points along the crest, selective logging on the lower slopes would scarcely be noticed from these high points.

In the light of these various conservational aspects it would appear that Clinch Mountain should be made a part of the public domain. As it perhaps forms too small an area to be suitable for a national forest unit, a possible alternative is its consideration as a regional forest. Though present conditions seem to relegate a State forest of this size to the status of a rather remote possibility, it is herein noted not only as a desirable potentiality, but as a State responsibility.

A tract of such attenuated character is restricted in the nature of its possible recreational usage; but, at the same time, it is readily available to a more widespread population than would be the case of a compact reservation of equal size. It is conceivable

that Clinch Mountain, along with such other areas as English and Chilhowee Mountains, and parts of the Cumberland Escarpment, might be a logical location for private resort developments. Leasing of suitable tracts for such use would be in accordance with established public forestry policies.

Short Mountain
[B-3]

Location: Hawkins County, Tenn., 12–14 miles air line north-northeast of Morristown.
Type: Developed scenic area.
Characteristics: Point 2,700 feet in elevation, highest in Tennessee Unit, valley views, second-growth woodland.

Short Mountain, rising 1,700 feet above its surroundings to a total height of 2,700 feet, reaches the highest elevation in the Tennessee Unit of the Clinch Mountain Forest. It is a narrow ridge only 4 miles long, connected by a spur to Stone Mountain, a minor ridge some 14 miles in length. Both are parallel to and a short distance south of Clinch Mountain. At the base of Short Mountain is Galbraith Springs, a resort hotel centered about mineral springs. From this point a steep trail affords the opportunity for an ascent to the summit. Along the trail, an occasional opening in the second-growth woodland of oak and pine allows glimpses of the Holston River and the valley knobs to the south. Although these vistas are frequently cluttered and obscured by foreground growth, a forest-management program emphasizing recreation could keep them open.

Scrubby growth again interferes with views from the summit. A temporary surveyors' tower permits one to obtain a view over the growth, and indicates

The sheer sides of Devil's Nose provide a stiff climb, and the summit offers excellent views.

---

[1] From a statement by Mr. I. C. Burroughs, TVA Forestry Division.

the potential range of vision that would be revealed from an observation tower such as would probably be a feature of a forest-management program. To the north the view extends over Stone Mountain, in the foreground, Clinch Mountain, immediately beyond, and the minor ridges of the Clinch-Powell River Valleys, to the distant Cumberland Mountains. Eastward one looks down a narrow valley into Rogersville. Toward the south one gets the full effect of views over the Holston River and valley knobs such as those glimpsed during the ascent.

The area is suited to little intensive recreational development aside from the essential features of a forest-management program. These would probably include an observation tower on the summit, an access trail leading to it, and additional fire trails.

Some 10 miles northeast of Stone Mountain is the Devil's Nose. An isolated mountain, 2,000 feet in elevation, its sheer sides have been popular with local hikers as a sporty climb rewarded by an excellent view. It is reached from Tennessee Highway 70 at a point 4 miles north of Rogersville.

The winding Holston River glimpsed between tall pines on the slope of Short Mountain.

33

CLINCH MOUNTAIN FOREST: VIRGINIA UNIT
[C-2]

Location: Extending northeastward from the Tennessee-Virginia
State line to Little Moccasin Gap.

Size: 88,000 acres.

Type: Wilderness; occasional outing areas, including developed scenic
and intensive-use areas.

Characteristics: Long wooded ridge with subordinate parallel ridges
and adjacent submarginal land. Attractive views over ridge and
valley land.

Clinch Mountain, within the Virginia Unit of the
forest, is a single narrow ridge. Except for a section
7 miles in length which runs due west from Big Moccasin Gap, it runs in a general northeast-southwest
direction. Its point of highest elevation in this section, 3,217 feet, is Big Knob east of Gate City. West
of Big Moccasin Gap the boundaries of the unit have
been extended to include portions of Pine Mountain,
Moccasin Ridge, and Copper Ridge—portions which
make up an area presenting a serious erosion problem.
The Clinch River thus becomes the boundary of the
unit for a considerable distance on the north, and the
Holston North Fork, for a short distance on the south.

In general, the same factors which make it desirable
that the Tennessee Unit become a publicly owned reservation, apply to the Virginia Unit. The mountain
has the same characteristics of forest growth, scenic
advantages, and erosion problems. A portion of the
mountain extending along the Russell-Washington
county line west of Little Moccasin Gap has been
recommended by the State Forester of Virginia for
acquisition as a State forest, but no State funds are
available for its purchase at the present time.

No points of marked recreational significance are
noted in this unit, but, as need arises for their development, numerous sites of varying recreational interest
may be found on ridge top, river bank, or in cove land.

GREAT KNOBS FOREST
[F-2]

Location: 2 miles south of Abindgon, Va.

Communities served: Abingdon, 2 miles.

Size: 5,550 acres.

Type: Wilderness.

Characteristics: Unusual topography and fairly complete forest
coverage.

The Great Knobs comprise 5,550 acres of wooded
knolls immediately south of Abingdon. Part of a belt
of such knobs extending along the South Fork of the
Holston River between Abingdon and Bristol, they
are the most characteristic and at the same time the
most noteworthy section of the belt. The growth is
predominantly of pine and is fairly uniform, although
some attempt has been made to clear and farm portions
of the area. Resultant farmsteads are definitely submarginal in appearance.

This fact suggests its suitability for a State forest.
Its value as a natural scenic reservation in such close
proximity to Abingdon would be great, although its
development primarily as a recreation area cannot be
justified by its inherent qualities. For this reason the
area is best suited for forest purposes with incidental
emphasis on wilderness forms of recreation.

BAYS MOUNTAIN FOREST
[C-3]

Location: Hawkins, Greene, Hamblen, and Sullivan Counties,
Tennessee.

Communities served: Kingsport, 2 miles; Bristol, 25 miles; Elizabethton, 33 miles; Johnson City, 25 miles; Greeneville, 15 miles;
Morristown, 30 miles; Rogersville, 8 miles.

Size: 94,050 acres.

Type: Wilderness, with limited developed scenic areas.

Characteristics: Interesting topography, rugged and rural scenery;
distant views; average tree growth.

Bays Mountain extends as a single ridge from Kingsport in a southwesterly direction to Tennessee Highway 70 between Greeneville and Rogersville. From
this point it continues as a series of knobs to Dand-
ridge and beyond. Only that portion which is north
of the Nolichucky River seems to have special recreational merit. A parallel, more disjointed ridge,
formed by Chimneytop, Fodder Stack, and Stony
Lump, lies slightly to the south of Bays Mountain
and a series of low, knobby ridges borders it on the
north. The mountain has an average elevation of
2,000 feet, and is cut by deep coves, pockets, and an
occasional gap which allows passage across it. Chimneytop, Fodder Stack, and Stony Lump, although
they combine to form a ridge, have a considerable individuality in themselves. Chimneytop, on a
clear day, affords views of the entire North Carolina-
Tennessee State line between Gregory Bald, in the
Smokies, and the Virginia line. In addition, the
view extends east as far as Whitetop, in Virginia.
To the north, the long, low contour of the Cumberlands extends above Clinch, Powell, and other
valley ridges. Immediately below, fields and woodlands pattern the valley floor. Chimneytop, when
viewed from the direction of Kingsport, presents an
aspect which has often been compared to Japan's
Mount Fuji. It rises to an elevation of 3,076 feet

to dominate the view from this direction. Fodder Stack and Stony Lump, with an elevation of 2,600 feet, and as stodgy as their names imply, contrast with it. These three are also covered with a good quality of second growth, where absence of clearing has permitted it.

An industrial plant in Kingsport owns a large part of Bays Mountain and manages the forest on a sustained yield basis. Such a policy insures the scenic protection of that part but does not necessarily provide for recreational use by the public. That such a forest policy is practicable indicates that timber growth is more rapid here than on other valley ridges. This assumption is corroborated by results obtained in the watershed of Kingsport reservoir, on the eastern extremity of the mountain. The isolation of the valleys and the submarginal quality of cleared land, moreover, indicates that forestry offers the best economic use of the area.

A public forest would recognize collateral use for recreation either of a wilderness type, or, in limited portions, a more intensive or resort type.

Paul Moore, Knoxville

The infra-red camera discloses unseen details of mountain and valley landscape. A view from the summit of Chimneytop, Hawkins County, Tenn., toward the Bald Mountains of Cherokee Forest.

From the edge of Chimney Rock the quiet waters of Lake Lure seem cradled in the foothills of the Blue Ridge.

The Asheville Area

GENERAL DESCRIPTION OF THE AREA

THE Asheville area comprises a large part of western North Carolina and a smaller adjoining portion of South Carolina. All areas and features in Tennessee, shown on the map, are described in chapter I. In 1930 the area had a sparse and generally rural population. Asheville is its largest city, with a population of about 50,000, according to the 1930 census. Asheville's 1936 population, including suburbs, was estimated to be slightly under 100,000, which does not take into account the extremely large transient population.

The Blue Ridge Mountains, extending through the Asheville area in a general northeast-southwest direction, form the drainage divide between the South Atlantic region and the Tennessee River Basin. The French Broad River and its tributaries form the principal drainage system in the area west of the Blue Ridge.

Within this area rise many of the highest mountains of eastern North America. Mount Mitchell, elevation 6,684, the highest peak east of the Mississippi, lies a few miles northeast of Asheville. Mountain ranges of the area which attain elevations over 6,000 feet are Pisgah Ridge, the Balsams, the Black Mountains, and the Craggy Mountains. The lower mountains form many cross ridges extending between these high ranges and the Blue Ridge, a striking contrast to the ridges of east Tennessee, most of which lie parallel with each other. Well covered with forest growth, the mountainsides of the area often rise abruptly from narrow, picturesque valleys

through which flow many streams made turbulent by frequent waterfalls and rapids.

Scattered throughout the maze of mountain ranges, the wider valleys and small plateaus form good farmlands. In the center of the area and surrounded by its mountains is the extensive, rolling plateau known as the Asheville Basin, which has a general elevation of 2,000 to 2,500 feet above sea level. Most of the basin is used for general agriculture. This is also true of the Piedmont country, just east of the Blue Ridge, which lies some 800 to 1,000 feet lower than the basin.

The heavy precipitation in the Asheville area is a primary reason for its abundant flora, full streams, and the opportunities for developing hydroelectric power. There are, however, marked variations in the amount of rainfall throughout the area. On the higher slopes and mountain tops precipitation is much heavier than in the valleys, especially along the eastern and southern slopes of the Blue Ridge, parts of which average more than 80 inches a year. A large part of the total annual rainfall, especially in the summer, comes from local showers and thunderstorms. Rainfall is heaviest during March, July, and August in all parts of the area.

Average annual temperatures also vary considerably within the area. At Linville it is 48.4°; at Asheville, 51.1°; and at Tryon, 59.5°. This partially accounts for the fact that Tryon is a winter and spring resort while resorts west of the Blue Ridge have their principal season during the summer.

Scattered throughout this section are many resorts,

the tourist and resort business being extensive enough to form an important source of income for a considerable part of the population. Many towns double their normal population during the summer months—Hendersonville, Waynesville, Brevard, Chimney Rock, Black Mountain, and Spruce Pine are among the more important resort centers in addition to Asheville. Private summer camps, both boys' and girls', are numerous and there are several assembly grounds for the summer conferences of various large church bodies.

The Asheville area constitutes the section of the Tennessee River watershed that is best known for its scenic resources. For years people have come here to spend their holidays at resorts and to enjoy the recreation areas and the many points of scenic interest that are found here. Although the national forest lands are located in the general west and north portions of the area, the mountains, lakes, waterfalls, and other scenic attractions are widely scattered within its borders.

More than one-third of the area is included within national forest boundaries. Thus it is unusually well endowed with publicly owned and administered recreation areas. This being the case, it seems reasonable to refrain from making many suggestions for additions to the public domain. Except for the larger reservoirs, the kinds of scenic interest which lie outside national forest territory may all be found in abundance within its boundaries.

The Asheville area serves as the eastern approach to the Great Smoky Mountains National Park, center of recreational interest in the Tennessee Valley. Many vantage points within the Asheville area command superlative views of the Smokies, rising west of the Balsams. Outstanding among such vantage points is Black Camp Gap, on the western margin of the park. The Blue Ridge Parkway, under construction through the Asheville area, is planned to become the principal recreational motor road in Eastern United States.

Fisher, Asheville

Black Camp Gap discloses the rugged wilderness which forms the eastern portion of the Great Smoky Mountains National Park.

EXISTING REGIONAL RECREATION AREAS

PISGAH NATIONAL FOREST
[C–5, G–1]

UNTIL recently, Pisgah National Forest was composed of four separate divisions. These units have been abolished, and the forest now consists of all the land in these old units, plus a great deal of intervening and adjacent land between and around them. The boundaries now include 1,178,000 acres, all of which are within North Carolina. Thus there is under one jurisdiction the largest recreational area within the Asheville area.

Pisgah National Forest consists in part of a tract of more than 85,000 acres, originally acquired by George Vanderbilt after he came to Asheville in 1890. Because of his interest in both forestry and game protection, the tract has been administered under scientific forest practice, and as a game preserve. In 1915 the Federal Government purchased all but 500 acres of this tract and established it as Pisgah National Forest. Near Mount Mitchell and Grandfather Mountain land for national forest purposes was first acquired in 1916. In 1921 these tracts were made a part of Pisgah National Forest. Additions were made to the old divisions, and new purchase units were created at various times until the present boundaries were established in 1936.

The old Vanderbilt tract, which lies south of Asheville, is characterized by steep, high mountains and narrow valleys. Parts of it were once cut or burned over, but most of it is again well-timbered and has an abundant undergrowth of laurel and rhododendron, demonstrating to a very marked degree the results of proper forest management. Pisgah Ridge, the dominant range, has an elevation over 5,000 feet for more than half its length. Of all the peaks on this ridge, Chestnut Bald, elevation 6,040 feet, and Mount Pisgah, elevation 5,749 feet, offer the most sweeping views of the surrounding country. The principal streams in the forest east of Pisgah Ridge are the Davidson River and the north and south forks of the Mills River. The smaller streams in the mountains descend rapidly, forming many falls, cascades, and rapids.

Lying west of Pisgah Ridge and extending to Soco Gap, west of Waynesville, is a triangular-shaped addition to the Vanderbilt tract. The southeastern and southwestern boundaries of this addition are Pisgah Ridge and Balsam Ridge, respectively. Each one rises over 6,000 feet, their highest peak Richland Balsam, reaching an elevation of 6,540 feet. Other prominent high peaks near these boundaries are Cold Mountain, Waterrock Knob, and Lickstone Bald. The northern boundary of the addition follows parts of North Carolina Highways 293 and 284 and United States Highways 19 and 23. Most of this area is drained by the Pigeon River.

The older sections of Pisgah Forest near Mount Mitchell include that portion of the Blue Ridge between Swannanoa Gap and Little Switzerland, all of the Black Mountains, except the section which is Mount Mitchell State Park, and a large part of the Craggy Mountains. The Black Mountains, highest and most rugged of these ridges, attain elevations over 6,000 feet for more than half the length of their main crest. The Craggy Mountains also rise to peaks higher than 6,000 feet. Streams in the Mount Mitchell section are rather small, and there are no large waterfalls. The slopes have all been cut over, but a good timber growth again flourishes on them.

The older parts of Pisgah Forest, southeast of Grandfather Mountain and those in Madison County along the Tennessee State line, although once cut over, also have healthy, vigorous stands of second-growth timber. The irregular mountain ranges southeast of Grandfather Mountain are relatively low. Only a few peaks rise above 4,000 feet, and their general elevation ranges between 2,000 and 3,000 feet. The principal streams are the Linville, the Johns, and the Yadkin Rivers. These headwater streams have tortuous courses following deep, irregular gorges.

The Bald Mountains in Madison County rise above 4,000 feet, attaining their highest elevation in Cold Springs Mountain, 4,889 feet. Camp Creek Bald and Rich Mountain are other high peaks on the State line. This area is drained by small streams which are tributaries to the Nolichucky and French Broad Rivers.

Of all additions to Pisgah National Forest, the section southeast of the Blue Ridge centering around Linville Gorge contains as beautiful mountain scenery as any part of the Asheville area. Small farming areas are found along the lower stream valleys, but most of the land in the vicinity consists of forested mountain ridges.

Adjacent to the North Carolina-Tennessee line in Watauga, Avery, Mitchell, Madison, and Haywood Counties is less interesting mountainous country. Most of the highest elevations occur along the State line, and it is here that the principal scenic interest occurs. Forest cover varies in its quality, but the land is well adapted to national forest use. Small towns, villages, and farms scatter along the narrow plains of the stream and lower mountain slopes. Several lofty mountain peaks rise here, the highest being Yellow Mountain, elevation 5,330 feet. Other prominent mountains are Beech Mountain, Haynes Knob, Naked Place Mountain, Chambers Mountain, and, along the boundaries, Roan Mountain, the Unaka and Iron Mountain ranges and Grandfather Mountain. A well known mountain, which has a toll road to its summit, is Max Patch, elevation 4,660 feet, in the western corner of Madison County. It commands fine views in all directions, particularly south toward the Smoky Mountains. The principal streams are the Toe, Elk, Watauga, French Broad, Cane, and Pigeon Rivers. Some of these rivers and tributary streams are polluted by industrial and mine wastes, which partially or totally destroy fish life.

The older divisions of Pisgah National Forest have had increasing recreational use since their establishment, and all of them offer potentialities for even greater recreational use in the future. Every appropriate form of recreation consistent with the protection and perpetuation of timberlands, watersheds, wildlife and other forest resources is encouraged and stimulated in the administration of the forest. Since the establishment of the CCC there has been notable progress in the construction of roads, trails, shelters, and camping and picnicking facilities.

Motoring is the type of recreation which probably has attracted the greatest number of people to Pisgah Forest. In the past few years, old roads have been much improved and new gravel roads opened, while

From the Yonahlossee Road motorists view a succession of mountain ridges fading into blue haze.

Overhanging trees grace the Davidson River in the Pisgah National Forest.

still others are planned or are being constructed. The proposed Blue Ridge Parkway, as planned by the National Park Service, will pass along the crest of Balsam Ridge and Pisgah Ridge southwest of Asheville and along the Craggy and Black Mountains and the Blue Ridge northeast of Asheville. If all these plans become realities, there will certainly be an adequacy of roads in Pisgah Forest.

Nearly every highway and road in Pisgah Forest is a scenic drive, but there are four existing roads with scenery so outstanding that they deserve special mention. Pisgah Motor Road, easily reached from Candler, on United States Highways 19 and 23, or by way of North Carolina Highway 284, follows close to the top of Pisgah Ridge for more than 6 miles, commanding sweeping views to the east. The Mount Mitchell Toll Road, a rough one-way drive, which leads off United States Highway 70 one mile east of the town of Black Mountain and winds 19 miles up to Camp Alice, near the summit of Mount Mitchell, is notable for views it affords of the Catawba River Valley and the Blue Ridge to the east. Passing through Little Switzerland, North Carolina Highway 26 follows close to the crest of the Blue Ridge for about 6 miles. Superb views extend east and south from Little Switzerland and from this highway. The Yonahlossee Road, United States Highway 221, between Blowing Rock and Linville is famous for beautiful views along its entire distance. It should be noted that three of these four outstanding scenic drives parallel the proposed Blue Ridge Parkway in their respective sections and may become a part of the parkway, at least temporarily.

All the older sections of Pisgah Forest now have hiking trails, camp sites, and picnic grounds with facilities for their use and enjoyment. Additional recreational facilities of this nature are planned. In several places the Forest Service program for development contemplates one or more small lakes for water sports and also areas to be made available for summer homes under a system of special permits.

Hunting and fishing, of course, play an important part in the recreational use of Pisgah Forest. However, the old Vanderbilt tract is a national game preserve, and two State game refuges are established in other sections of the forest. Definite restrictions on hunting and fishing apply to all these refuges. During the fall hunting season, which overlaps the fall and winter fire season, the national game preserve is entirely closed to the public, thus reducing the opportunity for poaching and minimizing the fire hazard. When deer are plentiful an annual hunt, restricted to

Roadside pines at Bent Creek Gap frame vistas of neighboring ridges in Pisgah Forest.

a day or two and limited in the number of hunters, is permitted. Fishing is allowed in the game preserve for short periods throughout the summer, but every fisherman must have a special permit.

A separate description of some of the most outstanding features of Pisgah Forest follows.

U. S. Forest Service

Cold Mountain and the Balsams dominate westward views from Mount Pisgah.

41

Mount Pisgah (Big Pisgah)
[C–4]

Mount Pisgah, one of the better known mountains of North Carolina, rises to an elevation of 5,749 feet. Forming a definite peak and standing slightly to the west of the main Pisgah Ridge, it dominates that whole ridge as it is seen from the Asheville Basin.

The popularity of Mount Pisgah is due to its easy accessibility, its freedom from toll charges, and the Forest Service recreational developments nearby. There is a large parking space on the Pisgah Motor Road near the crest. From this point a hike of about a mile brings one to the top. The views from the peak extend to the Smoky Mountains in the west, the Blue Ridge in the east, and the Black Mountains north of Asheville and the great Craggies.

Fisher, Asheville

Wrested from the rocky soil of the highlands, this tiny farm reposes at the foot of Mount Pisgah.

Fisher, Asheville

Lookingglass Rock rises domelike over a sea of trees, its naked walls of living granite defying the ravages of time.

Lookingglass Rock
[C-4]

Lookingglass Rock is an isolated mountain lying south of Mount Pisgah. It rises to an elevation of about 4,000 feet, standing 1,000 feet and more above its immediate surroundings. The rounded, bare granite cliffs of its north and west sides give the mountain a dome shape as seen from those directions. Such spheroidal weathering occurs in a few other places in the mountains of North Carolina, but Lookingglass Rock is the most impressive example of it. The name "Lookingglass" comes from the fact that, across the bare granite dome and down the side of the cliff, there is a wide fan-shaped waterfall which glistens mirror-like in the sunlight.

This landmark forms an interesting feature for the motorist and the hiker in that section of Pisgah Forest. Good roads have been opened on all sides of the mountain, making it easily accessible and affording splendid views of it and the surrounding country.

43

Lookingglass Falls
[C-4]

About half a mile from its junction with Davidson River, Lookingglass Creek falls in a straight drop of about 35 feet. On one side of this stream the new route of North Carolina Highway 284 passes close by the head of the falls in a way that somewhat mars the naturalness of its setting. A very steep, rocky mountainside with a profusion of laurel and rhododendron marks the opposite bank.

U. S. Forest Service

Lookingglass Creek dives 35 feet into a profusion of laurel and rhododendron.

Courthouse Falls
[B-4]

Near the headwaters of Courthouse Creek in the south end of Pisgah Forest several falls and cascades occur, the largest of which is an almost vertical drop of about 30 feet. Since Courthouse Creek is a rather small stream, these falls are not as spectacular as the others described here.

This section is reached by the surfaced Courthouse Creek Road, which passes within a quarter of a mile of the highest falls. A trail following an old logging railroad leads from this road down past the high falls. Camping and picnicking facilities are planned in this vicinity.

Pink Beds
[C-4]

On a small plateau lying between the main Pisgah Ridge and minor ridges east of it are the famous Pink Beds. Laurel and rhododendron are abundant throughout Pisgah Forest, but they attain widespread profusion on this plateau. Of the many places in western North Carolina noted for the showy display of laurel and rhododendron, this beauty spot is surpassed only by Craggy Gardens, described elsewhere in this chapter. The Forest Service roads through this area afford drives through the very midst of these laurel and rhododendron thickets. There is a large Forest Service campground on the plateau.

Lower falls of Courthouse Creek, a roaring chute between lichen-flecked walls.

44

Catheys Creek Falls
[C-5]

Perhaps the most beautiful waterfalls in this part of Pisgah Forest occur along the section of Catheys Creek where that stream rushes down through its steep, narrow valley in a descent totaling some 300 or 400 feet within a quarter-mile course. The most spectacular drop forms a series of sloping falls where the water descends about 125 feet in 300 feet.

The falls are located on the Catheys Creek road, 3 miles north of the point where it leaves United States Highway 64, 5 miles southeast of Brevard. This road is far enough from the falls to leave their immediate surroundings quite unspoiled.

The waters of Catheys Creek rush headlong down riffles of furrowed rock.

French Broad Falls
[C-5]

On the North Fork of the French Broad River in the south end of Pisgah Forest, there is a beautiful waterfall. It differs in character from other waterfalls described here, in that it is much broader than it is high, being some 15 feet in height and about 50 or 60 feet across. A small side stream joins the river immediately below the falls with a drop of equal height and beside it stands an interesting log water mill with a horizontal wheel.

Below these falls the river descends through a narrow valley in a series of cascades and rapids. Since this part of Pisgah Forest was not in the original Vanderbilt purchase, it has been cut over in recent years, so that it lacks the dense timber stands and luxuriant undergrowth of other sections of the area.

This rough-hewn grist mill draws power from a side stream at French Broad Falls.

The North Fork of the French Broad River cascades with formal abruptness over this 15-foot ledge in the Pisgah National Forest.

Craggy Gardens
[D-3]

Along the summit of Craggy Mountains between Craggy Dome and Craggy Flats lie the widely publicized Craggy Gardens. In this area, which is really a heath bald, the only vegetation is grass and low thickets of purple rhododendron, growing in great profusion. During the month of June when these shrubs bloom, Craggy Gardens becomes one of the most spectacular show places of the Asheville vicinity.

Apart from the blooming season of this natural rhododendron garden, this crest of Craggy Mountain has a great charm and appeal, commanding sweeping views to the east, south, and northwest. A good road leads to a point within half a mile of Craggy Flats, where there is an attractive picnic grove near the parking space. This road is reached from Asheville by way of Barnardsville.

Fisher, Asheville

Masses of the Catawba rhododendron form a natural garden of rich purples and lustrous greens on the high slopes of the Craggies.

Blue Sea Falls
[E-2]

Blue Sea Falls, on the headwaters of the Cane River, is close to Wilson Brothers' Motor Road up Mount Mitchell about 5½ miles south of the junction of this road with North Carolina Highway 695. It is not an exceptionally attractive waterfall, having a height of only 20 feet and a small volume of water, but it is easily accessible and well known for this reason. The herbaceous growth around the falls is beautiful and varied.

Blue Sea Falls, in Pisgah Forest, is easily reached from a road up Mount Mitchell.

Buck Creek picks an uncertain course through a tumble of rocks beside North Carolina Highway 104.

Buck Creek Falls
[E-2]

On Buck Creek, close to North Carolina Highway 104, 3 miles west of Lake Tahoma, there is an attractive waterfall composed of a series of several small falls about 40 feet in total height. The surrounding area offers an opportunity for an attractive wayside picnic spot that would be enhanced by a trail to the foot of the falls, with another pathway leading along the stream below it.

Clarkson Knob
[E-2]

Immediately northwest of the small resort colony of Little Switzerland is Clarkson Knob, a point on the Blue Ridge which commands a thrilling 360-degree panorama. A tower has been built here which serves as a fire lookout and as an observation platform. Many of the notable high mountains of North Carolina, including the Black Mountains, Roan Mountain, Yellow Mountain, Grandfather Mountain, and Tablerock Mountain, may be seen from here. The tower is accessible by a fairly good road, less than 2 miles distance from Little Switzerland.

From Kilmichael Tower on Clarkson Knob the full contour of the Black Mountains penetrates the haze.

Linville Falls and Gorge
[F-1, F-2]

The steep, narrow valley between the long ridge of Linville Mountain and Jonas Ridge is known as the Gorge of the Linville River. At the head of the gorge the stream has cut a passage down into and over a rock cliff, making a beautiful waterfall. The upper part of the falls is hidden from view because the water has worn its path through a crevice in the cliff. After making this initial fall, the water flows into view and over an almost vertical drop of about 40 feet. Points along the top of the gorge overlook the falls and its surroundings, which are quite unspoiled by intrusions of civilization.

The gorge below the falls is less known but fully as interesting for its scenic beauty. For more than 10 miles the river flows south between two well-wooded mountain ridges which in general rise 1,000 to 1,500 feet above it.

Jonas Ridge on the east side of Linville Gorge has two distinctive peaks, Hawksbill and Tablerock Mountains, each of which attains an elevation of approximately 4,000 feet. Hawksbill presents a sharp, pointed profile, while Tablerock Mountain has a broad and fairly level summit. A fire lookout station on the latter commands extensive views in all directions. A new road is being constructed to Tablerock Mountain from North Carolina Highway 181. Another road, planned to follow along the east side of Jonas Ridge, will make that whole ridge more accessible to automobiles.

North Carolina Highway 105, now a rough dirt road, follows close to the crest of Linville Mountain on the west side of the gorge. This "skyline" drive has fine views along and near it not only across Linville Gorge, but also west to the Blue Ridge and Black Mountains. Perhaps the best place to see the gorge is from a point called Wisemans View, which is about 4 miles south of Linville Falls and approximately a quarter of a mile from the highway across the gorge from Tablerock Mountain.

U. S. Forest Service

Tablerock Mountain clings to a precarious perch at the edge of Linville Gorge, across from Wisemans View.

49

Within the memory of man, Linville Falls has halved its height by undercutting its own crest to carve a new channel behind massive walls of granite.

Grandfather Mountain
[F-1]

The origin of the name of Grandfather Mountain, 5,964 feet, is attributed to two different sources; first, to its profile which resembles that of a bearded old man in a reclining position, and, second, to its age, which is placed by geologists as among the oldest on the North American Continent. In spite of its great age, Grandfather Mountain has a ruggedness and spectacular quality which is more characteristic of the younger mountains in the West than of other summits in the Appalachians. Three distinct peaks, each one sharply separated from the other, form the salient facial features of the fancied profile. The crest of each peak supports only mosses, lichens, ericaceous shrubs, and low conifers. Other portions of the mountain support a rich growth of black spruce at the higher elevations, and mixed hemlock and northern hardwood on its lower slopes. A dense rhododendron and laurel growth among rough, irregular boulders of gigantic proportions contributes to the almost universal wildness of Grandfather.

The various peaks of Grandfather offer panoramic

U. S. Forest Service

Balanced Rock, on the side of Grandfather Mountain, overhangs Yonahlossee Road.

Superlative views in all directions reward those who scale Grandfather Mountain.

views in all directions. In the north one may see Hanging Rock, and slightly west of it Beech Mountain; in the west Roan Mountain rises above the intervening Grassy Ridge Bald and Big Yellow Mountain; toward the south, the line of vision follows Jonas Ridge to Hawksbill and Tablerock Mountains.

A toll road to the base of the first peak has recently been built by the Linville Improvement Co., which owns the mountain. This toll road, a half mile in length, does not seriously impair the wild character of the mountain, for it stops at a point beyond which heavy cuts and fills would be necessitated. The spruce timber, however, is now being logged by a lumber company, and these operations do impair its forest beauty. By written contract, the company has agreed to reserve a 200-foot strip along the Yonahlossee Road (United States Highway 221), which skirts the mountain on the south.

Along the trail to the first peak of Grandfather Mountain an ominously overhanging cliff frames this mountain view.

Elk River Falls
[F-1]

Elk River Falls is a natural feature which at present is leased by a private fishing club which has used the vicinity for outings of its members. The falls drops 75 feet, pouring abruptly over the rim of a ledge of granite or crystalline rock into a broad, deep pool. From this pool the waters of the creek flow out over a shallow cascade into a boulder-strewn gorge whose slopes are covered with a growth of mixed pine and hardwoods. Well-worn paths in the vicinity of the falls lead to vantage points from which one may obtain excellent views.

Approach to the falls is from United States Highway 19 E at Elk Park, 2 miles east of the Tennessee State line, by way of a dirt surface road. In the 4½ miles of its length the road crosses and recrosses the creek by means of several fords which make the road difficult to travel in times of high water. Above the falls, the Elk Creek valley is cultivated in small farms of picturesque character. Small fields near the falls are suitable for camping and picnic grounds.

After plunging 75 feet over a sharp granite ledge, the waters of Elk Creek form a pool of unmeasured depth.

53

Dutch Creek Falls softens the bare rock outcrop like a mantle of finely-woven lace.

Dutch Creek Falls
[F-1]

Dutch Creek Falls, 90 feet high, is located 2 miles south of Valle Crucis, N. C., at the head of a small cove which is virgin in appearance, if not in fact. The stream drops almost vertically down the steep face of the cliff, which is sufficiently rough to break the fall and vary the texture of the water. Large hemlocks, beeches, and other cove hardwoods tower above a dense tangle of laurel and rhododendron. Only a few foot-worn paths give access to the falls through this tangled growth. Because Dutch Creek has a large watershed above the falls, the flow is fairly uniform the year round. Its entire atmosphere has an intimacy and charm which is unspoiled in spite of numerous visitors.

Below the falls, farm lands approach the entrance of the cove; above the falls, a narrow valley supports a few small farms. The falls may be reached from the Dutch Creek Road, which leads south from North Carolina Highway 194, at the Valle Crucis Episcopal Church. From a ford across Dutch Creek, one-fourth mile south of the church, a trail one-quarter mile long leads up the creek valley to the base of the falls. A quarter mile byond this ford, the road crosses Dutch Creek by means of a bridge. From the bridge a short trail gives access to the upper side of the falls.

Blowing Rock
[G-1]

Blowing Rock, 3 miles south of the resort town to which it gives its name, is an overhanging portion of a narrow ridge of rock high above the gorge of the Johns River. Peculiar wind currents sweeping up and over the rock from the gorge below give the rock its name and, according to legend, prevented the tragedy of another lover's leap. Indian tradition states that an unhappy brave, discouraged because of parental opposition to his efforts to woo his loved one, in despair, jumped from the rock only to

Plateau Studios, Asheville

Blowing Rock, where wind foils gravity, hangs over the Johns River Gorge, commanding a full view of Grandfather Mountain.

55

be wafted by the wind currents back to safety and his beloved's arms. Today, bits of paper, or even one's hat, may be returned to the rock by the up-draft of the air current. In the winter time the same currents reverse the usual trend of snowflakes and create an up-swirling snow storm.

Aside from these curious phenomena, the rock affords magnificent views of the Johns River Valley and the Grandfather Mountain to the northwest, over other parts of Pisgah National Forest to the west and southwest. Pines, mixed hardwoods, laurel, and rhododendron cover the rock with a profuse vegetation which, however, does not obstruct the view.

A property line following the crest of the ridge divides the rock between two private ownerships. On the one side, an admission charge during the season admits one to the rock. At the other side, free admission may be obtained to a souvenir stand and rustic observation tower from which one may look over the rock to the distant views.

MOUNT MITCHELL STATE PARK
[E-2]

The summit of Mount Mitchell, and a tract of 1,225 acres around it along the main crest and west side of the Black Mountains, is the only North Carolina State park in the Asheville area. Toll roads pass through Pisgah Forest, barely entering the park proper. Visitors must hike into it and most of them follow the trail leading up from Camp Alice, a small hotel located at the junction of the two toll roads.

As the highest mountain on the continent east of the Mississippi River, Mount Mitchell has a great tourist appeal. The elevation of its summit is 6,684 feet, and here a stone observation tower commands extensive views in every direction. Prof. Elisha Mitchell, who first explored the Black Mountains, is buried at the top of this mountain named for him.

The original forest in the park area was red spruce, a virgin stand of which still covers Mount Mitchell and the crest of the Black Mountains. Some of the

Cane River Gap offers this view of Mount Mitchell, highest peak in eastern America.

park has been cut or burned over at one time or another, but a good stand of hardwoods remains.

The only roads to it are the narrow, rough Mount Mitchell and Wilson Brothers toll roads. The former leads to the park from the south leaving United States Highway 70, 1 mile east of the town of Black Mountain, and the latter approaches from the northwest, from North Carolina Highway 695, and joins the Wilson road just south of the park.

TABLE ROCK STATE PARK
[C–5]

Table Rock Mountain stands out prominently along the Blue Ridge in South Carolina. The north side of this mountain lies within the watershed of Greenville Reservoir, described elsewhere. Two thousand four hundred acres along its southern slopes have recently been acquired by the South Carolina State Commission of Forestry and are now being developed as a State park. This development includes the construction of cabins, a lodge, camping grounds, trails, bridle paths, and a 40-acre lake.

S. C. Forestry Commission

Table Rock greets the visitor at the entrance of its namesake park.

The principal feature of the park is Table Rock Mountain, every side of which, except the west side, has very abrupt slopes exposing a great deal of bare rock. A part of the south side is a cliff almost 1,000 feet in height. The top of the mountain, having an elevation of 3,157 feet, commands extensive views across the Piedmont and the Blue Ridge.

The Blue Ridge, on the right, marches away into the hazy horizon in this panoramic view from Black Mountain toll road up Mount Mitchell.

PARIS MOUNTAIN STATE PARK

Paris Mountain Park includes approximately 1,000 acres on the southeast slope of Paris Mountain, 7 miles northwest of Greenville, S. C. It lies generally south of the area covered by the map accompanying this chapter and hence is not shown. The park, which is being developed at the present time, will serve a heavy industrial population in Greenville and the area within a 30-mile radius of the city.

Paris Mountain, although lower than the mountains of the Blue Ridge Province, is prominent above the general level of the Piedmont. Six miles of park drive climbing high on the mountain slope, afford panoramic views over the Piedmont and to the Blue Ridge in the northwest. Hiking trails, through the mixed pine and hardwood forest, offer access to other vantage points. The nucleus of park developments centers about three small lakes built several years ago by the Greenville city water department and abandoned in favor of the larger reservoir near Table Rock Mountain. The larger of these lakes, impounded by a stone dam, has been developed for swimming and an attractive stone bathhouse built near its shore. A group cabin area for underprivileged children will be built about one of the smaller lakes.

S. C. Forestry Commission

This sturdy dam creates a 19-acre lake in South Carolina's Paris Mountain State Park.

GREENVILLE RESERVOIR
[C-5

The city of Greenville, S. C., has a reservoir for its water supply on the South Saluda River in the northwestern corner of Greenville County. The county owns the watershed of 9,000 acres lying between Table Rock Mountain and Pinnacle Mountain on the south and the Blue Ridge on the north. The reservoir consists of a body of water some 420 acres in surface area and a quarter to a half mile wide. Beautiful views across it extend to the mountains on either side.

Recreational use of the watershed is limited by the necessity of protecting the reservoir from pollution. At present the watershed is fenced and trespassing is prohibited, but, under proper supervision, it might be possible to use the area for hiking and picnics. The area should appeal to visitors to Table Rock State Park, adjacent to it on the south.

North Carolina's Tablerock looms distantly above Lake James.

South Carolina's Table Rock Mountain towers above the rippled surface of Greenville Reservoir.

LAKE JAMES
[F-2]

The largest body of water in the Asheville area is Lake James, a reservoir for storage and hydroelectric power, created by damming three streams, the Catawba River, the Linville River, and Paddy Creek. A canal between the Catawba River arm of the reservoir and the Paddy Creek arm forms a connection necessary to make this a single large reservoir having a total water surface of approximately 6,500 acres

when full. This reservoir is uppermost in a series of Catawba River power developments, all controlled by the Duke Power Co. The primary purpose of Lake James is water storage, hence it is subject to considerable draw-down which, normally 20 and 30 feet, may amount to a maximum of 80 feet, September 1 to January 1 constituting the usual period for lowering the normal water level.

Because of its well-wooded shores and the fine views across it to nearby and distant mountains, Lake James has a beautiful setting; but, due to its fluctuation, it has little recreational use except for some fishing and boating. There are a few cabins and one large boys' camp near it.

The north shore lies within a recent addition to Pisgah National Forest and may sometime be developed by the Forest Service. A site for a park on its south shore is suggested later in this chapter.

LAKE TAHOMA
[E-2]

About 7 miles northwest of Marion on North Carolina Highway 104 is Lake Tahoma, created several years ago as the promotional feature of a resort development. The development consists of a few summer cottages around the lake, in addition to an amusement pier and boating and swimming facilities. The property around the lake lies entirely within a recent addition to Pisgah National Forest.

Lake Tahoma has a beautiful setting, with the nearby Blue Ridge and Black Mountains rising into full view above its well-wooded shores. A small hydroelectric generating station is located at the dam, but the draw-down is seldom more than 5 feet during the recreational season.

Wooded shores meet the waters of Lake Tahoma in Pisgah National Forest.

LAKE LURE
[E-4]

A popular and widely publicized lake in western North Carolina is Lake Lure, which serves as both a hydroelectric power development and a resort. The operation of the power plant is very closely dependent upon the surface level of the lake, so that the power generators cease operation when the water level falls as much as 6 inches below normal. In an emergency, the Southern Power Co., owners of this generating station, may lower the level more than this amount, but they have never done so. As a consequence, the lake is more suited than many others to recreation.

Lake Lure, with a surface area of approximately 1,500 acres, has a maximum length of 3 miles. Its winding shoreline outlines many narrow arms and small bays which lie in irregular valleys between the foothills of nearby mountains. Chimney Rock Mountain and Rumbling Bald dominate the views across the lake. Although the surrounding property has been subdivided for summer homes, only a small percentage of it has been developed. Summer camps, two resort hotels, and a bathing beach, however, attract visitors, and the lake is used extensively for boating and fishing. United States Highway 74 follows the southern shore rather closely.

Fisher, Asheville

Sunset intensifies the beauty of mountain-bordered Lake Lure.

CHIMNEY ROCK
[E-4]

Just as Lake Lure is the most widely publicized lake in western North Carolina, so is nearby Chimney Rock its most widely advertised rock feature. It is owned by the Chimney Rock Co., which operates a small hotel in connection with its well-maintained development of this mountainside. Open the year round, it is visited by hundreds of tourists.

Chimney Rock Mountain rises more than 1,500 feet above the Broad River, 1 mile west of the head of Lake Lure. The upper part of this mountain on the side facing the river exposes a bare rock cliff, three to four hundred feet high. The Chimney Rock proper, a rounded column of rock which gives the mountain its name, stands out from the main face of this cliff. A road leads up for about 3 miles to a parking space and to a small rustic hotel and a chain of cabins literally hanging to the mountainside and located near the base of Chimney Rock. The mountainside above this point is developed with an elaborate system of trails, wooden stairways, and overlooks. The trails, vantage points, and minor features are designated by various names, such as Appian Way and Moonshiner's Cave, to heighten their appeal to visitors. The views from the top of Chimney Rock and many other points above it on the mountain extend eastward across Lake Lure and far down the Broad River valley to the low foothills of the Piedmont.

About a half mile west of the Chimney Rock, a small creek drops over a bare rock precipice along the rim of the mountain in a thin, straight fall of more than 300 feet, known as Hickorynut Falls. Visible from the highway at the base of the gorge, this fall serves as an interesting objective for two of the main trails along the mountainside.

SUGARLOAF MOUNTAIN
[E-4]

On Sugarloaf Mountain, 3,967 feet elevation, the Blue Ridge rises to one of its greatest heights in the Asheville area south of Swannanoa Gap. The mountain top lies 8 miles by a rough gravel road east of Edneyville, a small settlement on United States Highway 64, between Hendersonville and Bat Cave. Near the summit is a small hotel, the owners of which charge the motorist a toll to drive to the top, where they have built an observation tower. The views from here are perhaps as fine as any in North Carolina, extending in all directions along the Blue Ridge, into the Asheville Basin on the west and across the Piedmont to the east. Except for the hotel and observation tower the mountain is undeveloped.

Fisher, Asheville

Beyond the western slope of Sugarloaf Mountain wooded crests toss wavelike across the Asheville Basin.

Harmonious development has retained the natural impressiveness of Chimney Rock.

SHUNKAWAKAN FALLS
[E-4]

Two miles east of Tryon Peak a small stream tumbles down the southeast side of Tryon Mountain in a series of steep cascades and falls, which are known as Shunkawakan Falls. The side of the mountain rises more than 1,500 feet above the Piedmont country making these falls, which are perhaps the highest in the Asheville area, visible for several miles. The top of the falls, seemingly on the skyline, may be reached by a road up Tryon Mountain, but the only recreational development of the area around them consists of the many miles of bridle trails maintained by the Tryon Riding and Hunt Club.

Only fishermen visit the secluded waters of Lake Turner, storage reservoir near Tryon, N. C.

LAKE TURNER
[E-4]

The Turner Shoals hydroelectric dam on the east side of the Blue Ridge on the Green River creates a reservoir known as Lake Turner. About 2 miles long and one-fourth of a mile in its greatest width, it lies about 5 miles south of Lake Lure on North Carolina Highway 192, a gravel-surfaced road forming part of a short route between Tryon and Lake Lure.

The well-wooded shores afford attractive views across the lake to Tryon Mountain and the Blue Ridge. Because of a considerable annual draw-down, there is no recreational development on this lake and little recreational use of it except for fishing.

LAKE LANIER
[E-5]

Lake Lanier, located 2 miles south of the town of Tryon, was created several years ago for a resort development of summer homes. Although a few such cottages have been built on its shores in addition to a resort hotel, the development as a whole has never progressed far. However, boating and swimming facilities are available to the public. The whole setting of Lake Lanier is attractive, with some fine views across its waters and wooded shores to nearby peaks on the Blue Ridge.

The open shores of Lake Summit, just south of Hendersonville, are popular for summer camps.

Lake Lanier, at the foot of the Blue Ridge, was created for recreational use.

PEARSON FALLS
[E-5]

The Tryon Garden Club owns a 325-acre tract around Pearson Falls on a small stream which flows from the west into the Pacolet River in its high, narrow valley west of the town of Tryon. The club maintains this area as a preserve for wild flowers, mosses, ferns, and other plants native to this section of the Blue Ridge. It is open to the public on payment of an admission charge.

Aside from the great variety of plants, the principal feature of this area is Pearson Falls, an attractive series of waterfalls about 75 feet in total height. It is reached by a minor road which connects with United States Highway 176, 5½ miles west of Tryon.

LAKE SUMMIT
[D-5]

Lake Summit is a hydroelectric power development situated on the Green River just across the Blue Ridge

south of Hendersonville, N. C. It extends between the two points where United States Highways 25 and 176 cross the Green River, and is thereby accessible from either end by roads along its north and south shores. The lake is about 2 miles long, nearly a quarter of a mile in greatest width and has a surface area of about 230 acres.

There are public bathhouses and swimming facilities on this reservoir, as well as cottages, most of which are on the south shore. The north side is largely undeveloped. The shores of the lake and the nearby hills are well wooded.

CAESARS HEAD
[C-5]

The south side of the Blue Ridge in Greenville County, S. C., is largely an escarpment, some 1,000 to 1,500 feet high. One of the highest points on the escarpment, known as Caesars Head, lies 16 miles southeast of Brevard, N. C., adjacent to United States Highway 276. The property along the top of this portion of the escarpment is used largely for private homes and cottages. There is a small picnic grove and an observation tower to which an admission is charged. The whole escarpment commands extensive views across the Piedmont country. Caesars Head, by the prominence of its position and easy accessibility, is the best known point on it.

CONESTEE FALLS
[C-5]

An unusually fine wayside scenic spot occurs on United States Highway 276, seven miles south of Brevard. Only 50 yards from the road, two streams literally fall into each other in a beautiful series of steep slides and straight drops which total approximately 100 feet. The falls are not visible from the highway and only a casual sign and a small refreshment stand indicate the trail entrance from the road. Although under its present ownership it may be freely visited by passersby, the falls is worthy of attractive entrance and access treatment and the preservation from despoliation that public ownership would afford it.

Maidenhair Falls, after a 30-foot drop, spreads fanlike over the rocks below.

old watermill and farmhouse about a half mile from the Federal highway. Although frequently visited by the people of the neighborhood, the falls are not widely known and remain unspoiled in their lovely wooded surroundings.

CASCADE LAKE
[C-5]

Cascade Lake is a reservoir created by the Brevard Dam of the Cascade Power Co. It lies in a narrow, winding section of the Little River Valley in low

Beautiful Conestee Falls is 50 yards from United States Highway 276, 7 miles south of Brevard.

MAIDENHAIR FALLS
[C-5]

A small stream with the unlovely name of Hogshead Creek drops down a narrow steep valley in the Blue Ridge Mountains 2½ miles southeast of Brevard near United States Highway 276. In a series of falls and rapids along a mile of its upper course, this creek makes its most abrupt drop in Maidenhair Falls, which makes a sheer plunge of about 40 feet just before spreading into a broader but shorter fall. The falls are reached by walking up a short steep trail from an

Cascade Lake, a 50-acre reservoir on the Little River.

66

mountains of the Blue Ridge, some 5 miles east of Brevard. Although about a mile in length and covering about 50 acres, its comparative narrowness makes it appear rather small. This reservoir is subject to considerable draw-down and largely for that reason has no recreational development. It might be included as a part of the Little River Falls tract immediately above it as a regional park development. This potential recreation area is described in another section of this chapter.

The access road to and along a part of the reservoir is rough and narrow, so that the lake is seldom visited. A small parking space is available for the few fishermen who go to the lake. By this road, the lake lies 5 miles south of United States Highway 64 and 6 miles north of United States Highway 276.

JUMPOFF MOUNTAIN
[D-4]

Jumpoff Mountain, 4½ miles west of Hendersonville, is the site of one of the most ambitious schemes for a resort ever attempted in western North Carolina. What was planned to be a 14-story hotel, Fleetwood Inn, stands today with only its full steel framework and its brick facing in place, forming a gaunt landmark visible for miles around. The hotel site commands fine views in all directions, especially across the Asheville Basin to the Pisgah Range and the Black Mountains, and east to the Blue Ridge. However, a more attractive spot for enjoyment of these views is the top of a low cliff, called Jumpoff Rock, a quarter of a mile northwest of the hotel and only slightly below the 3,141-foot summit of the mountain.

From Jumpoff Mountain, west of Hendersonville, the profile of Mount Pisgah tops the horizon.

67

LAKE LOGAN
[B-4]

On the West Fork of the Pigeon River about 7½ miles south of Woodrow, the Champion Fibre Co. has created a small reservoir for water storage purposes. This reservoir, known as Lake Logan, covers approximately 120 acres. It lies in a steep, narrow valley between two high ridges, Fork Mountain on the east, which rises to an elevation over 5,200 feet at High Knob, and the Balsam Range on the west. Except for the property immediately around it, on which there are several summer cottages and which will probably remain in private ownership, Lake Logan is surrounded by land which ultimately will be purchased by the Forest Service.

Since the primary purpose of the reservoir is storage, it is subject to draw-down during dry seasons. However, it provides swimming, boating, and fishing for the summer cottagers and a nearby boys' camp. An undistinguished development at present, it might well be made more attractive for the periods during which its normal pool elevation is maintained.

ASSEMBLY GROUNDS

The summer assembly grounds of several church bodies and other religious organizations are located in the Asheville area. These properties range in size from those of less than 100 acres to one containing 3,500 acres. Usually controlled by church organizations or affiliated associations, the grounds almost always include one or more buildings for holding the programs of the assemblies in addition to an assembly hotel and housekeeping cottages. There are provisions for outdoor sports and usually an artificial lake large enough at least for swimming.

The larger assembly grounds are briefly described here, although not all are shown on the map.

Fisher, Asheville

A dam impounds headwaters of the Pigeon River to form Lake Logan. This 120-acre lake lies in Pisgah National Forest.

Lake Junaluska

One of the larger assemblies is that held by the Methodist Episcopal Church, South, at Lake Junaluska 3 miles northeast of Waynesville. The assembly grounds on the north shore of this 175-acre lake consist of an extensive development of hotels, housekeeping cottages, and summer homes. Facilities for swimming and boating are available during the summer, and fishing is allowed if a special permit is purchased.

Lake Kanuga

The summer conference resort of the Episcopal Church lies 5 miles southwest of Hendersonville on Lake Kanuga, the church owning a 1,200-acre tract around this 30-acre lake. This attractive assembly development includes a club house, hotel accommodations, and numerous cottages. As originally developed, a larger lake was formed. After the floods of 1916 washed out the dam, the smaller lake was created by a lower dam rebuilt upstream and closer to the assembly grounds.

Montreat

The Mountain Retreat Association, affiliated with the Southern Presbyterian Church, owns a 3,500-acre tract lying between the main crest of the Blue Ridge and Walkertown Ridge north of the town of Black Mountain in Buncombe County. Montreat, a municipality within the association grounds, is the center of assembly activities. It has a large inn, open the year round, smaller hotels and many summer homes. A 2-acre lake provides swimming facilities.

Ridgecrest

At Ridgecrest on the west side of Swannanoa Gap the Southern Baptist Church conducts its summer assembly. There is a small lake here, but the setting of the assembly development is scenically less interesting than some of the others, as well as being bisected by a main highway.

Blue Ridge

Three miles southwest of Black Mountain the Blue Ridge Association, affiliated with the Y. M. C. A., has an assembly ground of some 1,600 acres in the Swannanoa Mountains. The main buildings have a particularly fine setting with splendid views off to the Craggy Mountains on the north. The Y. M. C. A. uses the grounds during the summer, and the newly organized Black Mountain College has taken them over for the rest of the year.

Fisher, Asheville

Sunset on Lake Junaluska, summer capital of Southern Methodists.

PROPOSED REGIONAL RECREATION AREAS

BLUE RIDGE PARKWAY
[B-4, F-1]

THE Blue Ridge Parkway, connecting the Shenandoah National Park and the Great Smoky Mountains National Park, is being constructed under the design, direction, and administration of the National Park Service from funds provided by PWA. The parkway consists of a strip of land averaging 2,000 feet in width which follows, for the most part, the crest of the Blue Ridge. Through this strip will run a two-lane motorway, along which camps, picnic areas, and golf courses will be developed at intervals. The parkway is designed to make the scenic features of the Appalachian Mountains available to motorists and to provide a recreational motorway between these two great eastern national parks.

The parkway enters the Asheville Area at Deep Gap on United States Highway 421, crosses this highway, and swings south along the Blue Ridge to Blowing Rock. From Blowing Rock to the Qualla Indian Reservation it lies entirely within Pisgah National Forest except where it crosses the Asheville Basin near Asheville. Between Blowing Rock and Grandfather Mountain the proposed location follows closely the alignment of the present Yonahlossee Road, although it will swing higher on the shoulder of Grandfather Mountain than does the present highway. Turning southwest from Grandfather Moun-

Fisher, Asheville

Views such as this from Buck Creek Gap will characterize the Blue Ridge Parkway.

70

tain, the parkway crosses Grandmother Mountain and then Linville River, just north of Linville Falls, which, according to present plans, may be developed as a related feature. It then follows the crest of the Blue Ridge in a southwesterly direction past Little Switzerland. Still following the crest of the Blue Ridge, it crosses Buck Creek Gap, Big Laurel Mountain, and continues to the junction of the Buncombe, McDowell, and Yancey county lines. At this point, it leaves the Blue Ridge and follows the southern crest of the Black Mountains to Balsam Gap, where it turns south along the east slope of the Great Craggy Mountains, around their southern extremity passing out of Pisgah Forest and on to Elk Mountain, east of Asheville. The parkway then descends to a comparatively low elevation which is maintained across the French Broad River at Biltmore. Upon entering the southern section of the Pisgah National Forest just east of the river, it rapidly ascends along the Buncombe-Henderson county line to Pisgah Ridge at Mount Pisgah. It then follows Pisgah Ridge to Tennessee Bald, where it swings northwest along the Balsam Range to Soco Gap, west of Waynesville. At Soco Gap it turns west through Qualla Indian Reservation to its terminus at the Indian village of Cherokee, near the boundary of the Great Smoky Mountains National Park.

.

PROPOSED JOSHUA MOUNTAIN STATE FOREST PURCHASE UNIT

[C-5]

Location: Transylvania County, N. C., adjoining the Pisgah and Nantahala National Forests.

Communities served: Brevard, 8 miles; Asheville, 32 miles; Hendersonville, 30 miles.

Size: 2,100 acres.

Type: Wilderness with occasional intensive-use areas.

Characteristics: High ridges broken by deep, narrow valleys; elevations from 2,000 to 3,500 feet; many small waterfalls; cool summer climate; some virgin timber.

The Joshua Mountain Forest, proposed for acquisi-

tion under the Fulmer Act, lies on the watersheds of the east and middle forks of the French Broad River in Transylvania County, N. C. A typical mountain watershed, its surface consists of high ridges broken by deep narrow valleys. The elevation ranges from 2,180 feet on the French Broad River to 3,548 feet on Sassafras Mountain, at the south end of the tract. Joshua Mountain, between the two forks, reaches an elevation of 3,163 feet to form the most prominent feature of the forest. The two streams have numerous small waterfalls and cascades which would be outstanding in a region less plentifully supplied with superlative falls. The original forest consisted of deciduous hardwoods with some pine and hemlock. The present forest shows a considerably higher balance of yellow pine. About 75 percent of the area has been cut over and subjected to severe and frequent burning. Game is scarce but the results of management in the nearby Pisgah Forest indicate that a similar program would serve to replenish the supply.

While naturally endowed with scenic and recreational resources which would be outstanding in country of average attractiveness, the Joshua Mountain Forest does not compare favorably with other nearby attractions. Superlative waterfalls, such as those on the Toxaway, Horsepasture, Whitewater, and Little Rivers, lie within a few miles of the tract. Higher elevations characterize the Balsams and Pisgah Ridge. Campgrounds and picnic areas have been developed in nearby national forests. For these reasons, there will probably be little demand for the development of intensive recreational facilities. If the area becomes stocked with game and its streams with fish, some demand may accrue for sportsmen's accommodations.

Note.—The Fulmer Act, referred to in connection with this and other proposed State forest purchase units, is an act of Congress providing Federal funds for the purchase of State forest lands. The money is loaned to the States with the provision that part of the earnings from the forests so created will go toward repayment of the loan.

POTENTIAL REGIONAL RECREATION AREAS

ELK MOUNTAIN PARK
[D-3]

Location: Crest of Elk Mountain, 2 miles north of Asheville.
Community served: Asheville, 2 miles.
Size: Approximately 100 acres.
Type: Developed scenic area.
Characteristics: Partly wooded mountain top with broad views of Asheville and vicinity.

ONE of the well-advertised drives in the vicinity of Asheville is the Elk Mountain Scenic Highway, which is also North Carolina Highway 694. This road follows the mountain's ridge so closely that it affords some of the best views of any road in the vicinity of Asheville. Since all of Elk Mountain and other ridges close to Asheville are in private ownership, one or two public parks on them seem highly desirable as places where people might come for a few hours' outing or picnic and enjoy the sight of rolling plateau country and distant mountains. A possible park site on Elk Mountain affords commanding views not only of Asheville, the Asheville Basin, and Pisgah Ridge to the south and east, but also north across the Walnut and Spring Creek Mountains to the North Carolina-Tennessee State line.

Fisher, Asheville

Views from Elk Mountain extend across the Asheville Basin to Pisgah National Forest.

LITTLE RIVER FALLS
[C-5]

Location: Transylvania County, N. C., 6 miles southeast of Brevard.

Communities served: Brevard, 10 miles; Hendersonville, 18 miles; Asheville, 40 miles; Greenville, S. C., 35 miles.

Size: 5,000 to 6,000 acres.

Type: Outing area, combining developed scenic and intensive-use areas.

Characteristics: Rolling plateau broken by deep stream valleys with beautiful waterfalls.

The Waterfalls on Little River, upstream from Cascade Lake, also described in this report, constitute an outstanding scenic attraction even in a land favored with as many beautiful falls as the Asheville area contains. For 3 or 4 miles this river flows through a privately owned tract known as Buck Forest, where three principal falls occur, all within a distance of 2½ miles. The upper falls is known as Bridal Veil Falls, the middle one as High Falls, and the lower one as Triple Falls.

In High Falls the river cascades down over steeply sloping rock in a total drop of more than 100 feet. Since the river at this point has a watershed of approximately 25 square miles, the volume of water which flows over the falls during the spring and summer is great enough to make High Falls perhaps the largest and most impressive in the Asheville area.

Bridal Veil Falls is approximately 1¾ miles above High Falls and about 60 feet high. Bridal Veil, however, carries a smaller volume of water than does the other, because High Falls receives the flow of an additional stream which joins the Little River between the two falls. Below High Falls the river flows through a steep winding valley down into Cascade Lake. Three-fourths of a mile downstream

The waters of the Little River cascade in complete abandon down the 100-foot face of High Falls.

is the third falls, Triple Falls, consisting of three successive short drops.

Buck Forest, which includes 5,000 to 6,000 acres, is a well-wooded area much of which is a fairly level or rolling plateau. This locality offers splendid opportunities for the development of active recreation areas, vacation camps, cabins, and camping grounds.

At present the tract is wholly undeveloped; a rough narrow road leads to High Falls, but the other two falls may be reached only by trail.

SPIVEY MOUNTAIN
[C-3]

Location: Buncombe County, 3 miles west of Asheville.
Community served: Asheville, 3 miles.
Size: Approximately 500 acres.
Type: Developed scenic area.
Characteristics: A wooded mountain top commanding extensive views across the Asheville Basin.

A short distance west of Asheville a low mountain ridge rises above the Asheville Basin so that two high points at the east end of it command extensive views in all directions. These two peaks are known as Spivey Mountain and Deaver View, the former having an elevation of 3,331 feet and the latter being about 200 feet lower. At present, a State fire tower surmounts Spivey Mountain, but there is no recreational use of the well-wooded slopes around and between the two peaks.

A small tract developed with trails, overlooks, picnic facilities, and cabins would offer an exceptionally attractive objective for a short drive from Asheville, and offer a scenic spot for picnics.

LAKE JAMES PARK
[F-2]

Location: South shore of Lake James.
Communities served: Marion, 10 miles; Morganton, 12 miles.
Area: 300 to 400 acres.
Type: Developed scenic area.
Characteristics: Well-wooded shore of the largest reservoir in North Carolina.

Lake James has been described in this chapter in the section on existing regional recreation areas. It was pointed out that there has been very little recreational use of this reservoir largely because its primary purpose is for water storage entailing a maximum draw-down of 80 feet, the usual period of draw-down falling between September 1 and January 1, and during occasional dry periods in other seasons. Thus, during most of the spring and summer, the great beauty of this lake with its wooded shores and views of distant

Slopes of the Swannanoas furnish views of the Craggy Mountains.

mountains is not seriously spoiled by any lowering of the water level.

Greater enjoyment of this reservoir would be possible if some area along its south shores were a park. It should be noted that the land adjacent to the north shore of the lake lies within a recent addition to Pisgah National Forest and may in the future be developed by the Forest Service. Picnicking, camping, and boating are the types of recreation for which a park on the south shore should make provision. A well-wooded site, traversed by North Carolina Highway 105A and easily accessible from United States Highways 70 and 64, seems most suitable.

SWANNANOA MOUNTAIN FOREST
[D-3]

Location: Buncombe County, east of Asheville.
Communities served: Asheville, 3 miles; Black Mountain, 3 miles; Hendersonville, 20 miles; Marion, 25 miles.
Area: Approximately 17,000 acres.
Type: Wilderness area with intensive-use areas for outing developments.
Characteristics: High, well-forested mountain range.

The Swannanoa Mountains between United States Highways 70 and 74 and North Carolina Highway 119 constitute a large, unified forest tract, all of which has been cut over at least once and seems adapted for acquisition and administration as a public forest. The crest of this mountain range rises to elevations of more than 4,000 feet and commands some extensive views of the valleys and mountains on both sides, especially of the Craggy Mountains and the Black Mountains. Near the foot of the Swannanoa Mountains and along its lower slopes on both sides are several areas which seem well adapted for intensive-use purposes, such as vacation camps. One such developed area already exists on the north side of the range, namely the 1,600-acre tract of the Blue Ridge Association, used as a summer assembly ground.

The Knoxville Area

GENERAL DESCRIPTION OF THE AREA

THE Knoxville area includes portions of Kentucky, Virginia, Tennessee, North Carolina, and Georgia. The principal city in the area is Knoxville, which lies on the Tennessee River, formed by the junction of the Holston and French Broad Rivers just above the city. Other principal tributaries of the Tennessee which lie partly within the area are the Clinch and Powell Rivers, in the north portion, and the Hiwassee and Little Tennessee Rivers in the south.

Generally speaking, the Tennessee River flows southwesterly through this section of the Great Valley, which is here some 40 to 50 miles wide. To the southeast lies the broadest part of the Blue Ridge Province, including most of the Great Smoky Mountains, and a portion of the Unakas. Northwest of the Valley are the Cumberland Mountains. Within the Valley itself lie numerous clearly defined ridges, running in the northeast-southwest direction so characteristic of the physiography of the Valley of East Tennessee. A fair amount of the land in the central valley is fertile farmland under cultivation, but there is a large proportion of marginal land. The greater part of the mountains is forested, but except for about 200,000 acres of virgin timber in the Smoky Mountains, the trees are second-growth. Elevations vary from 800 in the Tennessee River Valley to 3,550 (Cross Mountain) in the Cumberland Mountains, and 6,642 (Clingman's Dome) in the Great Smoky Mountains. In general, the Smokies are about twice the height of the Cumberlands. Summer temperatures in the highest mountains will average 10° to 12° cooler

than in Knoxville, and extreme maximum temperatures run 20° lower in the mountains.

Aside from Knoxville, the principal urban centers in the area are Middlesboro, Ky. (10,350), and the contiguous cities of Alcoa and Maryville, with a combined population of 10,213.

Knoxville, with a 1930 population of 105,802, is the fourth largest city in Tennessee, and is the general center of trading and industrial activity in the lower Valley of East Tennessee. (The 1937 city directory gives Knoxville a population of 158,000.) It is a railroad and highway traffic center of considerable importance, and will be the head of the 9-foot navigation channel in the Tennessee River.

Middlesboro is the largest city in southeastern Kentucky. It has a few industries, but is primarily a trading center for the coal-mining district in which it lies. Alcoa (5,255) and Maryville (4,958) are in effect one city. The former was built by the Aluminum Co. of America and is inhabited by employees of the two large aluminum plants. Maryville is essentially a local trading center, whose business district serves Alcoa and surrounding Blount County.

The Knoxville area is divided into three main geographic provinces, each of them having its own special significance in relation to scenic recreation. These provinces are: (1) The Blue Ridge Province (Great Smoky and Unaka Mountain Ranges); (2) the Valley Province, with its long ridges; and (3) the Cumberland Mountain Province.

(1) The Blue Ridge Province is the most spectacular

of the three, with elevations twice as high as the highest of the Cumberland Mountains, and six or seven times as high as the average of the Valley Province. Most of this land is in, or proposed for inclusion in, national parks or national forests. It is adapted to both outing and conservation types of recreation. Its scenic value is sufficient to draw people from all over the country, if not the world. At present, recreational facilities in the Blue Ridge Province are inadequate to meet the demand.

(2) Scenic recreational potentialities in the Valley Province lie chiefly in the series of existing and pro-posed reservoirs on the Tennessee River and its tributaries. Water areas are essential for any great recreational province, and, in varying degrees, the reservoirs will largely fulfill that need.

(3) The Cumberland Mountains within this area are somewhat like the Blue Ridge, but on a smaller scale. Coal mining activities, though rather extensive, have not, except in certain localities, appreciably affected the mountain scenery. Though very little of the virgin forest remains intact, second-growth timber covers most of the area, and it seems suited for wilderness recreation under national forest jurisdiction.

Thompsons, Knoxville

These placid waters of the Little River belie their origin on the steep slopes of the Great Smoky Mountains.

76

EXISTING REGIONAL RECREATION AREAS

GREAT SMOKY MOUNTAINS NATIONAL PARK
[E-5]

THE Great Smoky Mountains National Park was authorized by Congress in 1926, and was officially established in 1931. The Tennessee-North Carolina State line divides the park into approximately equal parts. The long dimension of the park runs nearly east and west, its maximum length being 54 miles. Included within the tentative boundary are 445,000 acres, or 695 square miles.

This tract comprises as great a concentration of unspoiled scenery as exists in the United States east of the Mississippi. More than 200,000 acres of the park are in virgin forest, including the largest and finest primeval hardwood forest in the country, and the largest virgin forest of red spruce, which reaches its southern limit of growth there. Aside from Mount Mitchell, elevation 6,684 (in Pisgah National Forest), the park contains the highest mountains in Eastern United States. There are 16 peaks which are over 6,000 feet high. The highest is Clingmans Dome, elevation 6,642. Mount Le Conte, elevation 6,593, is the highest peak from base to summit, east of the Mississippi, with a net height of 5,300 feet.

Thompsons. Knoxville

Broad-shouldered LeConte, best known peak of the Smokies, rises in austere majesty at the entrance to the national park.

Object of many hiking parties in the Smokies is this jutting precipice, known as Alum Cave.

Ramsay Cascades veil this giants' stairway on the slope of Mount Guyot.

The view from Clingmans Dome extends southward across the forested slopes of furrowed ridges which make up the Blue Ridge Province.

Misty Rainbow Falls refreshes a hiker on the Rocky Spur trail up Mount LeConte.

Hidden in the silent shadows of virgin forest on the side of Mount LeConte, Dome Falls enshrouds itself in an aura of mystery.

Carlos Campbell Knoxville

The dazzling brilliance of snowclad Clingmans Dome, stands out in sharp relief against a cloudless sky.

Carlos Campbell, Knoxville

Spence Field, a mountain-top meadow, characteristic of the many "balds" in the Smokies.

Thompsons, Knoxville

Pastoral quiet characterizes mountain-locked Cades Cove, deep in the Great Smokies.

Wylie Bowmaster, Knoxville

Patterned fields contrast with forest-textured mountain slopes—Cades Cove in the Great Smokies.

Carlos Campbell, Knoxville

The twin-peaked Chimneys push their rocky summits through a covering of rich foliage.

Sugarland Valley, ribbed by tree-clad ridges, stretches from the Chimneys toward Cove Mountain.

A natural swimming pool in the Great Smoky Mountains cooled by the splashing waters of Abrams Falls.

It is said that nowhere else in the temperate zone, within an area of equal size, is there as great a variety of plant life as is found in the Smokies. Of trees alone, 152 species have been identified, as compared with 85 known native species in all continental Europe. There is also a great variety of indigenous birds and animals, but many kinds have been greatly diminished in numbers, or exterminated by hunters. Restocking of a few nearly extinct species is contemplated. The protection which the park offers will make the tract a real sanctuary for wildlife, because—unlike many of the western national parks, where severe winters drive wild creatures down from the higher elevations into unprotected areas outside the parks—the mild climate of the lower sections of Great Smoky Mountains Park will assure protection from cold and molestation.

Both in substance and contour, the Smokies are among the oldest mountains in the world. In contrast to the predominating limestone of the ridges in the Great Valley, and the sandstone of the Cumberland Plateau, the geological formations of the Smoky Mountains are varied, including such sedimentary rocks as conglomerates, sandstone, shales, limestones, dolomites, and some metamorphic rocks derived from these. All the layers have been folded. Igneous rock is found just outside the boundary in North Carolina.

Unlike many of the western mountains, whose rocky summits are almost bare of vegetation, all of the highest peaks in this park are covered with dense forests of conifers. Mountains of intermediate height are overlaid with hardwoods. Some of the mountain tops, known as "balds", are covered only with grass. From these unobstructed vantage points, wonderful panoramic views are disclosed. Others of these mountains have an ericaceous or heathlike cover of laurel, rhododendron, and related shrubs.

As might be expected in mountains so richly clothed in vegetation, numerous streams tumble down steep, narrow valleys with frequent cascades and waterfalls. Among the latter are Rainbow Falls, on the north slope of Mount LeConte, with a direct drop of 82 feet; Ramsey Falls, 100 feet high, near Greenbrier, northeast of LeConte; and Abrams Falls, not exceptionally high but with a voluminous and continuous flow of water, on Abrams Creek below Cades Cove in the southwest section of the park.

Inasmuch as the minimum congressional requirement of 400,000 acres has only recently been reached, major development of the tract has not yet been started. Located relatively near the most populous sections of the United States, the park commands an attendance greater than that of any other national park except Shenandoah. For the year ending October 1, 1937, there were 727,000 visitors.

A large part of the Great Smoky Mountains consists of superlative and primeval wilderness areas. It is obvious that when the contemplated development has been completed, there will be vastly greater use of the park than at present. This fact places a great responsibility on those in authority to see to it that the park's irreplaceable wilderness scenic values will not be impaired. Fortunately plans for the park give evidence of recognizing this necessity. The whole east half will be retained in its primeval condition, reached only by wilderness trails. Roughly speaking, this half is separated from the western section by the Newfound Gap highway. This road and an 8-mile crest drive from Newfound Gap to Clingmans Dome were completed in 1936. Consideration has been given to the possibility of creating a lake in Cades Cove by the damming of Abrams Creek. Another potentiality is the damming of the same creek near its confluence with the Little Tennessee River.

More definitely planned projects include an administrative center near Gatlinburg, numerous foot and bridle trails (some already built), several vacation camp areas, picnic grounds, and shelters.

Carlos Campbell, Knoxville

From a rocky shoulder of LeConte two hikers survey Clingmans Dome, 7 miles distant.

QUALLA INDIAN RESERVATION
[F-6]

This reservation, which belongs to the Cherokee Indians, is located in North Carolina between the Great Smoky Mountains National Park and portions of the Pisgah and the Nantahala National Forests. It comprises 73 square miles of mountain land ranging in elevation from 2,000 to 5,000 feet. With the national park, it shares the watershed of the Ocona-lufty River, and also includes a separate smaller tract of mountain ridge southeast of Bryson City.

The reservation contains land of distinctly scenic character, but its recreational significance to the public is limited. Interesting spectacles for visitors are furnished by the annual Cherokee festivals, in which opportunities are given to view Indian games, dancing, and handcraft.

The fact that this is a public reservation should insure control over its scenic values, a fact which is of significance to motorists and to hikers in adjacent park and forest lands, from which the Qualla Reservation is visible. United States Highway 19 and North Carolina Highways 107 and 112 pass through or near the reservation.

Wrathful waters of Soco Falls have choked their own stream with tangled debris.

CHEROKEE NATIONAL FOREST
[G-4, C-6]

The Unaka Division of Cherokee National Forest which lies northeast of the Great Smoky Mountains

National Park has been described in chapter I. A description of the Cherokee Division southwest of the park follows.

The Cherokee Division extends in a southwesterly direction along the Tennessee-North Carolina line in Tennessee from the Little Tennessee River to the Georgia line. It includes the heavily wooded mountainous sections within Monroe and Polk Counties, Tenn. The Cherokee Division includes 459,573 acres in southeast Tennessee. The forest growth is varied, with numerous ecological or environmental groups.

The Cherokee Division does not have as spectacular scenery as other portions of the Blue Ridge Province, notably the Great Smoky Mountains National Park and the Nantahala National Forest. The peaks are generally lower, averaging 3,500 feet in height. A few peaks of greater elevation are found along the eastern boundary. Among the loftiest of these are: Big Fodderstack, 4,300 feet; Laurel Top, 5,300 feet; Haw Knob, 5,500 feet; Big Frog Mountain, 4,200 feet; and Oswald Dome, 3,200 feet.

Recreational uses of the forest are encouraged. Chief among these are hunting, fishing, hiking, camping, and picnicking. Several scenic drives have been constructed through the forest, and the use of fire and truck trails by pleasure cars is encouraged. The Tellico River drive extends from Tellico Plains for 22 miles along the Tellico River to the North Carolina line. Narrow and winding, the drive closely follows the river in grade and alignment. It is generally an attractive river valley road, but somewhat cluttered by private cabins on land not owned by the Forest Service. Close to the road is Bald River Falls, approximately 100 feet high. From the road, numerous trails and roads lead up tributary creeks and abutting ridges. One of these leads to a site for summer homes at Pheasant Field. This site has 15 lots available at a small annual rental for the erection of camps and homes whose plans meet standards established by the Forest Service.

The Kimsey Highway (Tennessee Highway 40) a very scenic but narrow, winding road, extending from Tennessee Highway 39 south of Etowah to Ducktown, affords magnificent views from various points. For a considerable distance it reaches an elevation of 3,000 feet in traversing the summit of Little Frog Mountain. Other through roads are the Joe Brown Highway from Tellico Plains to Murphy, N. C., and Tennessee Highway 68 from Tellico Plains to the Kimsey Highway at Harbuck.

The forest has considerable historical interest.

It was the favorite hunting ground of the Cherokee Indians and they had villages at Tellico Plains and at various points along the Little Tennessee River within the forest boundary. Just outside the forest is the site of Fort Loudoun, built in 1756–57 by the British to protect these Indian villages from the French. Fort Loudoun is described later in this chapter.

Just southeast of Tellico Plains, Laurel Creek has been dammed to make Tellico Lake, which covers about 15 acres. The lake and its environs are owned by a club with a small membership. There is a lodge and a few cabins. The feature is mentioned because it lies within the forest boundary, and might at some time be available for public ownership and use.

Bullet Falls, 10 miles airline distance, southwest of Tellico Plains, is an attractive waterfall, 25 to 30 feet

Tellico Lake, a private fishing reserve in the Cherokee Forest.

Provident nature furnishes this fishing pool at the foot of Bald River Falls in Cherokee National Forest.

Unchecked fumes from copper smelters reduced this area of 15 square miles in the Ducktown Basin to a barren wasteland—colorful in vivid reds and violets and yellows—yet tragic in its utter desolation.

high, with a good dry-weather flow. It is reached by a county road which runs up Starr Mountain.

Another feature within Cherokee Forest is the Parksville Lake, 15 miles east of Cleveland, Tenn., on United States Highway 64. Created by a power dam of the Tennessee Electric Power Co., this reservoir has an area of approximately 2,000 acres, subject to a considerable draw-down. A private hotel, with bathing and boating facilities, is included among the recreational developments of the lake.

A national game refuge of 30,000 acres is located on Big Frog Mountain between the Ocoee River and the Georgia line and between Tumbling Creek, Sylco, and Sheeds Creeks in Tennessee. Deer, wild turkey and other game are protected at all times, and fish are propagated in special pools within the area. The area is so located that game will spread from it into other parts of the forest.

A tract of 100,000 acres lying on the upper watersheds of the Tellico River and Citico Creek has been

The Kimsey Highway affords this sweeping view over the Ducktown Basin.

87

designated as the Tellico Fish and Game Management Area, a cooperative project between the Tennessee Department of Conservation and the United States Forest Service. A program of stocking and propagation will replenish the area with deer, other game, and fish. For 5 years hunting will be prohibited and fishing permitted only under special regulations. An exception to hunting prohibitions is the 2-week wild boar hunt conducted each year in November, the quarry being a mixed strain of domestic hogs and imported Prussian boar. This hunt, instituted in 1936, gives promise of becoming a nationally recognized sporting event.

A recreational center known as Lake McCamy is under construction near the top of Bean's Mountain. The development includes a dam 20 feet high and 225 feet long, creating an artificial lake of 12 acres which will be available for swimming. The elevation of 2,500 feet gives to the development a climatic advantage which is recognized in plans for a group of vacation cabins and a central recreational building. Other sites around the lake may be available for private lease under suitable restrictions. The development may be reached by way of the "Waterlevel Road", a Forest Service truck trail leading from Parksville Lake to Oswald Dome.

Below the dam Rock Creek drops quickly from the

This limpid pool on the lower Tellico River invites a cooling plunge.

top of the mountain to join the Ocoee River near the head of Parksville Lake. The stream is a series of 12 cascades, of which Benton Falls is the most outstanding. At this point, the flow of the stream spreads in a thin veil over the fractured face of the cliff over which it drops, forming a contrast between the vertical lines of the stream and the horizontal bedding of the rock. A luxuriant growth of rhododendron fills the stream valley and forms a setting for the falls. Trails leading from Lake McCamy or from United States Highway 64 follow the stream past Benton Falls.

Cecil Pearce, Knoxville

Casting for a big one in the boulder-strewn waters of the Tellico River in Cherokee National Forest.

In Ravenel Primeval Forest venerable hemlocks rise from a tangle of rhododendron.

NANTAHALA NATIONAL FOREST
[E-7]

Nantahala Forest, established in 1911, lies south of the Little Tennessee River entirely in North Carolina. A total of 1,349,000 acres is included in its boundaries.

The mountains in this forest are considerably higher than those in the Cherokee National Forest, and in general compare favorably in elevation with those of the Pisgah National Forest; though only a few peaks along the northeast boundary, which it shares with Pisgah Forest, attain anything like the heights reached by Pisgah Ridge and the Black Mountains in the Pisgah Forest, or with the altitudes of the Great Smoky Mountains. Richland Balsam Mountain, one of the Balsam Range, on the Pisgah Forest border line, has an elevation of 6,540 feet, the highest point in Nantahala Forest. Another high peak within the forest is Waterrock Knob, elevation 6,400 feet, on the same mountain range.

It is impracticable to note all the mountains in the Nantahala Forest that have distinct scenic interest, or from which remarkable views may be obtained. Therefore, only a few have been selected for special mention; either because they are physically outstanding in their localities, because they are easily accessible, or for some other unique characteristic. A partial list of the better known mountains includes Wayah Bald (5,300), west of Franklin; Standing Indian (5,500) and Pickens Nose (4,905), southwest of Franklin; Whiteside Mountain (4,930), northeast of Highlands; and Cheoah Bald (5,000), east of Lake Santeetlah, and Hangover Mountain (5,200) west of Lake Santeetlah. Wayah Bald and Whiteside are individually discussed and illustrated.

Although most of the wooded land in the forest is second growth, there are within its boundaries two areas of virgin timber: one a tract of about 4,000 acres, known as the Joyce Kilmer Forest, west of Lake Santeetlah, in the northwest extremity of the forest; the other a privately owned tract of several hundred acres known as Ravenel's Primeval Forest, near Highlands, N. C. The latter contains mostly hemlock, with scattered giant oaks; the former tract is chiefly significant for its huge tulip trees, 5 to 7 feet in diameter.

The Nantahala National Forest was established partly for the conservation of timber lands, and partly for the protection of the watersheds of navigable rivers. Among the chief tributaries of these rivers are the Little Tennessee, Nantahala, Tuckasegee, and Cheoah Rivers in the Tennessee River Basin, and the rivers in the Savannah River Basin. A number of artificial lakes have been created in the Nantahala Forest, some of which were built primarily for power production, and some for recreational use. None of them has received very extensive recreational development. But with increasing recognition of recreation as one of the major functions of national forests, the Nantahala Forest, because of its general scenic character and its many specific scenic features of more than local interest, is destined to play an important part in any recreational development program for the eastern Tennessee valley.

The Nantahala Forest might well be called the "Land of Waterfalls", containing, as it does, two dozen or so cataracts worthy of special mention. In addition to these more important falls, it is reported that nearly every creek has at least minor cascades, which in a region less plentifully supplied with falls might be considered noteworthy.

There is a marked difference in character between the falls in this territory and those of the Cumberland Plateau, as described elsewhere in this report. In the plateau, the relatively young sedimentary layers of sandstone and limestone are usually clearly distinguishable, with the result that streams either cascade over a series of distinct strata, or, where soft layers are present or the water has sufficient force, the falls may be more or less deeply undercut, resulting in a sheer drop. In the Nantahala Forest, however, the geological formations are much older, and individual strata of rock have metamorphosed into a uniform structure. Whiteoak Creek Falls is the only one that shows any suggestion of stratification in the underlying rock. Because of this general character of the rock, falls in the Nantahala Forest are typically either "slides", such as Onion Falls, a term used to describe the slipping of water down over a relatively smooth rock slope, or else a series of irregular cascades, such as Cullasaja Falls. There are very few cases where, as at Dry Falls, the water shoots out in a headlong drop over a ledge.

The forest is crossed by three United States Highways: 19, 23, and 64; the Blue Ridge Parkway will form its northeast boundary, and various improved State and Forest Service roads give further access to a large proportion of the territory.

Wayah Bald
[E-7]

Wayah Bald, 10 miles airline due west of Franklin, is one of the best known peaks in the forest and, at present, the most accessible. A surfaced Forest Service road runs from United States Highway 64 at

Fisher, Asheville

From this rocky clearing in Nantahala National Forest, Hangover Mountain crowns the horizon.

90

Fisher, Asheville

Wayah Bald, outstanding peak of Nantahala Forest, rises abruptly from a cove typical of the highlands.

a point 5 miles west of Franklin for 33 miles to Nantahala, in the Nantahala Gorge, on United States Highway 19. Fourteen and one-half miles from Franklin, at Wayah Gap, another Forest Service road leaves this one and winds up to the top of Wayah Bald, where there is a stone observation tower. Further development of the mountain top as a vantage point is contemplated by the Forest Service.

Wayah Bald is the northeastern extremity of a boomerang-shaped ridge of which Wine Spring Bald forms the middle point and Rocky Bald the northwest end. The views from Wayah Bald are superb; in all directions mountains extend to the limit of vision. A noteworthy feature of the mountain is its extensive growth of azaleas, which in the spring furnish a remarkable display of colorful bloom.

Including Wayah Bald, and stretching to south and east of it, is the Wayah State Game Preserve, covering about 15 square miles. This tract, established in 1928, is maintained cooperatively by the State of North Carolina and the Forest Service.

Whiteside Mountain
[F–7]

Whiteside Mountain lies 4 miles, airline distance, northeast of Highlands. Although its elevation is not exceptional, it rises so abruptly from its base and offers such commanding and magnificent views of its surroundings that it achieves primary importance from a recreational point of view.

Six miles northeast of Highlands on United States Highway 64, a road leads off to the south for a quarter of a mile to a marked but undeveloped Forest Service picnic ground. From here a well-defined trail goes up to the southwest extremity of Whiteside, and for three-fourths of a mile along its crest. A branch trail leads northward to a curious dome-like promontory, called the Devil's Courthouse.

The western slope of Whiteside is relatively gradual, but the eastern face is an abrupt cliff, perpendicular in places, with vertical striations recalling the basaltic formations of the western mountains. This same type of rock face is to be seen on other lower mountains and ridges which enclose Whiteside Cove, south-west of Whiteside Mountain.

The top of the mountain is sparsely wooded, mostly with chestnut, some of which still retains a feeble existence despite the recent blight. In no direction, however, are views restricted by tree growth.

Good views of Whiteside are obtainable from several nearby roads; notably from Bearpen Mountain, the top of which is slightly more than a mile north-east of Highlands over a fairly good gravel road; also from United States Highway 64 at Cowee Gap or Sunrise, as it is also called, 6 miles from Highlands; and again from United States Highway 64 about 3 miles beyond Cowee Gap, toward Cashiers. The most impressive views of the mountain, however, are from Whiteside Cove, where the sheer height of the cliffs is completely visible. Undoubtedly there are few mountains in the whole Blue Ridge Province that present as many varied aspects from different angles as does Whiteside. This fact, combined with the remarkable views obtainable from the mountain itself, give it a unique position among points of scenic interest in the area.

Whiteside Mountain is spectacular in its abrupt rise above the valley.

Sheer, barren cliffs of Whiteside Mountain, visible for miles, make it an outstanding scenic attraction of Nantahala Forest.

Highlands Falls
[F-7]

The Cullasaja River is one of the more important tributaries of the Little Tennessee River. In the few miles from its source at Cowee Gap, through Highlands to the mouth just above Franklin, it pursues a turbulent course, and contains five waterfalls worthy of special description in this chapter.

About 2½ miles, airline distance, northeast of Highlands, is Highlands Falls surrounded by a virgin hemlock forest. The falls begins as a slide but the lower portion takes an abrupt drop, altogether making a total height of about 100 feet. Though less than half a mile from United States Highway 64, it is at present rather inaccessible, being reached by about a 2-mile hike over trails through Ravenel's Primeval Forest from the north, or from Highlands to the south. From the road on top of Bearpen Mountain, about a mile away, one gets a fair view of the falls to the north.

Bridal Veil Falls
[F-7]

About 4½ miles northwest of Highlands, United States Highway 64 makes a sharp curve into a rock ledge in order to pass under Bridal Veil Falls. A combined slide and vertical drop in a small tributary of the Cullasaja, carrying no great amount of water, the falls is noteworthy because of the unique experience of driving underneath a waterfall.

To avoid a drenching, United States Highway 64 dodges behind the cataract of Bridal Veil Falls in Nantahala Forest.

93

Dry Falls of the Cullasaja River—so named because one may walk between the tumbling curtain of water and the deeply-undercut ledge.
United States Highway 64 runs within a few yards of the falls.

U. S. Forest Service

The course of turbulent Cullasaja River, in Nantahala Forest, is followed by United States Highway 64.

Over frothy Cullasaja Falls, the tormented waters of Cullasaja River take their final plunge.

Dry Falls
[F-7]

A mile northwest of Bridal Veil, the Cullasaja drops about 75 feet over Dry Falls, so-called because the river, having considerably undercut the rock below the falls, rushes precipitately over a ledge in such a way as to make it possible to walk without difficulty behind it. The Forest Service has constructed an easily traversable path from a large roadside parking area down to this falls.

A short distance below Dry Falls is Van Hook Glade, a small but much-used forest tent campground.

Cullasaja Falls
[F-7]

Ten and a half miles from Highlands and 10 miles from Franklin, the river forms Cullasaja Falls, a series of cascades totaling 100 feet or more of fall. The falls are readily visible to the passing motorist.

The furious waters of Tuckasegee River crash over High Falls in a mighty display of power.

Onion Falls
[F–7]

The Tuckasegee River is the largest tributary of the Little Tennessee River. In the upper reaches of the West Fork, which has its source just north of Cowee Gap, there are two important waterfalls, Onion Falls and High Falls.

Onion Falls, also called Engrons Falls ("engron" being the local name for the wild onion), is located close to North Carolina Highway 106, 9 miles north of its intersection with United States Highway 64. It is a good example of the waterslide, about 100 feet in height.

High Falls
[F–7]

The High Falls of the Tuckasegee unquestionably rank among the three or four most beautiful and impressive cataracts in the Tennessee Valley Region. Located only about a quarter of a mile below Onion Falls, High Falls is concealed from North Carolina Highway 106 by a ridge. On the north side of a gap about a half-mile north of Onion Falls, an obvious trail leads over a low ridge and down the other side for another half a mile or less to the base of the falls. The main fall is about 125 feet to a great protrusion of rock on which the sheer mass of water is shattered. The water plunges through the balance of its descent in several separated cascades. Above the falls steep rapids account for an additional drop of 50 feet or so. For sheer turbulence this cataract is hardly surpassed by any of those visited in connection with this survey. A good stand of hemlock and hardwoods form the immediate setting around the falls, but the neighboring lands are covered with unimpressive second-growth timber.

Rainbow Falls
[G–7]

The Horsepasture River glides some hundred feet down a sloping rock face to form Rainbow Falls, 40 feet high. The face is smooth and unbroken, imparting to the water an unusually impressive appearance of swift, gliding motion. Even at times of comparatively high water, this almost oily smoothness characterizes the flow.

The falls lie in a narrow valley, wooded with mixed hardwoods, white pine, and hemlock, through which is scattered a rich undergrowth of rhododendron. The Boheynee Road, a dry-weather county road of dirt surface, leads past the falls, 2 miles south of the United States Highway 64 at Oakland Post Office.

Below Rainbow Falls, the Horsepasture River forms three more falls of distinctive character. The first below is a tumbling cascade whose churning waters contrast markedly with the smooth swiftness of Rainbow. The crest of the second is hidden beneath an overhanging ledge, permitting the spectator to watch the water move swiftly below him and be violently discharged outward and downward from a fissure at one side. It makes a total drop of some 40 feet. Still farther downstream the River makes its fourth and final plunge in a semi-cascade over a 60-foot cliff. An open glade below it permits unusual views.

The swift waters of the Horsepasture River race into a restless pool below Rainbow Falls.

Toxaway Falls
[G–7]

Toxaway, a most interesting falls of the slide type, lies immediately below the old damsite of Lake Toxaway, which was an artificial lake created 25 years ago as the central feature of one of the most attractive resort developments in the southern Appalachians. Flood waters, released when the dam gave way in 1916, stripped the gorge below it bare of vegetation, which has not been appreciably restored since that time. The exposed rock surface, in great planes, has weathered a mellow grey.

The face of this 125-foot falls is convex, like a quarter-dome, almost architectural in its perfection. The profile curve of the dome is interrupted one-third of the way from the top by a vertical offset 15 feet high, above which the same curve of the dome is carried to its crown. The dome is set in a corner between the end wall and side wall of the gorge which meet at right angles at the center of the dome.

97

The rock face of the falls is softly rippled, causing the flowing water to assume the familiar arrowhead pattern. A few potholes near the base break the otherwise smooth flow.

United States Highway 64 crosses Toxaway River at the top of the falls and at this point affords views to the north across the old lake bed to Panthertail Mountain and Tennessee Ridge. It is necessary to leave the highway and descend to the gorge in order to obtain adequate views of the falls.

Toxaway River, below the crossing of United States Highway 64, slides 125 feet down this bare quarter-dome. Stripped of soil and vegetation in 1916 by the rampaging waters from a burst dam, the rocks remain naked.

Whitewater Falls
[G-7]

Among the more spectacular waterfalls of the Nantahala National Forest is Whitewater Falls, lying in a remote portion of the forest near the South Carolina line. The falls is more than 325 feet in total height, but it is broken midway by a sloping shelf over which the stream cascades with considerable show. Although the immediate vicinity of the falls has been heavily cut over and frequently burned, forest growth is returning to a healthy appearance.

The falls may be reached by way of the Boheynee Road past Rainbow Falls, a dry-weather county road of unimproved dirt surface. The road leads past the base of the falls, but a short hike to adjacent vantage points will obtain better views.

Whiteoak Creek Falls
[E-7]

Several miles east of United States Highway 19, the Nantahala-Wayah Bald Forest Service road winds up the valley of Whiteoak Creek. It passes close to an attractive waterfall, consisting of six stepped cascades, totalling about 30 feet in height. Mention has already been made of the fact that such stratification is unusual in this territory. The falls has a setting of considerable natural charm despite its utilization as the source of power for a small watermill.

Whitewater Falls, a seldom-visited wonder of Nantahala Forest.

The lower portion of Glen Falls glides between borders of flowering rhododendron.

Queens Creek Falls
[E-6]

The section of the Forest Service Nantahala-Wayah Bald Road, immediately east of United States Highway 19, is called Winding Stairs because of the course that it takes in ascending the east side of Nantahala Gorge. Near the top of this ascent, the road passes two falls on Queens Creek, a few hundred feet apart. Both are irregular water slides with the upper one the more impressive. There is a total drop in the two falls of perhaps 150 feet, the upper falls contributing two-thirds of that height. The surroundings are not particularly attractive, showing evidence of considerable grading for the road, clearing of ground cover, etc. Also a power line crosses directly over the creek at this point. This swath will always detract from the falls, but restoration of natural plant growth under forest management will considerably improve the setting of the falls.

From the hairpin turn on United States Highway 129, just before that road begins its descent of the west side of Nantahala Gorge, a glimpse may be had of Queens Creek Falls, about 2 miles away.

Glen Falls
[F-7]

Glen Falls, one of the best known cataracts of the Nantahala Forest, is located on the East Prong of Overflow Creek, a tributary of the Chatooga River, 2½ miles, airline distance, southwest of Highlands. About 2½ miles from Highlands, on the Forest Service road to Dillard, Ga., a fair gravel road branches off to the south. Then, after a little over a mile along this road, a fork leads to the right, continuing as a trail to the waterfall. The upper 50 feet of Glen Falls consists of cascades; the lower 100 feet of a slide.

Cheoah Lake
[D-6]

Second of the Aluminum Co. power lakes, Cheoah Lake lies on the Little Tennessee River in Graham and Swain Counties, N. C., south of the Great Smoky Mountains National Park. Covering 700 acres, it is 7 miles long but, like Calderwood, seldom over a few hundred feet wide. On the south it is bordered by the Nantahala Forest, but on the north a strip of private land intervenes between the lake and the national park boundary. Its steep shores are almost completely forested with second-growth hardwoods, but the narrow valleys of tributary creeks support a few farms whose owners guide fishing parties on the lake. A

hotel and cabins at Tapoco, N. C., below the dam, afford accommodations for visitors. The chief recreational significance of the lake, however, lies in the views of it from nearby vantage points. United States Highway 129 crosses the Little Tennessee immediately below the dam, and North Carolina Highway 288 skirts the northern shore.

Calderwood Lake
[C-6]

Calderwood Lake is the lowest of the chain developed in the Little Tennessee River by the Aluminum Co. of America. It lies in Blount and Monroe Counties, Tenn., and Graham and Swain Counties, N. C. The area around it is sparsely settled. Covering some 500 acres, the lake is 9 miles long but seldom more than a few hundred feet wide, for at no point does it extend far beyond the original river channel in a narrow, steeply walled valley. The lake is accessible from United States Highway 129, a portion of the "Outer Loop", a scenic highway around the Great Smokies. The Cherokee and the Nantahala National Forests border the lake on the southwest.

Although the lake is used somewhat for fishing, there are few boats on the lake, and the steep banks invite little intensive recreational use. The chief scenic and recreational significance derives from views of the lake from nearby roads and mountain peaks.

Carlos Campbell, Knoxville

Mountain shadows close in on deep-set Calderwood Lake as the sun silhouettes two hikers.

Lake Santeetlah
[D-6]

The only large lake in this territory at present is Lake Santeetlah. This major storage reservoir in the hydrogenerating system of the Aluminum Co. of America covers some 2,700 acres in the northwest corner of Nantahala Forest. Formed by damming the Cheoah River, a tributary of the Little Tennessee, the lake has a beautiful setting, surrounded as it is by high mountains. At its normal water level, the lake is a thing of beauty in itself, because of its rambling shore line and dark green water. However, as a storage reservoir, it is subject to a maximum draw-down of over 40 feet. Thus, in dry periods the exposed mud flats are not only unsightly, but also form a hindrance to recreational use of the water. Consequently, although there is a limited number of summer cabins, the effect of summer draw-down has been to retard resort development. Although good fishing is reported in the spring and early summer, extensive and rapid fluctuations of the water level are unfavorable

Matterns', Knoxville

Nantahala Forest holds many attractive campsites—this one is on the shores of Lake Santeetlah.

to fishing in other seasons of the year.

United States Highway 129, a through highway from Knoxville to the south, winds along the eastern shore of the lake for about 10 miles, and offers varied views of numerous coves and wooded promontories.

Thompsons, Knoxville

Many-armed Lake Santeetlah, high in the mountains of Nantahala National Forest, beckons the adventurer

Hiwassee Lake
[C-7]

TVA has commenced construction of a dam on the Hiwassee River below the town of Murphy. Hiwassee Lake, created by this dam, will lie in a narrow mountain gorge with a tortuous, interesting shoreline. Several long arms will flood creeks and tributary rivers. At normal elevation this reservoir will have an area of about 6,300 acres, with a shoreline of 150 miles. There will be an extreme drawdown of 111 feet and lesser fluctuations will occur frequently. This factor may restrict recreation on the reservoir to fishing, or to other recreational uses only when the reservoir is full.

The land forms around Murphy and along Hiwassee Lake are ridges and knobs, not parallel, of a continuous character which tend to be monotonous, and from which no particularly sweeping views are obtained. Murphy, at the junction of Valley River and Hiwassee River, is on United States Highways 19, 64, and 129. A TVA access road leads to the dam site from the junction of North Carolina Highways 68 and 294; the latter road and the Joe Brown Memorial Highway cross embayments of the reservoir. Except for these points, access will be difficult.

Lake Emory
[F-7]

Lake Emory, slightly over 100 acres in extent, is formed by damming the Little Tennessee River a few miles north of Franklin. This lake forms part of the power system of the Nantahala Power & Light Co., but siltation has become so serious as to impair the usefulness of the reservoir. This fact also limits its present and future recreational value.

Lake Sequoyah
[F-7]

Lake Sequoyah is the reservoir for the Highlands Municipal Power Plant. A concrete dam, close to United States Highway 64, backs up the Cullasaja River to form a 46-acre lake in an attractive wooded setting. The town owns all the land around the lake and is selling to private purchasers for building sites, apparently without reserving any portion for public park purposes. As yet, however, no considerable amount of private development has taken place.

Aptly-named Lake Sapphire sparkles in a verdant setting.

Private Recreational Lakes

Several small lakes have been created within the Nantahala National Forest for private or restricted commercial use. Lake Fairfield, the largest of these, covers some 37 acres and is used by patrons of Fairfield Inn and a private camp for girls on land leased from the owner of the inn. A 5-acre lake adjoins High Hampton Inn south of Cashiers. On the upper Chattooga River adjacent to the village at Cashiers, a lake of 27 acres has been developed for recreational use, although such use is apparently slight at the present time. Its shores are marshy and scenically undistinguished. There is, as yet, no effect of plant growth such as would normally be found about a natural body of water. The Country Club at Highlands has a 9-acre lake on its grounds. Lake Sapphire of 27 acres and Ravenel Lake of 23 acres are included within the grounds of private estates.

Scenic Motorways

United States Highway 64 is especially scenic during most of its course through the Nantahala Forest. Noteworthy points and sections are views from Glade Gap, Wallace Gap, and Cowee Gap; the gorge of the Cullasaja River, between Franklin and Highlands; and, in general, that part of the road between Cowee Gap and the eastern boundary of this area.

United States Highway 19, south of the Little Tennessee River, offers good views of the Smoky Mountains at several points. The portion of this highway which follows the river through Nantahala Gorge is well known to motorists.

United States Highway 23, at Watauga Gap, between Franklin and Dillsboro, provides a good view of the mountains to the north.

United States Highway 129, from the Tennessee-North Carolina State line to Robbinsville, at the south extremity of Lake Santeetlah, is as scenic as it is circuitous. At the place where it begins the descent to Nantahala Gorge, the view is well worthy of further development of the present inadequate observation point.

North Carolina Highway 288 runs from United States Highway 129 to Bryson City, following the north bank of the Little Tennessee River very closely for nearly the whole distance. Although very winding, the drive offers a worth-while scenic trip.

The United States Forest Service road from Franklin to Nantahala has already been referred to several times. Though not of superlative scenic interest, its varied character and well-maintained gravel surface makes this a very pleasing road.

Lovely Lake Fairfield blends with its setting.

U. S. Forest Service

From Wallace Gap, on United States Highway 64, wave after wave of sun-flecked forest rolls away toward the northeast.

Nantahala Gorge, invaded by rail, highway, and power lines, has surrendered much of its once-wild beauty.

Virgin yellow poplars of tremendous size dwarf a varied undergrowth in Joyce Kilmer Forest.

CHATTAHOOCHEE NATIONAL FOREST
[A–8, F–8]

The Chattahoochee National Forest,[1] comprising 1,165,000 acres of forest land in north Georgia, was formed in July 1936 from portions of the Nantahala and Cherokee National Forests, which prior to that date extended into Georgia, together with additional land around the two. Located almost entirely in highlands, it is bounded on the north by the North Carolina State line, on the east by the Chattooga River, forming the South Carolina State line, on the south by the Piedmont Plateau, and on the west by the Great Appalachian Valley. It encloses within these boundaries the southern extremity of the Blue Ridge province, a region of rugged mountains heavily forested and intersected by narrow coves and valleys which are drained by swiftly cascading streams.

The mountains for the most part, aline themselves in narrow ridges which display no pronounced directional lines. Occasional peaks, either isolated or rising above the general contour of the ridges, break the skyline and impart an appearance of greater height to the mass. The highest elevations in the forest are associated with the Blue Ridge which describes a huge semicircle through the forest, enclosing the watershed of the Hiwassee River. Brasstown Bald, or Enotah, 4,768 feet and highest mountain in Georgia, leads as a spur from the Blue Ridge. Rabun Bald, 4,750 feet, and Hightower Bald, 4,567 feet, on the Ridge near the North Carolina line; Big Bald, 4,120 feet, at the opposite extremity; Tray Mountain, 4,398 feet; and Blood Mountain, 4,463 feet, are the highest points on the Ridge itself, which averages over 4,000 feet for most of its distance within Georgia. Other mountain groups, including the Cohuttas in the west, the Amicalolas in the south, the Tallulah Mountains in the east, and Duncan Ridge in the interior, may reach elevations up to 4,100 feet but in general average approximately 3,500 feet.

Narrow coves, valleys, or gorges between the mountains offer slight invitation to clearing. Slopes are precipitous and flood plains narrow or entirely absent. Occasionally, however, advanced erosion has created intermontane basins such as those around Hayesville and Ducktown. Agriculture has cleared a high percentage of the rolling upland within these basins, which have been excluded from the forest boundaries.

The forest is the source of major tributaries of the Tennessee, Savannah, Coosa, and Chattahoochee Rivers. Their headwater character is reflected in the swift, often precipitous, courses of the numerous streams. Waterfalls are frequent; cascades and rapids almost inevitable. Watermills at intervals along many of the smaller streams and power lakes on the rivers testify to the economic water resource within the area. Dense forest cover, still luxuriant despite having been almost completely cut over, insures a permanent flow in the stream courses.

Forest types vary from the southern hardwoods at the lower elevations bordering the Piedmont, to the more northern conifers on mountain slope and summit. Although the forest lies entirely beyond the southern limit of spruce and balsam, white pine and hemlock grow on the north slopes, yellow pine on the south. Redbud, dogwood, azalea, mountain laurel, and three rhododendron species give rich floral displays during May and June. Natural heath or grass balds cap several mountain peaks; their character is implied in the names of many. The Toccoa experimental forest is conducting forest management studies on a 4,000-acre tract in Union County.

Wildlife within the forest includes all native upland species except wolf and mountain lion, which disappeared during the past century. Deer, bear, and fox are increasing in number under the Forest Service management, and smaller species abound. Streams continue to offer good fishing, and are being restocked by the Forest Service. A game refuge managed by the State in cooperation with the Forest Service on Federal lands affords protection to all species of native game within the boundaries of its 14,000 acres.

The Chattahoochee, ancestral hunting ground of the Cherokee Indians and their refuge in time of war, was first explored by the white man in 1539 when De Soto established a winter camp in the Nacoochee Valley. Traders from Virginia and the Carolinas came into the area a century later, and, under the treaty of 1777, large grants were given to Revolutionary War veterans from Carolina. In 1835 the Indians were removed to Oklahoma and the whole block was acquired by the whites. Soon afterwards, a few settlers began to penetrate the mountains and to make permanent homes in the wilderness, although exploitation of timber resources did not get under way until the latter part of the nineteenth century. Purchases by the Forest Service followed passage of the Weeks Law in 1911. The culture of the Cherokees remains indelibly imprinted on the Chattahoochee in the names of mountains, streams, and many villages. Many tangible remains include Indian mounds in

[1] Information on the Chattahoochee Forest is from the U. S. Forest Service, TVA Forestry Division, and published material.

the Nacoochee Valley, bathhouses in caves along the Soque River near Clarksville, Track Rock near Blairsville, and the ruins of Fort Mountain.

Northern Georgia was among the first highland areas to receive intensive recreational development. Before the Civil War, planters from Savannah and Charleston, seeking to escape the humid, feverish summer climate of the coastal plain, brought their whole establishments to the higher altitudes of the Blue Ridge Province. Difficult access prevented their going far into the interior and summer colonies sprang up in the vicinity of Nacoochee Valley and Tallulah Falls. Slaves were set to digging gold, so vacations proved profitable as well as enjoyable for the owners. Improved access allowed further penetration to later resort sites at Mountain City, Lake Rabun, Clayton, and outlying localities. Climate and scenery still hold many people to the vicinity, although newer summer colonies have sprung up in the greater elevations of western North Carolina.

Included within the boundaries of Chattahoochee Forest are seven power lakes, six of them forming a related development by the Georgia Power Co. on the Tugaloo and Tallulah Rivers. The seventh is a storage reservoir developed by the Tennessee Electric Power Co. on the Toccoa River. The recreational possibilities of these reservoirs have only recently been fully explored. Under the influence of the Forest Service, the Emergency Conservation Work program has made them more available to the general public with improved access roads and the development of active recreational facilities.

Burton Lake
[E–8]

Its 2,775 acres make Burton the largest of the six related Georgia Power Co. lakes. Primarily used for storage, it is subject to draw-downs of 40 or 50 feet from its normal pool elevation of 1,866 feet. Although recreation on the lake is neither encouraged nor discouraged, the low, wooded mountains around it permit good camping and hiking. Recent Forest Service roads have improved its accessibility, formerly available only at the point where United States Highway 76 crossed one of its narrow upper arms. It is the farthest upstream of the six reservoirs.

Lake Nacoochee
[E–8]

The level of this lake of 560 acres was barely raised from the former river channel by its 60-foot dam.

Steep wooded banks permit only occasional beach facilities which have been taken advantage of in recent years by an increased number of summer homes. A one-half mile section of lake frontage has been developed as a public beach and picnic area by the Forest Service in cooperation with the ECW program.

Lake Rabun
[E–9]

This lake of 834 acres and a pool elevation of 1,690 feet has been more intensively developed than any other of the chain. Many private cottages and estates have been built along its shores. Recently a beach, picnic, and camping area has been developed by the Forest Service. By agreement with individuals in the summer colony, the power company recognizes such recreational use and restricts its draw-down during the summer months. Both Lake Rabun and Lake Nacoochee have attractive settings beneath the Tallulah Mountains which rise 1,500 feet above them at the south.

Tallulah Falls Lake
[E–9]

The smallest of the six lakes, this reservoir includes only 63 acres. It is primarily devoted to power purposes, for it commands a head of 608 feet. It stands at the head of the former Tallulah Falls which was more than 400 feet high, and diverts the water around the natural falls in order to obtain increased head.

Tugalo Lake
[F–9]

A dam across the junction of the Tallulah and Chattooga Rivers creates Tugalo Lake of 557 acres. Its western arm lies at the bottom of the spectacular Tallulah Gorge, 600 feet deep and 2 miles long. The power developments have destroyed much of the naturalness of the gorge but it still remains an objective for hiking and horseback riding from the nearby resort developments in Tallulah Falls and on Lake Rabun and Lake Nacoochee.

Yonah Lake
[F–9]

This 425-acre lake is the lowest of the chain, and lies outside the boundaries of the forest. Although it may be subject to a draw-down of 10 feet, its shore line is adapted to recreational development which may come about in connection with the Northeast Georgia Upland Park.

Toccoa Lake
[B–8]

This lake, largest in the forest, serves as a storage reservoir for the Tennessee Electric Power Co. lakes on the Ocoee River. Covering 3,530 acres at its normal pool elevation of 1,690 feet, it is subject to a considerable draw-down. The lake occupies a basin 11 miles long and averaging more than a mile wide. Many small coves serve to create an illusion of increased size. Its setting embraces the low, forested hills at the south end of the Ducktown Basin. Recreational development is confined for the most part to roadhouses and fishing camps along United States Highway 76, which crosses the dam.

Amicalola Falls
[B–9]

Perhaps the most striking series of waterfalls in the entire southeast are those at the headwaters of Amicalola Creek on the boundary of the forest in northwestern Dawson County. The creek plunges a total of more than 700 feet in less than one-half mile down the precipitous face of Amicalola Mountain. It includes three major cascades and many smaller ones from 10 to 25 feet high. Although the flow of the stream is small, its regularity and clearness compensate. Until recently the falls have been isolated to all but the foot traveler. The Appalachian Trail passes within one-fourth mile of the top of the falls, and recently a Forest Service road has been constructed along the path of the trail so that one may drive to a vantage point above the falls. This point, in a setting of dense hardwood forest, affords a view down the steep course of the stream and out onto the broad Piedmont Plateau which spreads out below the falls.

High Falls
[C–9]

Within the State Game Refuge No. 2, in Fannin County, a high cascade drops from Little Rock Creek into Rock Creek, tributary of the Toccoa River. Its densely forested setting is remote although a trail leads up Rock Creek, by the base of the cascade.

Frogtown Creek Falls
[D–9]

Several cascades tumble from the side of a spur of Blood Mountain into Frogtown Creek on the south slope of the Blue Ridge. In wet weather they afford a spectacular display visible from United States Highway 19 south of Neels Gap.

Goslin Falls
[E–9]

This 80-foot cascade near Lake Rabun is typical of many shelved cascades found on other streams of the Chattahoochee Forest.

Estatoah Falls
[F–8]

In spite of an extremely variable flow, this falls has year-round interest in the large cliff over which it flows. It is visible from the Dillard-Highlands road, which ascends the gorge of Mud Creek.

Betty Creek Falls
[E–8]

Betty Creek cascades the length of a small but rather broad valley from the slopes of Pickens Nose in North Carolina into the Little Tennessee River. A Forest Service road borders the stream and permits ready access to the valley.

War Woman Creek Falls
[F–8]

A 40-foot fall is the highest of a group of several cascades near the headwaters of War Woman Creek, a tributary of the Chattooga River. The falls lie in a wooded cove one-half mile from War Woman Dell, Forest Service picnic area 4 miles east of Clayton.

Big Bend Falls
[F–8]

These falls are on the Chattooga River in the extremely wild northeast border of the forest. They are a low falls but have a considerable flow.

Brasstown Bald
[D–8]

The highest mountain in Georgia, Brasstown Bald, or Enotah, reaches a height of 4,768 feet on the boundary of Union and Towns Counties. Its broad summit is a natural bald permitting unobstructed vistas, and its position on a spur of the Blue Ridge permits glimpses through the Ridge and out to the Piedmont to the south. To the north it overlooks the Young Harris valley at its base and on clear days views extend as far as the Great Smokies.

Rabun Bald
[F–8]

Second highest in Georgia, Rabun Bald towers above the Blue Ridge and the headwaters of the Little

Fisher, Asheville

Hikers up the slopes of the Blue Ridge in Georgia rest to gaze across a sea of trees toward Rabun Bald.

Tennessee River in the northeast corner of the forest. To the north one may look along the Blue Ridge into western North Carolina; to the southeast over the broad, predominantly forested valley of the Chattooga; to the southwest over the cove of Mill Creek, with its heavy mantle of virgin pines, and beyond to successive mountain ranges of the Georgia Highlands. Forest Service drives lead nearly to the top of Rabun Bald from Clayton and the Dillard-Highlands road.

Glassy Mountain
[E-8]

Great faces of bare ledge, shining in the sunlight, give their name to Glassy Mountain, 3,521 feet high. It rises above the shores of Burton Lake and affords unusual vistas over water and forest to the long line of the Blue Ridge beyond. A Forest Service road

leading 7 miles from Tiger permits automobiles access to the lookout station on top of the mountain.

Black Rock
[E-8]

Black Rock forms the western wall of Rabun Gap. Its sheer stone face rises 1,700 feet above the floor of the gap to a total elevation of 3,700 feet. A road to its summit permits easy access to the vistas which it affords over the pastoral scenery of the valley below.

Yonah Mountain
[D–9]

Only 3,173 feet high, Yonah is none the less outstanding, for its position 4 miles out from the main mountain mass affords grandstand views over the entire forest south of the Blue Ridge. A cliff on the

110

west side of the mountain is associated by legend with the Cherokee Indians, one of whose number is supposed to have jumped from the top of its 600-foot face to the jagged rocks below. A Forest Service road leads from the Nacoochee Valley to a fire observation tower on the summit.

Lake Winfield Scott
[C-9]

This lake of 22 acres lies near the headwaters of Coopers Creek west of Blood Mountain. It is provided with picnicking and camping facilities, and summer home sites will be designated. The vicinity is heavily forested, but occasional clearings occupy small areas in nearly level coves along Coopers Creek. The access road, leading from United States Highway 19 at the lake in Vogel State Park, passes through Sosebee Cove below Wolf Pen Gap. In this cove a 60-year-old stand of yellow poplar shows examples of this species which are noteworthy in the entire southeast.

Grassy Mountain Lake
[A-8]

An earth-fill dam impounds a 17-acre lake near the headwaters of Mill Creek on the slopes of Grassy Mountain, 3,200 feet above sea level. The vicinity is heavily forested with hardwoods and white pine. Nearby is the gorge of the Conasauga River whose 1,000-foot walls are clothed with a luxuriant growth of white pine. Fed by the perpetually flowing waters from 11 natural outlets known as Tibb's Springs, the lake will be stocked with fish and will be suitable for swimming and boating. Vacation cabins will be built on the shore of the lake. A steel fire tower on the nearby summit of Grassy Mountain commands views over the Great Valley to Chattanooga and into the Blue Ridge Province in Georgia, North Carolina, and Tennessee.

SUMTER NATIONAL FOREST
F-8]

Sumter National Forest includes three divisions, all in South Carolina. Of these, only the Oconee Division, lying inside and along the northwest border of the State, is included in this inventory. The oldest division of the forest, Oconee was severed from Nantahala Forest in 1936 and placed under joint administration with two recently established divisions on the Piedmont to form the Sumter National Forest.

The division lies in Oconee and Pickens Counties in

the foot-hills along the eastern boundary of the Blue Ridge and extends for a short distance onto the Piedmont. Contiguous to the Chattahoochee and the Nantahala National Forests, it lacks their high altitudes and rugged topography. Its highest elevation, 3,548 feet, is found on Sassafras Mountain on the northern border; other elevations seldom exceed 2,500 feet. Chattooga Ridge, parallelling the long axis of the forest, leads from the vicinity of Highlands, N. C., to form the backbone of the forest.

With few exceptions, streams of the Oconee Division drain into tributaries of the Savannah River, the most prominent being the Chattooga. They present little similarity to streams of the Chattahoochee National Forest. The major valleys are broader, and minor streams short with fewer waterfalls. Forest growth is similar to that of Chattahoochee, although southern types predominate because of the lower elevations.

CUMBERLAND NATIONAL FOREST
[B-1]

As a forest blanket averaging 25 miles wide and 135 miles long, the Cumberland National Forest extends in a nearly north-south line across the State of Kentucky. It follows closely along the western margin of the Appalachian Plateaus between the Tennessee-Kentucky State line and the Ohio River. Only the southern extremity, in Whitley and McCreary Counties, lies within the Knoxville area. Scenically, the forest is a continuation to the north of the same general plateau characteristics which are evidenced in Tennessee. The southern part in particular has been severely dissected by advanced conditions of erosion, whose heroic scale is reflected by isolated mesalike tables, nearly segmented headlands, and deep boulder-strewn gorges. The heavily cut-over forest stand has been reduced to a characteristic pine association on the plateau surface, interlined by evergreens in gorges.

APPALACHIAN TRAIL
[B-9, G-4

The Appalachian Trail, a wilderness footpath leading along the crest of the Appalachian Mountains from Mount Katahdin in Maine to Mount Oglethorpe in Georgia, passes through the Knoxville area as well as the Upper Tennessee Valley and the Asheville areas. The trail is sponsored by the Appalachian Trail Conference, an association made up of various local hiking groups along its route. Individual members maintain this trail for the most part, although the work has been taken over within several public reservations by the CCC under the ECW program.

The Appalachian Trail enters the Knoxville area from the east on the North Carolina-Tennessee State line near Hot Springs, N. C. With minor deviations it follows the line westward through the Great Smoky Mountains National Park to Deals Gap, where it swings south and east through the Nantahala National Forest to join the Blue Ridge at Standing Indian Mountain. It then follows the Blue Ridge into Georgia and through the Chattahoochee National Forest to its terminus on Mount Oglethorpe in Dawson County, Ga.

Within the Smokies, the trail reaches the highest altitudes of its entire length, seldom dropping below 5,000 feet above sea level in the 78 miles of its course within the park. East of Newfound Gap the trail traverses an area of virgin spruce and fir, the wildest setting in its entire distance. West of the gap it is parallel for 7 miles to the Clingmans Dome Skyway, and beyond that point passes into hardwood forests and over the open grassy and heath balds which make up the west end of the park.

The trail leaves the State line at Deals Gap to cross the Little Tennessee River below Cheoah Dam. On entering the Nantahala National Forest, it turns east along the crest of Yellow Creek Mountain, then south into the Cheoah Mountains and ascends Cheoah Bald. After crossing the Nantahala Gorge at Wesser, N. C., it follows the crest of the Nantahala Mountains southward over Wayah Bald to Standing Indian. This portion of the Appalachian Trail, though at consistently lower elevations than those of the Smokies, ascends the outstanding peaks of the vicinity to command such superb panoramas as those from Cheoah Bald, Wayah Bald, and Standing Indian, as well as more restricted vistas along its length.

Within Georgia and the Chattahoochee National Forest the trail follows the crest of the Blue Ridge to its southern tip, and then swings on to a spur, Amicalola Mountain, which it follows to its southern extremity on Mount Oglethorpe. The trail links together many of the highest and most scenic spots in north Georgia. It crosses Hightower Bald, Tray Mountain, Blood Mountain, and passes close to Brasstown Bald. Near it are Nottely Falls, in the Vogel State Park, and Amicalola Falls.

Carlos Campbell, Knoxville

Haze-shrouded mountains rise in a succession of choppy waves in this view north from the Appalachian Trail at Cheoah Bald.

112

OCONEE STATE PARK
[F-8]

Located in Oconee County, S. C., approximately 10 miles north of the town of Walhalla, Oconee State Park comprises 1,165 acres lying at an average altitude of 1,800 feet above sea level. The park, surrounded on three sides by property of the United States Forest Service, has little inherent scenic interest except in the wooded shores of its 19-acre lake; but it seems suited to the intensive use for which it is designed. The recreational features of the park include 15 overnight cabins, trails, picnic areas, and a large combination boat and bathhouse which provides facilities for swimming and fishing.

S. C. Forestry Commission

Oconee State Park, S. C., centers around this sparkling 19-acre lake.

VOGEL STATE PARK
[D-9]

Vogel State Park consists of four tracts scattered along United States Highway 19 on each side of Neels Gap in Union and Lumpkin Counties, Ga. Small tracts include, respectively, the summit of Blood Mountain, Nottely Falls, and a 5-acre lake. The largest section, 200 acres in size, includes the vicinity of Neels Gap. In total, the tracts aggregate 252 acres. The State park service protects 4,500 acres additional forest land surrounding these units. Though privately owned, these acres serve as a protective belt for the park and as a game preserve.

The partially bald summit of Blood Mountain, 4,463 feet above sea level, is well known as a vantage point embracing superlative views over the mountain wilderness which forms the southern terminus of the Appalachians. No road leads up the mountain but hikers may use a 2-mile portion of the Appalachian Trail which follows the crest of the Blue Ridge across Neels Gap, up the slope of Blood Mountain, and on to the southwest. The 100-foot Nottely Falls is a headwater fall of small but fairly constant volume of flow. The falls lies close to United States Highway 19, although not visible from it. The 6½-acre tract surrounding the falls has been intensively developed with paths, trails, and an auto parking lot. A recreational lodge of stone, together with vacation cabins, has been built in Neels Gap. More vacation cabins, in addition to swimming and boating facilities, surround the lake.

NORTHEAST GEORGIA UPLAND PARK
[E-9]

As a land utilization project, the Farm Security Administration is taking options to a total of 50,000 acres within boundaries enclosing approximately 100,000 acres in Habersham and Stephens Counties, Ga. Known as the Northeast Georgia Upland Park, the area will be devoted largely to recreation. Although its location on the Piedmont affords a maximum elevation of only 1,600 feet, the topography within the park is extremely rugged and variations of 800 feet in elevation occur within short distances. The Chattahoochee Ridge extends along its western border and various tributaries of the Tugaloo River drain rapidly down the east slope of the ridge. Toccoa Falls, 217 feet high, lies at the head of the gorge of Toccoa Creek in the east center of the area.

According to plans, public recreational facilities typical of outing parks will be developed at various places within the tract. Most of these developments will include small recreational lakes to be constructed at natural sites, around which vacation cabins and facilities for boating and bathing will be constructed. A similar development is planned with frontage on Yonah Lake. Wayside parks and picnic areas will be developed at intervals along the highways within the area. The entire area will serve as a game preserve and it is hoped to develop an arboretum which will include all species of trees indigenous to the United States that will grow there. Such a development will be carried on over a period of years, and it is hoped that after 20 years the area will pay its own way.

BUFFALO SPRINGS FISH AND GAME PRESERVE
E-3

In Grainger County, Tenn., 26 miles, airline distance northeast of Knoxville, a fish and game preserve is being developed. Its purpose is twofold: To serve as a wild fowl hatchery, and to furnish good fishing for devotees of that sport.

The tract contains approximately 375 acres. Buffalo Creek, which is chiefly fed by Buffalo Spring located within the preserve, flows along the eastern edge. Even in dry months, the flow of this spring is several thousand gallons a minute and in the spring months, as much as 40,000 gallons. Near the eastern corner of the tract is a large old watermill, built in 1796, and still operating. It will be preserved as a historical feature. Below this mill the slopes of Buffalo Creek are wooded with good second-growth timber, but the central and western sections of the area are largely cleared land, with some scattered wooded areas.

The game hatchery consists of some 200 acres of the upland cleared and wooded area. The quail hatchery, which is the largest in the United States, includes an incubator, and a brooder with an estimated annual capacity of 100,000 birds; quail pens; and fields for raising food for the birds. About 50 acres will be devoted to the propagation of wild turkeys. Experiments will be made in raising wild duck, ruffed grouse, and California and Red Valley quail.

Eight or ten dams will be constructed on Buffalo Creek, creating 11-acre, 4-acre, and 3-acre ponds, and several smaller ones. Except for the largest one, these ponds, to be stocked with game fish, will be primarily for fishing. The 11-acre pond will have a bathing beach and bathhouse, boating facilities, week-end and vacation cabins, and picnic grounds nearby. Trails will be built through the woods and along the creek, with shelters as needed. There will be a public lodge, and houses for the superintendent and three assistants.

The nearest approach to the preserve from Knoxville is by way of United States Highway 11 W, 28 miles to Joppa, then 4 miles southeasterly on a good gravel road. It may also be reached by United States Highway 11 E to Jefferson City, Tennessee Highway 92 for a few miles, and then a county road.

MORGAN STATE FOREST
[B-3]

Lying across the Anderson-Morgan County line is the Morgan State Forest, a tract of 8,368 acres bought by the State because of its coal deposits. On an adjacent tract of 3,000 acres, administered by the State Department of Institutions is the Petros State Penitentiary, whose prisoners mine coal from the State land. A CCC camp has built fire trails in the forest, but any planning for recreational use is unlikely.

A 60-foot fire tower on top of Frozen Head, elevation 3,300 feet, provides panoramic views of the surrounding mountains and valleys. The tower is reached from Tennessee Highway 62 over 2 miles of unpaved road to Petros, several miles of curving two-way gravel road to the gap between Frozen Head and Fodderstack Mountain, and about 3 miles of narrow forest road to the tower. There is considerable use of this narrow road on weekends, and the quality of the views which may be obtained from the tower would seem to justify widening.

The only other possible recreational use of the forest might be a trailway running through the Cumberlands, perhaps passing this way in order to include the fire tower as a feature of interest.

NORRIS LAKE
[D-2]

The most widely known single feature of the TVA program is Norris Dam, named for Senator George W. Norris, "Father of TVA." Impounding the waters of the Clinch and Powell Rivers, important headwater tributaries of the Tennessee, Norris Dam creates a lake of some 34,000 acres at normal level. Norris Lake is primarily a storage reservoir whose enormous capacity permits it to serve the triple purposes of flood control, navigation, and power production. Its presence in a locality lacking in large natural lakes gives it special recreational significance.

The setting of Norris Lake is the rugged ridge and valley country of upper east Tennessee, a setting which has molded the body of the lake into thousands of tiny coves and through narrow valleys between wooded slopes. The irregular shore line extends for more than 700 miles. The surface of the lake has become popular for all water sports and its waters have afforded excellent fishing. To counteract the effect of an extensive draw-down, special facilities have been provided along its shores. Three areas, Norris and Big Ridge Parks, and Norris Lake Forest, are subsequently described in detail.

Norris Dam ranks, with others of the Nation's huge and recently constructed dams, as a popular sight-seeing attraction, being visited by an average of several hundreds of persons daily. These visitors come from all parts of the United States. An immense structure of gravity concrete construction, it is 265 feet high and 1,872 feet long. Across its crest a two-lane roadway forms a link in the Norris Freeway, leading west to Coal Creek, Tenn., or south to Norris town and Knoxville. Parking facilities are provided at each abutment of the dam and at the powerhouse.

Although built primarily as a dam construction road the Freeway is of permanent design and serves as the only means of access to Norris Dam. It represents an innovation in the design of rural roads, in that it is a two-lane roadway within a right-of-way of 250-foot minimum width. This wide right-of-way serves as a protective strip, restricting access from abutting land to a limited number of designated points and thus increasing the safety and efficiency of the road; the right-of-way and agreements with owners of abutting land prohibit the erection of billboards and business structures along the road. In this manner, the pleasing rural character of the road is preserved. Several informal picnic grounds have been provided at designated points within the protective strip.

The dam lies 20 miles north-northwest of Knoxville. It may be reached from Knoxville by way of Tennessee Highway 33 and the Norris Freeway, or from United States Highway 25 W at Coal Creek by way of the Freeway.

Along narrow ravines and around tiny coves, Norris Lake describes its tortuous 700-mile shoreline.

NORRIS LAKE FOREST
D-21

Surrounding Norris Lake 118,000 acres of land have been bought by the TVA for protective purposes—especially to prevent direct siltation of the reservoir through erosion. This whole tract is managed by the TVA Division of Forestry as a forest unit. As such, it recognizes recreation as one of five primary functions—the other four being timber production, crop production, fish and game production, and provision for grazing. Between 60 and 75 sites, totaling some 4,000 acres, will be selected along the shores of Norris Lake, and within these areas permits may be made to individuals and organizations for construction or use of cabins, camps, and other recreational features. These will, of course, be subject to control,

115

including approval of architectural design of structures. In addition to these areas, there will be provided, as needed, boat landings, trails, picnic areas, and fire towers. On the peninsula, which is near the center of the forest unit, it is probable that no construction will be permitted because of its relative inaccessibility. Some areas there, as elsewhere, however, will permit restricted hunting, and there will be certain tracts set aside for game breeding and for wildlife sanctuaries. One island in the lake is left entirely untouched, in order to study the uninfluenced processes of nature.

Although there is no scenery of superlative character in Norris Lake Forest, there is much that is very pleasing. The 705 miles of lake shore line, with its many wooded ridges and coves, will offer innumerable vistas to hikers and boaters, and, to a limited extent, to motorists and equestrians.

Certain tracts such as Big Ridge and Norris Parks within or adjacent to the Norris Lake Forest have already been specifically designated as recreation areas, descriptions of which follow. Another area, the Norris Town Forest, is recognized as an entity, but holds no special recreational significance. This tract of 7,000 acres, lying between Big Ridge and Norris Parks will receive somewhat more intensive forestry use than other parts of the unit, and its first forest maintenance community of 10 or 12 families is now established at Sequoyah Landing.

Some other sections of the forest, because of their strategic location and character, suggest special emphasis on recreational uses. Two of these are Caryville Lake, and the island west of the new bridge over the Clinch River on Tennessee Highway 33, the latter tract being tentatively called Beech Island. These two locations are discussed subsequently among the proposed or potential areas for development.

Four small dams have been built at the heads of small coves, and four more are planned. These are intended to produce ponds of from 2 to 26 acres in extent in locations where constant flows of fresh water will provide conditions favorable for breeding and rearing fish. Although any recreational use of these ponds will be subordinated to fish propagation, it is probable that swimming by the public will be permitted in some of them. Because of the smallness of the water areas, and because no special swimming facilities are to be provided, such use will doubtless be confined to local patronage.

Only the widening wake of a tiny boat disturbs the glassy surface of Norris Lake.

BIG RIDGE PARK
[D-2]

A tract of 4,592 acres of TVA property, lying adjacent to Norris Lake, 19 miles airline distance due north of Knoxville, has been designated as Big Ridge Park. It is bounded on the northwest and northeast by the Norris Reservoir, on the southeast by the crest of Wallen Ridge, and on the southwest by the reservoir taking line which cuts across Big Ridge and Lone Mountain. Parts of both of these ridges are included in the largest unit of the park which is almost entirely separated from the mainland by the lake.

On one of these arms, a concrete dam 200 feet long and 50 feet high has been built, thus forming a 45-acre lake of constant level, fed by springs, and unaffected by fluctuations of the reservoir below this dam. Around this lake, which has been stocked for fishing, are concentrated the intensive recreational uses which pertain to the functions of an outing park. Provisions for water sports include a bathhouse, a sand bathing beach, and a boat and canoe house; and 19 cabins have been built for vacation use near the lake. A picnic area, with tables and benches, a shelter, and over 100 log seats, occupies a wooded point overlooking the lake. The nearby park lodge contains a lounge and cooking and dining facilities. A 10-acre playfield near the picnic area provides for group games. Two parking spaces are conveniently located in relation to the above mentioned features. A trail leads around the lake and across the dam. Overlooking the latter, on the highest knob adjacent to the lake, is an observation point with a shelter.

The peninsula previously referred to as being almost an island is set aside as a nature-study area. It will be stocked with game and will remain undeveloped as a laboratory for the study of natural sciences. In order to protect game, the entire park will be fenced.

Land access to the park from the south will be by means of Tennessee Highway 61 which at present ends at the park. A county road connecting with the Norris Freeway reaches the park from the southwest. The entrance to the park is 25 miles from Knoxville by way of Tennessee Highway 33 (18 miles) and Tennessee Highway 61 (7 miles).

Cool, clear water and excellent swimming facilities draw daily crowds to Big Ridge Park.

A small boat feels her wings on the deep-blue water
of Big Ridge Lake.

NORRIS PARK
[C-2]

Norris Park is a tract of 3,887 acres in Anderson
and Campbell Counties, extending from the town of
Norris to the south extremity of Norris Lake. It
includes the land adjacent to both sides of Norris
Dam and runs for 2 miles along both sides of the
Clinch River below the dam, which is the center of
interest in the park.

That part of the park developed for intensive use
lies eastward of the east abutment of the dam. Here
the Norris Freeway enters a circle which, on the west,
gives access to the road over the dam, and on the north
leads to the main developed area of the park, containing a vacation cabin area, a tenting area, and picnic
grounds. Within the cabin area are 25 cabins (5 of
them double), a superintendent's lodge, and a public
lodge. At no great distance from these lies the
tenting area and trailer camp, equipped with water
and sanitary facilities as well as electricity. At the
nearby stable, horses may be rented, in order to utilize
for riding as well as walking the 18 miles of trails
which have been built on the east side of the lake.
The picnic grounds lie nearest to the dam and contain
numerous tables and benches and a large shelter.
Parking space is provided for all of the above features.
Below the cabins, at the edge of Norris Reservoir,
there is a floating boat landing.

Speeding motorboats cleave the waters of Norris Lake just above the dam.

At the east end of the dam, parking space is provided in close proximity to the abutment. At this point there is an information booth, refreshment stand, and a handcraft display shop. Below the dam on the east bank of the river are several fish-breeding pools, operated by the TVA Forestry Division, in cooperation with the United States Bureau of Fisheries. A large parking area accommodates visitors to both fish hatchery and powerhouse. Near the fish pools is the tree crop nursery of the TVA Forestry Division.

On the west side of the river, 4 miles of foot and bridle trails have been built, with several shelters which afford some of the best views of the lower face of the dam. Above the dam on the west side, in the site of the former stone quarry, a steel barge serves as a boat landing for TVA and private craft. On the hill over the west abutment of the dam a parking space and an observation point overlook the dam, powerhouse, and their associated developments.

On Reservoir Hill, one of the highest knobs in the park, is the underground reservoir of the Norris town water supply. On this area considerable work has been done in the way of recreational development. An extensive overlook, retained by high stone dry walls, offers excellent views of Norris Dam and Norris, of the Cumberland Mountains and, on very clear days, of the Great Smoky Mountains. Here are two parking spaces, a shelter, water and toilet facilities, and tables, benches and ovens for picnickers. Trails lead from here to various other sections of the park.

KENTUCKY RIDGE FOREST
[D–1]

The Kentucky Ridge Forest, a tract of 11,700 acres, adjoins Pine Mountain State Park in Bell County, Ky. It includes most of the watershed of Big Clear Creek, on the south slope of Pine Mountain, and the north slope of the north ridge of Log Mountain.

The area was purchased by the Farm Security Administration primarily for land utilization. However, some recreational development of outing park nature has been undertaken. Plans are underway to coordinate these facilities with those in the Pine Mountain Park, and there is a probability that the management of the two areas may be merged in the near future.

INDIAN CAVE
[E–3]

Indian Cave is one of the outstanding limestone caves in this part of the country. The entrance to it lies close to the Holston River, 23½ miles, airline

distance, northeast of Knoxville. It is reached over 7 miles of gravel road from Blaine, which is 21 miles from Knoxville on United States Highway 11 W, or else from United States Highway 11 E at New Market, over 5½ miles of gravel road, and a ferry across the Holston.

Exploitation of the cave was begun 4 years ago. Fortunately very little has been done to modify the original interior. An easy sand path, without steps, follows for the most part an underground creek for a distance of a mile and a half. Fifteen miles of electric cable provide an indirect system of lighting which reveals the cave without being obtrusive. Traditional use of the cave by Indians is evidenced by smoke-blackening of the ceiling and of the stalactites and stalagmites in one or two of the larger chambers.

Several simple and rather attractive rental cabins have been erected on the river slope near the cave entrance. Other development around the cavern entrance is, however, less pleasing.

GRAND CAVERNS
[C–4]

Grand Caverns, which were opened to the public in 1929, are located in western Knox County, 13 miles, airline distance, from Knoxville. They are reached from Knoxville by way of Ball Camp Pike and the county road through Byington, over 13 miles of hard surfaced road and 3 miles of a good macadam road leading to the Solway Bridge over the Clinch River.

The cave has not been as extensively developed as has Indian Cave and although the direct lighting system sets off the formations to less advantage than does indirect lighting the stalactite and stalagmite formations in Grand Caverns seem to be more extensive and more varied than in Indian Cave. Limestone formations predominate but there is some onyx present. There are many leads in various directions that have not yet been made accessible.

LEA LAKE
[D–3]

About 1790 one Major Lea built a substantial brick house in the cove enclosed by the butt of Clinch Mountain. In recent years this house, which served as a haven for travelers in pioneer times, was purchased and remodeled and enlarged in the spirit of the original structure. This structure, now called Lea Lakes Lodge, forms the nucleus of a private summer residential development of high caliber. A number of cabins and lodges have been built of logs or siding which are, for the most part, of simple straightforward design. As a feature of the resort, Lea Lake was built by damming up a spring-fed stream. This lake of 9 acres extent is the first of about five which it is proposed to build. A bathhouse and diving platform have been provided. In the vicinity of the lodge are several kinds of mineral springs.

Quiet Lea Lake is the center of a secluded resort development.

SAVAGE ROCK GARDENS
[C-3]

Savage Rock Gardens are located in Anderson County, Tenn., 20 miles airline northwest of Knoxville. The area consists of many acres of woods on the south bank of Coal Creek whereon frequent waterworn limestone formations rise as much as 20 feet above the ground. Many of the rocks have a curiously contorted and gnarled appearance. The owner, Mr. Savage, has planted and encouraged the growth of many native wild flowers and rock plants so that in the spring months the area is a mecca for people from many miles around. Some garden varieties of flowers such as iris and longspurred columbine have also been introduced in some profusion. These exotics, however inherently attractive they may be, strike an inappropriate note in the woodland setting.

The public is welcomed at all times. Numerous winding woods trails give access to various parts of the tract. Very little maintenance is provided and so in summer the area is claimed by weeds, with very few midseason wild flowers in evidence. The woods are cool and attractive, however, and the rock formations of sufficient interest to attract many visitors even when there is no floral display.

SHEEP PEN BLUFF
[C-4]

Sheep Pen Bluff is a tract of 30 acres located in Blount County, Tenn., 13 miles airline southwest of Knoxville, on the south bank of the Tennessee River. It is owned by Maryville College and is located a mile or so from the town of Louisville. Like Peter Bluff, but considerably less high, it is a dissected rocky cliff. At its maximum it is perhaps 100 feet above the river. Views are localized but attractive. At one point in the bluff, one may walk through a short passageway in the rock and emerge onto a shelf which has the character of a small cave.

This tract is open to the public and is considerably used locally for picnicking. It is reached from the town of Louisville by taking the road toward the old ferry and turning left just before reaching the river. From Louisville, it is about 2 miles to the point where one leaves the road and follows a trail for about three-quarters of a mile to the bluff.

PROPOSED REGIONAL RECREATION AREAS

CUMBERLAND GAP NATIONAL PARK
[D-1]

Location: At intersection of Tennessee, Virginia, and Kentucky State lines.
Size: 14,000 acres.
Type: Wilderness park, outing park combining developed scenic and intensive-use areas.
Characteristics: The most historic dry gap in the Appalachians; magnificent views from the rocky summit of The Pinnacle; 100-acre Fern Lake, surrounded by wooded mountains; two caves.

CUMBERLAND GAP and its environs have been proposed to Congress for establishment as a national park. The scenic values of the tract are exceptionally fine, but the chief justification for national park status seems to be a historical one. The gap was used more than any other in the Appalachian Mountains as a passageway for the early pioneers spreading westward from the frontier of the Eastern States. It also played a prominent part as one of the strategic points in the Civil War. The pass was discovered and named in 1750 by a party of Virginians under Dr. Thomas Walker.

Included in the proposed park would be about 22 square miles, consisting chiefly of the wooded slopes of the long ridge called Cumberland Mountain. The high point of this ridge within the proposed park area is The Pinnacle, elevation 2,465, from which, it is claimed, six States can be seen on a clear day. However this may be, there are magnificent views from this elevation in all directions except east, where the view is cut off by Cumberland Mountain. The

Well-concealed on the north slope of Cumberland Mountain, yet less than a mile from Middlesboro, is Fern Lake.

Luxuriant forests grace the slopes of the Cumberland Mountains in Kentucky, Tennessee, and Virginia. Jewellike Fern Lake nestles high in this mountain setting.

top of The Pinnacle is reached by a good gravel toll road which winds up to the summit from Cumberland Gap, 1,000 feet below. Part of the land is owned by nearby Lincoln Memorial University, and leased to the corporation which opened the road in 1929.

Another feature of interest in the proposed park is Fern Lake. This body of water, formed by damming the waters of Little Yellow Creek, was created to serve as the water supply for Middlesboro. It lies in an attractive setting at the foot of the north slope of Cumberland Mountain. An earth dam with a concrete spillway impounds the lake, which is about 100 acres in extent.

Boating was formerly permitted by the Kentucky Utilities Co., which owns the lake and its watershed, but a boating accident which resulted in a lawsuit caused the owners to withdraw the tract from public usage. The fact that use by a private fishing club with 100 members is permitted indicates that some recreational use of the lake is not inconsistent with its major purpose. It is conceivable that, with

proper restrictions, some future use of the lake by the public might be possible, particularly if the lake and its watershed were acquired for inclusion in a national park or national forest. Such use might well include development of pleasure drives, hiking trails, and picnic areas, and arrangements for boating and fishing.

Two caves lie within the proposed park boundary, both of them on the 2,000-acre tract belonging to Lincoln Memorial University. The entrance to Soldiers Cave is close to United States Highway 25 E, on the south slope of Cumberland Mountain. This cave, which is open to the public for a fee, contains formations of average interest. It is lighted and penetrable for a distance of a quarter to half a mile.

King Solomon's Cave, higher up the mountain, and something over a quarter of a mile from the other cave, is more spectacular but is not open to the public. Students are admitted on certain occasions. An underground stream which it contains serves as the water supply for the university, and for the towns of Cumberland Gap and Harrogate.

Historic Cumberland Gap is flanked on one side by the Pinnacle, towering above the knobs of Powell Valley.

123

SAND CAVE
[E-1]

Location: The southwest corner of Harlan County, Ky., near Virginia State line; 4 miles north of Ewing, Va.

Size: 12,000 acres.

Type: Wilderness area, with some outing features.

Characteristics: Large shallow cave with sand floor; surroundings of virgin timber with a dense undercover of laurel, rhododendron, and other flowering shrubs; adjacent to White Rocks, elevation 3,451 feet, the highest point on Cumberland Mountain; extensive views.

Sand Cave, in matter of size alone, is an outstanding scenic feature in the Southern Appalachians. Located on the north slope of Cumberland Mountain at the edge of a 10,000-acre tract of virgin timber, the cave lies immediately beneath White Rocks, the highest point on the mountain. Although the cave may be approached only with considerable difficulty, several hundred people visit it annually. These visitors consist, for the most part, of local people, as it is not widely known.

The cave consists of a single chamber, with a dome-shaped ceiling and a sloping sand floor. The great entrance arch has a span of 300 feet and its highest point reaches more than 100 feet above the floor. The floor area, one acre and a quarter in extent and covered with fine yellow sand estimated by geologists to be 250 feet deep, slopes steeply from the entrance toward the rear. The ceiling rises like a vaulted half-dome from points 8 feet above the floor at the rear to more than 100 feet at the crest of the arch comprising the entrance. Veins of different-colored sandstone, ranging through dark brown, purple, and deep red to light tan and yellow, are exposed in the side walls and ceiling of the cave. Individual sand or crystals in the floor may repeat these same colors. The total effect, however, is that of dark brown walls and ceiling sur-

An arch, 300 feet wide and 100 feet high, shapes the opening of Sand Cave.

mounting a brilliant white-yellow floor. Foot prints and other irregularities in the floor surface resemble miniature sand dunes.

Virgin hemlocks, estimated to be 400 years old, grow close to the entrance of the cave. They are but specimens of similar growth extending over the 10,000 acre tract on which the cave borders. This tract is owned by the Kentenia Coal Co., which holds the land for its mineral rights rather than for the timber. Although the timber has been somewhat damaged by fire, a tangled growth of rhododendron and laurel forms the ground cover. This growth is particularly profuse near the cave and forms a veritable thicket on the mountain above.

Vandalism has somewhat injured the cave, but such damage has not attained serious proportion at the present time. Its principal form is the scraping of various colors of sand from the walls in order to make up bottles of varicolored sand for sale as souvenirs in nearby towns. Fire, picnic refuse, and broken shrubbery are other evidences of misuse.

Any proposal for a national park at Cumberland Gap should include Sand Cave. The inclusion of Sand Cave in the currently proposed Cumberland Gap National Park would increase the acreage from 14,000 to 36,000 acres. This latter acreage would include the Kentenia tract in Kentucky, an additional 2,000 acres to the east of Sand Cave, and 10,000 acres on the Virginia side of the mountain. The park would thus combine the scenic and primitive interest of Cumberland Mountain with the historical interest of Cumberland Gap.

Sand Cave may be reached by a 4-mile hike or horseback ride up a steep trail from Ewing, Va. This trail is a partially graded fire trail, but its upper reaches are steep and involve some rock climbing. The trail emerges on the top of the mountain near White Rocks, turns slightly to the west and leads one-half a mile down the Kentucky slope of the mountain to the cave entrance.

PROPOSED PLATEAU PURCHASE UNIT
[C-1]

Location: On the Cumberland Plateau, bordering the Tennessee Valley on the northwest.
Size: 1,916,850 acres.
Type: Wilderness with occasional outing areas.
Characteristics: Broken and folded plateau; second-growth forest with some virgin timber; distant views.

Most of the nearly 2,000,000 acres included within the Proposed Plateau Purchase Unit falls within the Chattanooga area, but its most rugged portion overlaps the western margin of the Knoxville area. This portion is a region of irregular mountains and tight, narrow valleys. It includes such outstanding Cumberland peaks as Cross Mountain, Pilot Knob, Fodder Stack, and Brushy Mountain. Geologically its structure is the same as the plateau, but is older and more affected by erosion which has destroyed all semblance of plateau surface and produced some buckling and folding into irregular ridges. A distinct escarpment forms the southeast border and affords spectacular vantage points, such as Eagle Bluff and McLean Rock. Palisades which characterize the escarpment carry back in some instances into the interior to produce such cliff and gorge forms as the Cumberland Palisades near Jellico.

The Knoxville portion of the unit is drained almost entirely by tributaries of the Cumberland River, but small tributaries of the Clinch and Powell lead down the southeast escarpment and in some cases penetrate the interior. These stream courses are steep but seldom produce the cascades or falls which characterize the plateau.

Forest growth has been almost entirely cut over although some virgin growth remains in inaccessible coves and gorges. The cut-over forest is predominantly a pine-hardwood association; gorge growth includes hemlock, rhododendron and cove hard wood. Some game remains in the forest but the stock has been severely depleted by uncontrolled subsistence hunting and by repeated fires. Restoration of game will necessitate an adequate management program.

Cumberland Palisades
[C-1]

Location: Campbell County, Tenn., 4 to 6 miles east-southeast of Jellico, near United States Highway 25 W.
Type: Developed scenic area.
Character: High wooded bluffs and cliffs; stream valley, with numerous tributaries.

A few miles east of Jellico, along either side of United States Highway 25 W for a distance of over 2 miles, rise the Cumberland Palisades, or—as they are locally known—High Cliffs. On the north side of the highway, in the vicinity of Laurel Creek, these escarpments are topped by high, vertical or overhanging rock bluffs. Elsewhere the slopes rise in series of stepped cliffs. The road winds along the south bank of Clear Fork of the Cumberland River, which is fed by several other streams within a space of a few miles. This valley is somewhat marred by the rather crude alinement and profile of the highway and the accompany-

Cumberland Palisades, with their jutting cliffs, give canyonlike appearance to the valley of Laurel Creek.

ing line of telegraph poles; but most of the area's exceptional scenic value remains unimpaired.

Detailed and unhurried inspection of the cliffs could be made possible by the construction of turnouts and parking spaces, from which trails would lead among and up onto the bluffs.

Eagle Bluff
[C–2]

Location: Campbell County, Tenn., 1½ miles north of Jacksboro.
Type: Developed scenic area.
Character: Sheer rock cliffs offering fine views across the valley to the south; 2-acre artificial lake, spring-fed.

Although Eagle Bluff does not have a very high elevation—only slightly exceeding 2,000 feet—it is given special note because of its sheer cliff character, which assures unrestricted views over the valley to the south, and because the existing resort development has some scenic interest. A mile north of the Jacksboro Courthouse, approached by a good gravel road, the Eagle Bluff Springs Hotel stands in a clearing at the foot of the mountain. The hotel, which is no longer open to the public, is a simple frame structure, of considerable size. A few hundred feet southeast of the building, a 2-acre lake, fed by 11 mineral springs, lies in a setting which, with some grading and planting, could be made very attractive. Some

rather crude facilities are present, including bathhouses and a diving platform. Tree growth in the vicinity is rather good, consisting predominantly of pine. From the hotel winding trails lead to the springhouse and to Eagle Bluff.

McLean Rock
[D–1]

Location: Claiborne County, Tenn., 35 miles airline north of Knoxville.
Type: Wilderness.
Characteristics: Cliff-topped ridge, with one of the highest elevations on the south escarpment of Cumberland Mountain; superlative views in all directions.

About halfway between Cumberland Gap and the town of La Follette, Tenn., McLean Rock projects outward from the general line of Cumberland Mountain, permitting salient views thereof in both directions. With an elevation of 2,960 feet, 500 feet higher than The Pinnacle at Cumberland Gap, it is the highest point on the mountain for a distance of 45 miles. To the south the Great Valley stretches out in vast expanse, with House Mountain and the Butt of Clinch Mountain clearly visible. To the north, wave after wave of forested wilderness extends to the horizon, completely free of evidence of human occupation or manipulation, except for the not too evident fact that the woods are all of second growth.

The tree-clad slope of Eagle Bluff is reflected by the smooth surface of the lake at its base.

McLean Rock, projecting from Cumberland Mountain, affords magnificent views.

McLean Rock itself is an escarpment extending some distance along the crest of the mountain. No trees obstruct the view within an angle of perhaps 250 degrees, but the summit back of the cliff is fairly well wooded. A few hundred yards to the northwest a wooded knoll appears to be slightly higher than the rock. An existing trail leads to the summit of McLean Rock from the south side. Although occasional glimpses of the valley appear along the up-trail, one is unprepared for the breath-taking view from the crest—a spectacle surpassed by few, if any, panoramas in the whole Tennessee Valley outside of the Blue Ridge Mountain Province.

Cross Mountain
[C-3]

Location: Campbell and Anderson Counties, Tenn.; 24 miles airline northwest of Knoxville.

Type: Wilderness.

Characteristics: Cleared mountain top dominating the surrounding territory, with 360-degree panoramic view.

Cross Mountain, with an elevation of over 3,600 feet, is the highest point in the Cumberland Mountains west of the highlands in Harlan County, Ky. It consists of a long ridge, with spurs, and forms part of the dividing crest between the Tennessee and Cumberland River Valleys. The mountain, like nearly all of this part of the Cumberlands, has very little cleared land, but all the timber is second growth. The high, rather flat-topped knob on which is located a United States Geological Survey triangulation station, elevation 3,550, is cleared, except for the southwest edge. Summer grazing by cattle keeps the tree growth down. Superlative views unfold in all directions: mountains more than half a mile high in the northwestern 180 degrees, Cumberland Mountain in the northeast, and the Great Valley across the balance of the view. The Great Smoky Mountains, something over 40 miles distant, are visible on clear days, with House and Clinch Mountains, 27 and 29 miles away, normally prominent features in the eastern panorama. Norris Dam lies only 8 miles, airline distance, from Cross Mountain, so that a distant view of Norris Dam and the winding shoreline of the lake above it is available from this vantage point.

Access to the top of the mountain is by means of a new county road extending from the south edge of Coal Creek to Swag Gap, which is about 2 miles from the top. From here a trail, which is used by several miners' families who live on the mountain, leads to the summit.

CUMBERLAND STATE FOREST
[E-1]

Location: On Cumberland Mountain, in Virginia, extending along the Virginia-Kentucky State line northeast of Cumberland Gap.

Size: 15,000 acres.

Type: Wilderness with some developed scenic areas.

Characteristics: Steep to sheer slope of Cumberland Mountain, clothed with mixed pine and hardwoods and affording magnificent views over valley land to the south.

Cumberland State Forest has been proposed by the Virginia State Forest Service, but no funds are available for its acquisition at the present time. It lies on the steep southern slope of Cumberland Mountain, where it extends for a distance of some 20 miles in a northeast-southwest direction; quite attenuated in shape, its maximum width is scarcely 2 miles. For the most part, the cover is composed of second growth mixed pine and hardwoods, although some original growth remains on the steeper portions of the slope.

Protection of the slope is important from the standpoint of control over the watershed of the Powell River which lies at the base of the mountain. Should the entire mountain be denuded, the erosion problem, already serious on the lower slopes, would be greatly increased. Impairment of the scenic aspects of Cumberland Mountain near Cumberland Gap would be a tragic circumstance; uncontrolled cutting would result in such impairment. The Cumberland Mountain Forestry Association, a local organization, working with private land owners, has taken steps to prevent such an occurrence. The crest of the slope affords views over rolling farmland at the foot. Apparently one is standing on an isolated mountain crest, for the valley ridges, prominent when seen from their immediate surroundings, become dwarfed by comparison with the height of Cumberland Mountain, which has a general elevation of 2,500 to 3,000 feet, 1,500 feet above the valley floor. To the north one looks over forested plateau land only slightly lower than the crest of Cumberland Mountain. Recreational use of the forest would probably consist chiefly of hiking or horseback riding, with more intensive-use facilities developed in the vicinity of two special features of interest, Sand Cave, adjoining the forest on the Kentucky side of the mountain, and White Rocks, the point of highest elevation.

At the western end of the proposed forest, Lincoln Memorial University owns a 2,000-acre tract, a gift for forest experimental purposes. The university, however, does not possess sufficient funds for adequate management of the tract, although, through the Cumberland Mountain Forestry Association, it is insuring a program of fire and scenic protection. The proposed Cumberland Gap National Park which has been discussed previously in this chapter also overlaps a portion of the forest.

White Rocks
[E-1]

The name White Rocks is given to the point of highest elevation on Cumberland Mountain, 3,451 feet. The White Rocks themselves form a palisade 300 feet high and a half mile long on the crest of the mountain one-half mile east of the actual high point. From a distance, the cliffs appear to be sharp and angular with great plane surfaces, but on closer inspection they are found to be more rounded and softened, as is to be expected from their formation of sandstone and conglomerate. Although blackened at the present time by smoke stains and lichen growths, when first seen by early white settlers the rocks must indeed have appeared white. Used both as a signal point and ceremonial ground for tribal dances by the Indians, White Rocks had a special significance to these early settlers and became a permanent landmark of the time.

The high point is rounded and slopes in an easy grade up from the Kentucky side to drop more sharply into Virginia. Three hundred acres along 3 miles of the mountain's crest, including both the high point and the cliffs, in the past, have been cleared of forests and pastured by sheep. The resulting appearance is now that of a natural bald, which contrasts with the heavily wooded Virginia slope of the mountain and the virgin forests in the vicinity of Sand Cave. White Rocks embraces views in all directions: toward the south, the observer looks down into the intensively cultivated Powell Valley, then across the lower ridges of the Great Appalachian Valley beyond which loom the Great Smoky Mountains on the North Carolina-Tennessee State line; on the other hand, the heavily wooded mountains on the Kentucky side contrast sharply with these.

White Rocks may be reached by a 4-mile hiking and horseback trail from Ewing, Va., a trail which has an easy grade for the first 2 miles but which becomes steeper and involves some rock climbing as it nears White Rocks. The trail emerges on the crest between the cliffs and the high point. A second trail, 18 miles long, leads along the crest of the mountain from Cumberland Gap to White Rocks. Both trails are part of the forest protective program of the Cumberland Mountain Forestry Protective Association.

White Rocks, 3,451 feet above sea level, are the highest points on Cumberland Mountain, the boundary between Kentucky and Virginia.

Three hundred feet high and half a mile long, White Rocks were used by the Indians as a signal point and ceremonial ground.

PROPOSED CAMPBELL STATE FOREST
PURCHASE UNIT
[C–2]

Location: Campbell County, Tenn., in the Cumberland Mountains.
Communities served: Clinton, 20 miles; LaFollette, 8 miles; Knoxville, 35 miles.
Size: 61,000 acres.
Type: Wilderness, with occasional intensive-use areas.
Characteristics: Rolling to mountainous country, well forested, and permitting extensive views over adjacent valley lands.

Proposed for establishment as a State forest purchase unit under the Fulmer Act, the Campbell Forest overlaps the area included in the proposed Caryville Game Preserve. It also includes a portion of the land proposed for inclusion in the proposed Plateau Purchase Unit. Comprising a total of 61,000 acres, approximately 25,000 acres drain into the Clinch River and the remainder into the Cumberland. Topographically of plateau formation, the area has been severely dissected until it more nearly resembles folded mountains.

Elevations range more than 1,000 feet, keeping for the most part, between the 1,500- and 2,500-foot contours. Slopes are precipitous and mountain ranges exhibit no pronounced directional lines. Points of high elevation embrace views over adjacent mountains, out into the Powell Valley, and across Norris Lake. Walnut Mountain, 2,800 feet high, overlooks the entire area. The forest consists of varied hardwoods and pine from which the best timber has been culled by hand-logging, leaving a residual stand of fair quality.

At the southern tip of the area, Caryville Lake will provide the opportunity for intensive-use facilities. Other recreational significance of the tract attaches, for the most part, to vantage points along the southeastern escarpment. Outstanding among these is Eagle Bluff, which is described elsewhere in detail. A game refuge on part of the tract should restock the remainder with deer, grouse, turkey, and other upland game species, to provide for hunting.

Although the tract is recommended for acquisition as a state forest under the provisions of the Fulmer Act, final studies may indicate that the slower purchase program of the proposed Plateau Purchase Unit will be more desirable. The two proposals in no way conflict from a recreational standpoint, for the significance for recreation would be the same under either State or Federal ownership.

CARYVILLE LAKE AND GAME REFUGE
[C-2]

Location: Campbell County, Tenn., east and north of Caryville.
Communities served: Coal Creek, 7 miles; LaFollette, 8 miles; Clinton, 16 miles; Knoxville, 35 miles; Oneida, 35 miles.
Size: 6,500 acres.
Type: Outing park, combining developed scenic area and intensive-use areas.
Characteristics: 210-acre lake with background of mountains.

At the town of Caryville, where United States Highway 25 W and Tennessee Highway 63 intersect, an arm of Norris Lake necessitated relocation of sections of both of these highways. In order to prevent mud flats from occurring at Caryville during periods of even slight reservoir draw-down, a concrete dam was built east of the town just below the confluence of Cove and Dog Creeks. This dam creates a lake of constant level, similar to, but considerably larger than the one formed at Big Ridge Park. This lake has a beautiful setting, with the high ridge of the Cumberland Mountains on the west rising 2,000 feet above the lake; the end of Fork Mountain to the northwest, 1,100 feet above the lake; and Cumberland Mountain, at the same elevation, stretching to the northeast as far as the eye can reach. The lake is about 210 acres in extent. It has been proposed that an outing park be developed on the protective belt of land surrounding the lake. On land adjacent to Caryville, a playfield and boathouse for use primarily by the people of Caryville is suggested. Across United States Highway 25 W, on the knob which will be bounded by that highway and the confluence of the two creeks, TVA studies have indicated a desirable site for a tourist camp area with facilities for boating and fishing. This knob of about 20 acres is rather bare at present, but the setting is exceptionally attractive, and planting of trees would remedy the present deficiency. There would be water access to the main lake under the highway bridges on United States Highway 25 W.

A bond issue of $15,000 has been approved by Campbell County to purchase a tract of 5,300 acres which includes Fork Mountain. This area with the adjacent lake tract would make a total of some 6,500

acres. It is probable that the combined tract will be developed by CCC labor, in cooperation with the Tennessee Department of Conservation.

This area assumes recreational importance beyond its local and regional significance because of its location directly on one of the main tourist routes.

Caryville Lake, an arm of Norris Lake, lies at the base of Fork Mountain.

BEECH ISLAND
[D-2]

Location: Norris Reservoir near crossing of Tennessee Highway 33 over Clinch River.
Size: 45 acres.
Type: Outing park.
Characteristics: Island in Norris Lake, connected with mainland by a short causeway; sharp-topped ridge spurs, mostly covered with good second-growth timber.

Just west of the new bridge over which Tennessee Highway 33 crosses the Clinch River, the impounded waters of Norris Lake create a 45-acre island of irregular shape. It consists of connected ridges, those in the east end, rather sharp-edged, and predominantly wooded with good second-growth timber including a number of specimen beech trees. Except for one valley southwest of this island, the ground slopes away steeply, therefore draw-down of the water level will not create extensive mud flats.

Because the island lies near the point at which one

of the main north-south tourist routes crosses a major arm of Norris Lake, it would be desirable to recognize this significant location by a development which would enable travelers to get some benefit from the lake in passing. A preliminary study by TVA suggests use of the island for tent camping and picnic grounds. Motor roads would be restricted to the west half, foot-trails serving the balance of the tract. Access to the island would be obtained by raising the present road to form a causeway 100 yards long. Southeast of the island, and separated from it by an embayment of the reservoir, a small peninsula abuts on Tennessee

Highway 33 a few hundred yards south of the bridge. For this site is proposed a small tourist cabin development, with a gas station and restaurant, and a boathouse with a floating dock.

The scenic value of this tract is well above the average. From the island, of which one ridge is nearly a hundred feet above the normal water level, lake views a mile or more in extent will be obtainable to the north, east, and west. These facts, combined with the strategic location of the island, seem to make it potentially one of the most significant areas on Norris Lake for recreational use.

Where Tennessee Highway 33 crosses the Clinch River arm of Norris Lake, Beech Island offers an attractive site for a tourist camp.

WATTS BAR LAKE
[A-4]

Location: Rhea, Meigs, Roane, and Loudon Counties.
Size: 42,600 acres—approximately 67 square miles.
Type: A reservoir planned primarily to maintain a navigable channel on part of the Tennessee River.
Characteristics: A long, winding body of water in a setting of wooded and agricultural land; level of the lake will fluctuate.

Three proposed dams in the TVA program for the development of the Tennessee River lie within the Knoxville area. These water-control projects are

known as the Watts Bar, Coulter Shoals, and Fontana dams.

The site of the proposed Watts Bar Dam has been tentatively chosen at a point which lies about 6 miles airline southeast of Spring City, just below the present ferry crossing of Tennessee Highway 68. The lake will extend up the Clinch and Emory rivers as well as up the Tennessee River.

The Watts Bar Lake will somewhat resemble Norris Lake, winding through a similar ridge country, though the ridges are not as high or steep. The lower part of it from Kingston to the dam site will parallel the Cumberland Escarpment and the valley ridges, with four arms reaching back to the base of the escarpment. From Kingston up to the Coulter Shoals dam site the lake will cut across the ridge and valley formations. Two distinct areas, of different character from a recreational standpoint, will thus be found.

This reservoir and Chickamauga Lake below it offer recreational possibilities which may not be surpassed on any of the other TVA reservoirs. The combination of wooded ridges on the lower section of Watts Bar Lake and its closeness to the escarpment, together with the size of the water body, will make this area extremely important for the development of recreation. Wooded ridge country adjoining the reservoir offers distinct possibilities for camps, outing areas, cabins, and summer home developments.

A forested tract of about 20,000 acres in the vicinity of White Creek is believed worthy of consideration for State or Federal forest purchase. Reservation of such a tract would provide outstanding recreational opportunities related to the reservoir.

As in the case of other TVA reservoirs between Chattanooga and Knoxville, there may be expected an important use as a water travelway. Private boating, fishing, and swimming in connection with outing areas are the other principal types of water recreation to be expected on the main river reservoirs.

The reservoir will be accessible by road at numerous points. The relation of such access to possible outing areas, camp, and cabin sites, etc., and to vantage points on ridges, remains to be further studied.

Watts Bar Lake will enhance this pleasant rural setting southwest of Knoxville.

FORT LOUDOUN
[C-5]

Location: In Monroe County on west bank of the Little Tennessee River immediately south of Niles Ferry Bridge on Tennessee Highway 33.

Communities served: Knoxville, 36 miles; Loudon, 15 miles; Lenoir City, 20 miles; Maryville-Alcoa, 18 miles.

Size: Up to 600 acres.

Type: Monument; outing area combining developed scenic and intensive-use areas.

Characteristics: Site of Fort Loudoun, colonial fort built in 1756; pastoral scenery; mountain and river views.

Fort Loudoun, the first English settlement west of the Allegheny Mountains, was built in 1756 and 1757 as protection from the French and Spanish who were seeking to acquire dominion over the southern coast and the interior of the present United States. The fort was in the heart of the territory occupied by the "Over the Hill" Cherokees and was built at their request. The construction of the fort was attended by great difficulties not only in transporting men, materials, and equipment 150 miles across narrow mountain passes, but also in gaining effective cooperation between authorities in Virginia, North Carolina, and South Carolina. It was built by William de Brahm, chief engineer, and garrisoned by militia from the three colonies. When it was first built the Cherokees were friendly to the English, but gradually the garrison found itself in hostile territory.

Fort Loudoun was never taken by assault but was finally surrendered to the Indians by pact in 1760 after a long siege during which no help came from the colonies. After surrender, the garrison was ambushed and slain in its first camp on the homeward march. As a result of this treachery, the angered English warred on the Cherokees, burned their towns, and laid waste their fields. The territory of Tennessee was thus opened to colonization.

At the present time the site of the fort is a knoll wooded with hardwoods, some of which are gigantic in size. Rolling agricultural land surrounds the knoll, except on the side toward the river which swings in a wide curve around the site, with high bluffs falling away to the river at several points. To the south are views of the mountains.

Culminating 20 years of effort by various patriotic organizations, restoration of Fort Loudoun is now under way. A road has been built to the site by WPA and actual reconstruction of the buildings is to be undertaken following complete examination of the premises for evidence of the colonial occupation. The title to the actual land on which the fort stood,

5.72 acres, is held in escrow by the Fort Loudoun Association, chartered in 1933. A tablet was erected on the site in 1917 by the Tennessee Society of Colonial Dames of America.

COULTER SHOALS LAKE
[C–4]

Location: Loudon, Blount, and Knox Counties.
Size: 11,900 acres—approximately 18½ square miles.
Type: A reservoir planned primarily to maintain a navigable channel on the uppermost section of the Tennessee River.
Characteristics: A long, winding lake in a setting of undulating agricultural country; level of the lake will fluctuate.

The site of the proposed Coulter Shoals Dam lies about 4 miles east of Lenoir City. This dam will back the Tennessee River beyond Knoxville to points just above the confluence of the Holston and French Broad Rivers, where they form the Tennessee.

Coulter Shoals Lake will be smaller than other main river lakes, having a total surface area of only 18½ square miles. The greatest expanse of water in it will be near Concord, with an area between 2 and 3 square miles in a length of 2 miles of lake. The average normal width of the reservoir will be less than half a mile. The shore line will be varied by the number of coves and stream valleys into which the water will back. Maximum draw-down will be 11 feet, but the effect of this draw-down on the recreational use of the shores cannot be estimated until detailed surveys can be studied.

The meandering Tennessee, flanked by wooded bluffs and rolling cornfields, is churned to foam by the splashing of a stern-wheeler and its barge near Knoxville.

The lake will lie in a rolling section of country where the ridges are not pronounced and where a high percentage of the land is in farms, with only a few large forested tracts. Its proximity to Knoxville gives it particular significance for recreation. Several highways and county roads will make it easily accessible to the population of Knoxville, Maryville, and Alcoa. United States Highways 11 and 70 generally parallel the reservoir at distances of 2 to 6 miles. Tennessee Highway 33 from Knoxville to Maryville passes close to it on the southeast side near Topside and the Little River.

Several striking bluffs occur within a few miles of Knoxville and will be the principal scenic features of this reservoir. They offer opportunity for development as outing areas to serve Knoxville, Maryville, and Alcoa. Sites for summer camps, summer homes, and vacation cabins could be developed within easy distance of Knoxville, and facilities should exist for increased boating activities.

FONTANA LAKE
[D-6]

Location: On Little Tennessee River, in Swain and Graham Counties, N. C.

Size: Approximately 9,200 acres at normal pool elevation.

Type: Flood storage reservoir with considerable fluctuation of water level.

Characteristics: Irregular lake in a mountain setting; a generally steep shore line, wooded with second-growth timber.

Fontana Dam, proposed by the TVA in its plan for the unified development of the Tennessee River, will create a lake of 9,200 acres on the Little Tennessee River immediately above Cheoah Lake. Its setting is perhaps unrivaled among lakes in the Tennessee Valley. Above it on the north rise the heights of the Great Smoky Mountains National Park; on the south, the slightly lower peaks of Nantahala National Forest.

Except for the higher summits of the Smokies, most of the vicinity has been logged, but a good quality of second growth prevails around the proposed lake with little farmland intervening. From the dam site, 20 miles airline west of Bryson City, N. C., the lake will extend nearly to the city's outskirts, a river-channel distance of 30 miles. Several large arms and numerous coves will vary the shore line of the lake and visually increase the actual width of 1 mile.

Only extensive highway relocations will render accessible the main body of the lake, below the confluence of the Tuckasegee River and the Little Tennessee. United States Highway 19, which crosses the Nantahala and Little Tennessee arms of the lake, will make the upper reaches with gentler shore lines readily available by motor. Boats may provide the most feasible access to other parts of the lake.

Complete realization of the recreational potentialities of Fontana Lake will depend on a number of factors remaining to be determined. Adjacent to the national park, it will lie near the center of recreational interests in the Tennessee Valley; and unless special recreational lakes are provided elsewhere, a considerable demand will probably arise for facilities along its shore. The degree to which this demand may be fulfilled will depend on conditions of access and on water level fluctuation. Solution of the problem can come only through the close cooperation of the United States Forest Service, National Park Service, TVA, and other agencies involved.

135

POTENTIAL REGIONAL RECREATION AREAS

CHILHOWEE MOUNTAIN FOREST
[D-5]

Location: Blount and Sevier Counties, Tenn.

Size: 175 square miles—112,000 acres.

Type: Outing area, including developed scenic and intensive-use areas.

Characteristics: Long ridge, with broken mountains and valleys east of the Little River. Superb views of Great Smoky Mountains and the Great Valley.

CHILHOWEE Mountain is an attenuated ridge, beginning at the Little Tennessee River and extending northeast for 31 miles toward the valley of the Little Pigeon River. From the northwest side is visible the Great Valley with its minor ridges and valleys and the winding Tennessee River. Northward stretch the Slate Knobs, a rather monotonous succession of topographic waves. To the southeast lies the long chain of the Great Smoky Mountains. Eastward rises English Mountain, a continuation of the same ridge that forms Chilhowee, but cut off from it by the valley of the Little Pigeon. The elevation of Chilhowee varies from a third to half the height of the neighboring Smoky Mountains with the highest point, something over 3,200 feet, lying 3 miles from the northeast end of the mountain.

Covered with second-growth forest, the slopes of Chilhowee are steep, and in places there are sheer rock cliffs. Few streams of any importance have their origins on the mountain's slopes, though several mineral springs, such as Allegheny Springs, Montvale Springs, and Dupont Springs on the northwest slope, and Doyle Springs on the southeast, once gave rise to now vanished resort hotels. Unlike Clinch and Cumberland Mountains and the minor ridges in the Great Valley—all of which run consistently parallel with the main rivers—Chilhowee lies more or less crosswise to the principal water courses, such as the Little Tennessee, Little River, and Little Pigeon River. The water gaps of these rivers furnish the approaches through Chilhowee to the higher ranges to the southeast. From the crest of Chilhowee, superb views open out over the Great Valley. This vantage point also affords extensive panoramic views of the Great Smoky Mountains.

Because of its elevation and consequent favorable summer climate, together with its proximity to the Great Smoky Mountains National Park, Chilhowee Mountain appears to be a promising location for resort development. The map of the Knoxville area indicates that to the ridge itself there has been appended a large tract, bounded on the northwest by Chilhowee Mountain, on the south by the national park, and on the east by the Little Pigeon River. This area, largely forested, and mountainous to a minor degree, is eminently suited for recreational use. Two streams of considerable size, Walden Creek and Cove Creek, flow through the area, and it would be worth investigating the possibilities of damming one or the other to create a recreational lake of considerable size. Such a body of water would supply the present lack of opportunities for water sports in this locality.

On the map this whole area, designated as Chilhowee Mountain Forest, has been indicated as a potential regional forest. This suggestion does not mean that this form of jurisdiction is the only suitable one, but rather that the general character and size of the tract suggest preservation of the forest cover under some form of unified control, such as that offered by a publicly owned forest.

ENGLISH MOUNTAIN FOREST
[F-4]

Location: Sevier, Cocke, and Jefferson Counties, Tenn.

Size: 85,000 acres.

Type: Wilderness with occasional intensive-use areas.

Characteristics: English Mountain, elevation 3,800, offering distant panoramic views of the Great Smoky and Unaka Mountains; Webb Mountain, elevation 2,807, offering closer views of the mountains; second-growth woodland of mixed hardwood and pine; rural scenery.

English Mountain Forest would include 85,000 acres of land in a corner between the boundaries of the Great Smoky Mountains National Park and the Cherokee National Forest. Within the boundary are English Mountain, elevation 3,800 feet, and Webb Mountain, elevation 2,807 feet; both offering panoramic views of the Great Smoky Mountains. Between the two mountains the land is knobby, badly dissected, and marginal or submarginal from an agricultural standpoint. Clearings are confined to narrow strips along streams, and farms are isolated.

English Mountain forms a long ridge divided near its center by a gap of 2,300 feet in elevation. West of the gap the elevation of this ridge averages 2,500 feet. East of the gap the elevation varies between a maximum of 3,800 feet at the Pinnacle and 2,500 feet at the eastern extremity. From the Pinnacle the view to the north extends across a pattern of woods and fields traversed by the French Broad River, to

136

English Mountain, dominating a landscape of woods and fields, is suggested as a forest purchase unit.

The State Forestry Division, under the authority of the Fulmer Act, has proposed as a State forest a smaller tract, 43,478 acres in extent and lying only on English Mountain itself. Webb Mountain and intervening valley lands are omitted. The investigations by foresters indicate that private ownership is unable to realize a profit from the land or to adequately protect and maintain it. Much of the land is tax delinquent and could be brought into public ownership with little loss to the tax base of the counties involved.

CLINCH MOUNTAIN FOREST: TENNESSEE UNIT
[E-2, G-1]

Location: Extending northeastward from the intersection of Grainger, Knox, and Union Counties, Tenn., to the Virginia State line.

Size: 125,000 acres (partially in the Upper Tennessee Valley area and partially in the Knoxville area).

Type: Wilderness; outing area, including developed scenic and intensive-use areas.

Characteristics: Long wooded ridge, supplemented by lower parallel ridges in some places and widening out to form an enclosed cove at its southwest butt. Superb views over surrounding countryside to distant mountains.

the ridges of Bays Mountain, Clinch Mountain, and the Cumberlands. To the south lies a panorama of the Great Smokies with a foreground consisting of Webb Mountain and low wooded knobs. A closer view of the Smokies dominated by Mount Guyot and Mount LeConte may be obtained from Webb Mountain.

Sinking Creek, draining the northeast slope of English Mountain, is a cascading stream with one 30-foot waterfall. It flows in a rhododendron-filled gorge. Several mineral and freestone springs feed it and other streams to maintain a fairly constant flow. Groups of these springs formed the basis for old-time resorts at Glenn Alpine, Carson's, Carter, and Fain Springs, all on the slope of the mountain. Blowing Cave, near Glenn Alpine, is another feature of note.

Although not of superlative scenic character, except for English and Webb Mountains, the area is accessible by good highways: Tennessee Highways 35 and 75 and the new road along the northern boundary of the Great Smoky Mountains National Park; also, a rock surfaced county road from Sevierville to Cosby crosses the area. This factor of accessibility would enable the tract to be developed as a means of relieving the likely pressure of too intensive use within the national park. Camps, resorts, or picnic areas might be developed at various places. The park area itself would then be readily accessible by foot, horseback, or motor. Public management would, in turn, provide natural areas in the immediate vicinity of these developed areas and, as has been mentioned in connection with the potential Chilhowee Mountain Forest, this would insure the preservation of attractive views from the park.

Clinch Mountain is the longest and highest ridge in the Upper Tennessee Valley between the ranges of the Blue Ridge Province and the Cumberland Mountains. From its southwestern extremity—about 18 miles, airline distance, northeast of Knoxville—it stretches for 150 miles northeast, thus extending well into Virginia where it terminates in its highest elevation of 4,724 feet. Within the Knoxville area its crest varies from 2,000 to 2,500 feet elevation. The highest point in the area outlined on the map is found on adjacent Short Mountain which is over 2,700 feet high.

Several factors make it highly desirable that Clinch Mountain and some of the adjacent ridges be included in some form of publicly owned reservation. These ridges are the source of many streams that flow into the Clinch and the Holston Rivers. Heavy uncontrolled cutting and repeated forest fires have taken place on the ridges in the past and are continuing. For the present, however, timber cutting is definitely drawing to a close, due to the rapidly decreasing supply of merchantable material. But these two factors, fire and indiscriminate logging, have already had a decidedly detrimental effect on the watershed protection value of the area and have resulted in considerable erosion and consequent silting of the Clinch and the Holston. It is highly probable that this unwise treatment of the resources will continue as long as the area remains in unstable ownership. However, this is not to be interpreted to mean that selective logging of salable timber under proper forest management cannot be carried on in the future. Present information indicates that in the main this area represents a forest site of such low productivity that private forest management is economically unsound, and the area is, therefore, a public responsibility.

Considered from its scenic aspect, Clinch Mountain occupies such a dominating place in the Great Valley that it is mandatory that forest fires, destructive logging, and overgrazing be prevented if its scenic values are to be maintained. Permanent forest logging under skilled management would be feasible here, however, if properly conducted in relation to the recreational use of special areas and should, in fact, improve the appearance of the area in general. Moreover, as the chief scenic value lies not in the mountain itself but in the many beautiful panoramas which unfold from certain vantage points along the crest, selective logging practice on the lower slopes would not be conspicuous from these distant points.

In the light of these various conservational aspects it would appear that Clinch Mountain should belong to the public domain. It forms too small an area to be suitable for a national forest unit, therefore, a possible alternative is a State forest.

The attenuated character of the Clinch Mountain tract restricts the nature of its possible recreational usage; but, on the other hand, it is more readily available to the adjacent population than would be the case with a compact reservation of equal size.

It is conceivable that Clinch Mountain, along with such other areas as English and Chilhowee Mountains and parts of the Cumberland Escarpment, might be a logical location for private resort developments. However, leasing suitable tracts for such use would be in accord with established forestry policies.

The butt of Clinch Mountain rises in sharp contrast with the plain below.

Bean Gap
[E–2]

Location: Grainger County, Tenn., where United States Highway 25 E crosses Clinch Mountain.
Type: Wayside development.
Characteristics: One of the important gaps across Clinch Mountain; panoramic views from United States Highway 25 E.

Bean Gap is mentioned as a feature of Clinch Mountain because of its accessibility by means of United States Highway 25 E. Views from the gap are probably no better than from many other places along the mountain, but the highway makes them readily available, as well as forming a logical take-off or stopping-point for future trails developed in connection with potential forest recreational use.

Distant valley ridges show jointly in this roadside scene below Bean Gap, United States Highway 25 E.

Signal Point
[D–3]

Location: On the butt of Clinch Mountain at the southwest extremity of the ridge.
Type: Outing area, combining developed scenic and intensive-use areas.
Characteristics: 360-degree superb panoramic view from highest point; valley completely enclosed by wooded, rocky, mountain ridges; springs; two waterfalls.

The butt of Clinch Mountain is composed of several isolated knobs and spurs of various elevations. The highest of these is Signal Point, so called because of its use during the Civil War for relayed communication with Chattanooga. It rises 1,200 feet above its base to a height of over 2,300 feet. Looking from it toward the south on a clear day, the long profile of the Great Smoky Mountains may be seen; while northward, Cumberland Mountain stretches in an unbroken line across the horizon. To the east, Clinch Mountain extends to the limit of vision; while westward, in the near foreground, House Mountain looms up as an isolated peak with the minor valleys and ridges of the Great Valley lying beyond and on both sides of it. Because Signal Point is almost bare of trees, the view in all directions is unrestricted. Kitts Spur, running southeast from Signal Point at a lower elevation, offers approximately the same views except toward the north; even though rather well wooded with pines and hardwoods, these do not at present materially obstruct the views from the spur.

Completely enclosed by the above mentioned knobs, by the main ridge of Clinch Mountain to the north, and by the considerably lower Poor Valley Knobs on the east, lies an open cove where several springs form a stream that joins another branch flowing from the valley between Clinch Mountain and Poor Valley Knobs. This enlarged creek flows through a narrow gap at the east side of the butt, to join a tributary of the Holston River. In the small spring-fed stream which retains water even in the upper reaches except during serious droughts, there are two waterfalls. The upper one, about 40 feet high, is broken in two

by a rock ledge; the lower one forms a series of cascades and minor falls, totaling 100 feet or so. An existing trail winds up past these waterfalls to the top of the ridge where forks of the trail lead to Signal Point and Kitts Spur. The cove contains two possible sites for creating spring-fed lakes; one of about 30 acres and another of 10 acres or less. In this cove also lies the Lea Lake private development, which is described in this chapter.

HOUSE MOUNTAIN FOREST
[D-3]

Location: 14-16 miles airline northeast of Knoxville.
Size: 3,600 acres.
Type: Wilderness.
Characteristics: Isolated wooded peak, 2,129 feet elevation, affording views over rural country to the Cumberland and Great Smoky Mountains.

House Mountain is a natural feature which gains value by its proximity to a large city. Only a half-hour drive from Knoxville, it provides for a quick transition from urban surroundings into a place which

House Mountain rises abruptly from the valley in this scene reminiscent of a New England countryside.

is essentially a wilderness, although from the mountain one may always look out over a cultivated rural landscape. The mountain rises 1,100 feet above its base. To reach the top of its ridge, a stiff climb is necessary, whereupon a 2-mile hike along the crest offers continually changing vistas.

To the northeast the view is up the Great Valley between parallel ridges, the end of one of which, Clinch Mountain, is less than 5 miles away; while in the opposite direction, one looks down the length of low ridges to Knoxville. To the north, above the intervening ridges, rises Cumberland Mountain, and toward the south, on clear days there unfolds a complete panorama of the peaks of the Great Smoky Mountains National Park, with the lesser peaks of other mountains extending on either side.

House Mountain, in its present natural state, will increase in value with the growth of Knoxville. It should be acquired as a public reservation, perhaps as a State forest. Because of its comparatively small size, it might become a unit of the potential Clinch Mountain Forest. It should be administered with a minimum of trails and forest management, for neither the mountain nor its surrounding land is suited to intensive recreational use.

The mountain is best reached from Knoxville by way of Washington Pike or from United States Highway 11 W, east of Skaggston.

ANDREW JACKSON LAKE
[C-4]

Location: Knox County, Tenn., 11½ miles airline west-southwest of Knoxville.

Communities served: Knoxville, 13 miles; Lenoir City, 14 miles; Loudon, 20 miles; Clinton, 20 miles; Alcoa, 27 miles, Maryville, 29 miles; Coal Creek, 29 miles; Sweetwater, 32 miles; Harriman, 34 miles.

Size: 500 acres.

Type: Outing park.

Characteristics: 40-acre lake, natural in appearance, lying in rolling valley area; 100 acres of unusually good woodland with variety of undergrowth.

On the site of the present lake, a spring-fed stream once flowed through a 25- to 30-foot gorge and disappeared underground in a marshy area. But in 1910, an ill-fated horse is said to have found its way into this swamp and was drowned. The carcass was discovered and removed, but it had in some way disturbed and blocked the natural outlet of the stream. A lake began to form and soon had assumed the approximate contours of the present body of water which received the appellation of "Dead Horse Lake." Some years later when this lake and its environs were

Andrew Jackson Lake, with potential opportunities for water sports, is only 13 miles from Knoxville.

bought by some Knoxville men with the idea of promoting its recreational use, the somewhat malodorous name was changed to Andrew Jackson Lake; this title being adopted because of the tradition that "Old Hickory" had once owned part of this property. The former outlet was located by the new owners who assured its permanent closure by plugging it with several hundred bags of cement and clay. The water is clear, and its level only very slightly affected by dry seasons.

The deepest part of the lake, whose long axis runs due east and west, lies north of a promontory which juts out midway along the south shore. This promontory has been the location for such slight development as has been done and is the logical site for concentration of features pertaining to intensive recreational use of the water. Except for this promon-

A natural picnic grove near the shores, Andrew Jackson Lake.

140

tory and a small area at the west extremity of the lake, the south shore is entirely wooded with exceptionally good second growth amidst which remain scattered specimens of the original forest. The undergrowth, composed of small trees, shrubs, and herbs, is unusually varied, and along the lake shore occur frequent outcrops of interesting water-worn rock formations. Scattered through the woods and around the lake are a dozen smaller ponds, the largest of which, several acres in extent, has been increasing in size for several years without affecting the water-level of the large lake.

The woods extend unbrokenly for more than a mile, south, east, and west of the lake and would lend themselves admirably to a typical outing park development with trails, picnic areas, and vacation cabins and camps along the lake shore.

The tract is reached from the center of Knoxville by going 12½ miles west on United States Highways 11 and 70 and then northward on half a mile of gravel road. Accessibility and close proximity of the tract to Knoxville and other urban centers, combined with its natural advantages, make this area outstanding as the most desirable type of outing park.

GRAVESTON POND
[D-3]

Location: 15 miles airline north-northeast of Knoxville.
Size: 140 acres or less.
Type: Outing area for intensive-use.
Characteristics: Existing 7-acre pond, fed by several large springs; view of Butt of Clinch Mountain; small tract of good woods, rocky ridge.

Graveston Pond was formed by damming the flow of a very large spring and one or two lesser ones; the strongest spring still bubbles up appreciably above the normal water surface. The pond is from 75 to 200 feet wide, and a quarter of a mile long, with its widest portion at the upper end, where the springs are. Land in the vicinity is predominantly submarginal, and frequent longitudinal outcroppings of rock indicate a shallow soil. One rather good second-growth patch of woodland of about 25 acres lies not far from the pond, but for the most part the surroundings appear rather open, though dotted with numerous scattered red cedars, and, along the shore, fringed by sycamores and other riparian trees and shrubs. From the top of the bank at the upper end of the pond a good view of the Butt of Clinch Mountain may be obtained. The dam which forms the pond is a somewhat crude affair made of planks, and should

Graceful sycamores frame a tranquil picture of Graveston Pond.

be replaced in case of any recreational use of the area.

Notwithstanding its negligible size in comparison with such large bodies of water as Norris Lake and the future Coulter Shoals and Watts Bar Reservoirs, the spring-fed Graveston Pond might fit usefully into the future recreational picture as a county reservation because of the potentialities that it offers for swimming. It might be an appropriate location for a boys' or girls' camp, as well as a limited number of summer cottages. It is readily accessible from Knoxville by the old Tazewell Pike which runs alongside—and in places, rather too near—the pond.

RED KNOB
[D-4]

Location: 6 miles airline southeast of downtown Knoxville.
Size: 400 acres.
Type: Outing area, combining intensive-use and developed scenic areas.
Characteristics: Low bluffs along the river; high, partly wooded knob with good river and mountain views; good streams, with low waterfall; springs.

Red Knob is reputed locally to be the highest elevation in the vicinity of Knoxville. At any rate, the hill does rise considerably above its surroundings, permitting a very broad view of the whole extent of the Great Smoky Mountains. To the north and east lies the valley of the French Broad River with Paint Rock Bluffs beyond the first reverse loop of the river, while in the distance loom House and Clinch Mountains. The wooded north slope of Red Knob terminates in minor bluffs which rise perhaps 75 feet above the river. West of the knob runs a fair-sized stream, in which there is a cascading waterfall with about a 5-foot drop, and two good springs flow from the west slope of the hill. The tree growth is of average character.

The greater part of this tract as outlined on the map is wooded, and not suited to agriculture. Its best use appears to be recreational. Because of its proximity to Knoxville this tract would make a good county reservation for day or part-day outings. A road winding to the top of the knob would make available to Knoxville motorists a nearby place to which they might drive and park while enjoying an extensive, leisurely view of the Smoky Mountains—something which is not now provided for. The woods would be ideal for picnicking and hiking. Short boat trips could be made to nearby Michael Bluff and Paint Rock Bluffs.

Red Knob is approached from Knoxville by way of Island Home Pike. Along the pike, 4 miles from the south end of the Gay Street bridge, a gravel road turns east at a right angle; 2 miles farther, on this road, the base of Red Knob is reached at a point near the waterfall, which is the limit of approach by car.

CHEROKEE BLUFFS
[D-4]

Location: South bank of Tennessee River, 1¼ miles south-southwest of Henley Street bridge, abutting on the city limits of Knoxville.

Size: 220 acres.

Type: Outing park, combining intensive-use and developed scenic areas.

Characteristics: High river bluffs, wooded knob, views over Knoxville.

Cherokee Bluffs are outstanding among the cliffs located along the upper Tennessee River. Standing 200 feet or more above the river, they combine sheer rock cliffs with steep slopes to the water level. Tree growth is predominantly of oak and pine, with dogwood and redbud below, and—what is rare between the Smokies and the Cumberlands—a considerable undercover of rhododendron and laurel. In addition, the slopes and rocks are particularly rich in wild flowers and ferns in great variety.

Behind the bluffs are ridges, considerably broken up into individual knobs, predominantly wooded. There are few habitations within the area of 220

An unfamiliar view of Knoxville obtained from Cherokee Bluffs.

acres indicated on the map, but the bluff land is held by a few individuals who hope to sell it for high class residential property. However, a tract of this quality, lying so close to Knoxville, would be a great asset as a park and perhaps it should not be allowed to become unavailable to the public. Although it should probably be under city or county jurisdiction, its nature gives it regional significance.

Suitable development of the area as a park would consist chiefly of trails and picnic areas. A small artificial spring-fed pond of several acres' extent should be considered as a decorative rather than useful feature. Access to the park by a boat landing might be justified, but the bank is so steep as to discourage the provision of extensive aquatic facilities.

The present approach to the bluffs from the east is over a gravel byway that leaves the Maryville Pike (Tennessee Highway 33) in Vestal, passes under the railroad, and comes to an end in a row of cottages at the base of the bluff. From this point a graded trail leads along the hillside to a draw that contains the pond, then ascends to the top of the bluffs and continues westward. Another approach to Cherokee Bluffs is by a road from the southeast, leaving the Maryville Pike a mile or so south of the first one and winding upward to the top of a ridge from which the Smokies may be seen to the south, with a view of the river and Knoxville to the north. From here this road descends to join the first one just west of the railroad underpass.

LOONEYS ISLAND BLUFFS
[C-4]

Location: Knox County, Tenn., 3¾ miles airline southwest of Knoxville.
Characteristics: Sheer cliffs, wooded on top; river views.

Rising sheer from the river about 2½ miles down river from Cherokee Bluffs, and beginning just below Looneys Island, three cliffs, shaped roughly like the sliced end of a loaf of French bread, tower some 200 feet or more above the river and are crowned with a thick tree growth. It is nearly a mile from end to end of the three cliffs.

The nearest point of access to Looneys Island Bluffs is the new Knox Airport road (Tennessee Highway 33 A) which passes within a few hundred yards of the bluffs. Private residential development above the bluffs, however, will prevent access from that road. Therefore, as a scenic feature, it is probable that the bluffs will be available to the public only through views from the river and from the north shore.

MICHAEL BLUFF
[D-4]

Location: 4½ miles airline east-southeast of downtown Knoxville on the west bank of the French Broad River.
Size: 450 acres.
Type: Outing area for intensive-use.
Characteristics: River bluff, 75 feet high; exceptionally fine cedar growth.

Michael Bluff extends for nearly half a mile on the west side of the last northward bend of the French Broad River before it joins the Holston to form the Tennessee River. The sheer cliffs offer attractive views of the immediate river valley. Aside from the interest in the bluff itself and its views, an exceptionally fine growth of cedars occupies the ground running back from the bluff, the boles of a number of these superb specimens measuring a foot or even 18 inches in diameter. The very rocky soil is obviously too shallow to be of any use for agriculture. All things considered, it seems worthwhile to recommend a tract of 450 acres, extending back for a mile from the bluff to Island Home Pike, as a public recreation area. At the present time, the nearest approach to the bluff is by way of the Island Home Pike. At about 4 miles from the intersection of Main and Henley Streets, Knoxville, shortly after the pike crosses the railroad at the marble quarry, a stone road branches to the left and ends at a farmstead a quarter of a mile from the bluff.

PAINT ROCK BLUFFS
[D-4]

Location: 6 miles east of downtown Knoxville, on the north bank of the French Broad River.
Size: 100 acres.
Type: Developed scenic area.
Characteristics: Wooded, rocky bluffs with river and mountain views.

About 3½ miles above its confluence with the Holston River, the French Broad River makes a northward loop, on the north side of which for a distance of three quarters of a mile, rock bluffs rise in places from 100 to 200 feet above the river. Although the cliffs support many red cedars, pines, and hardwoods, these bluffs reveal good views up and down the river, as well as glimpses of the Great Smoky Mountains. Back of the eastern half of the bluffs, cleared land comes close to the bluff line; but between the western half and the county road lies a tract of very rocky ground largely covered with red cedars. This tract is worthless for agriculture but would be satisfactory as a recreation area. For this reason, and because the best approach to the bluffs is through this cedar woods,

Above its junction with the Holston River, the French Broad swings past Paint Rock Bluff.

an extensive cliff, it rises impressively from the river as a dissected rocky acclivity forming irregular cliffs reaching a height of 200 feet or more above the river and revealing fine views up and down the river and across the farmland and ridges of the Great Valley to the mountains in the southeast. Behind the rocky projections of the bluff, a wooded hill rises an additional hundred feet. West of the bluff a small valley will be partially flooded by the waters of the proposed Coulter Shoals Reservoir; this cove should then offer a strategic and convenient location for the development of facilities for water-sports.

The area is approached by a good crushed stone road that loops down into the cove already mentioned. This road at its nearest point to the bluff is 20 miles from Knoxville via United States Highway 70 and Concord. Two miles west of Concord on the Lenoir City Road, turn left on to a good stone road; after 2 miles turn right; and at another 1½ miles turn right again. One mile farther is the cove west of Peter Bluff, to which a lane leads from the road. When the proposed Coulter Shoals Dam has been completed, Peter Bluff would probably make a very satisfactory county or TVA Park.

a tract of some 100 acres including the cliffs is indicated on the map as being desirable as a future county or municipal reservation.

The bluffs are easily reached by motor as follows: Leave Tennessee Highway 34 about three-fourths mile east of Boyd's Bridge over the Holston and take the paved county road through Marbledale. At 2½ miles on this road, turn south through a gate onto a rough but passable local road southeast for half a mile. At this point the road curves to the south, and a foot trail leads straight on to the river. This trail extends eastward the full length of the bluffs.

PETER BLUFF
[C-4]

Location: Knox County, 18 miles airline southwest of Knoxville.
Size: 100–150 acres.
Type: Outing area combining intensive-use and developed scenic areas.
Characteristics: Wooded rocky bluffs with river and mountain views; adjacent cove for access to water facilities.

On the north side of a loop of the Tennessee River, about 1½ miles upstream from the site of the proposed Coulter Shoals Dam, stands Peter Bluff. Though not

MEREDITH CAVE
[C-2]

Location: On Shanghai Branch of Norris Lake, 6 miles south of La Follette, Campbell County, Tenn.
Type: Developed scenic area.
Characteristics: Large limestone cavern of undetermined depth; probable recent geological origin.

Meredith Cave opens from a hillside above Shanghai Branch of Norris Lake, one-fourth of a mile from the shore. The natural entrance, an arch 30 feet across and 10 feet high, gives access to a corridor which slopes back and down on a 15 percent grade. Beyond the entrance corridor a succession of roomy, high-ceiled chambers are connected by a confusion of winding passages. The cave has been worn from soft limestone, the absence of stalactites, stalagmites, and other water-deposited formations suggesting that it is young in the geologic calendar. Although parties have penetrated its interior for more than 2 miles, the cave has never been fully explored.

The cave has some historical significance in connection with saltpetre operations and would be worthy of visit if adequately lighted and its natural setting left undisturbed. A road leading from La Follette to a boat landing on Shanghai Branch passes through a portion of Norris Lake Forest close to the cave.

Sentinel Peter Bluff overlooks farm and woodland along the Tennessee River below Knoxville.

Falls Creek Falls Park derives its name from this spectacular cataract. Altogether 257 feet high, the sheer drop alone is nearly 100 feet greater than the height of Niagara.

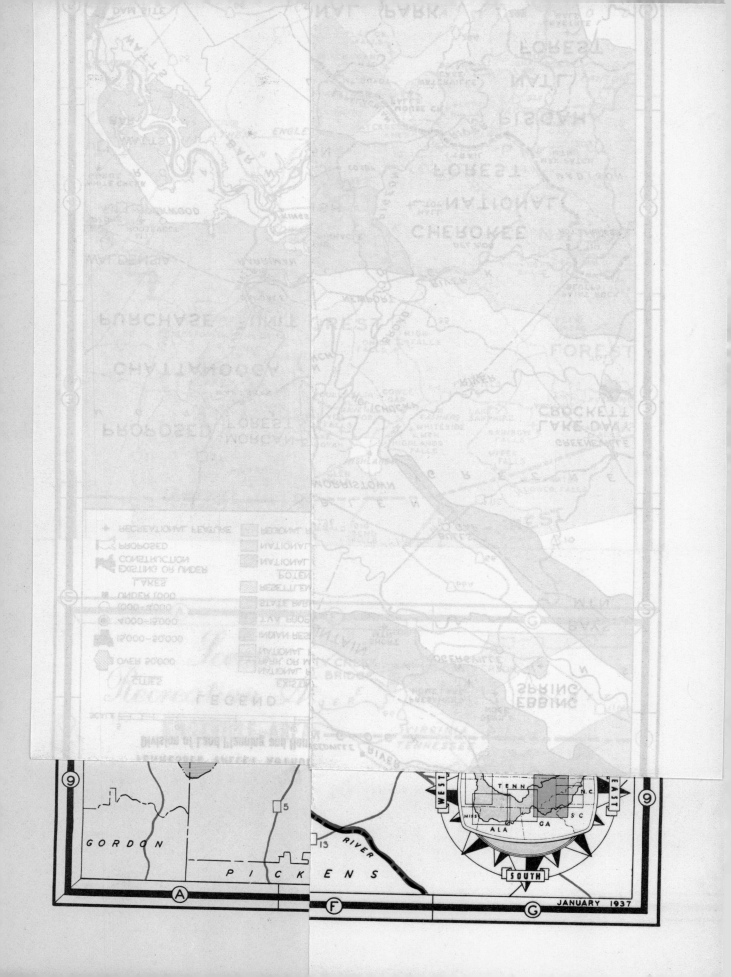

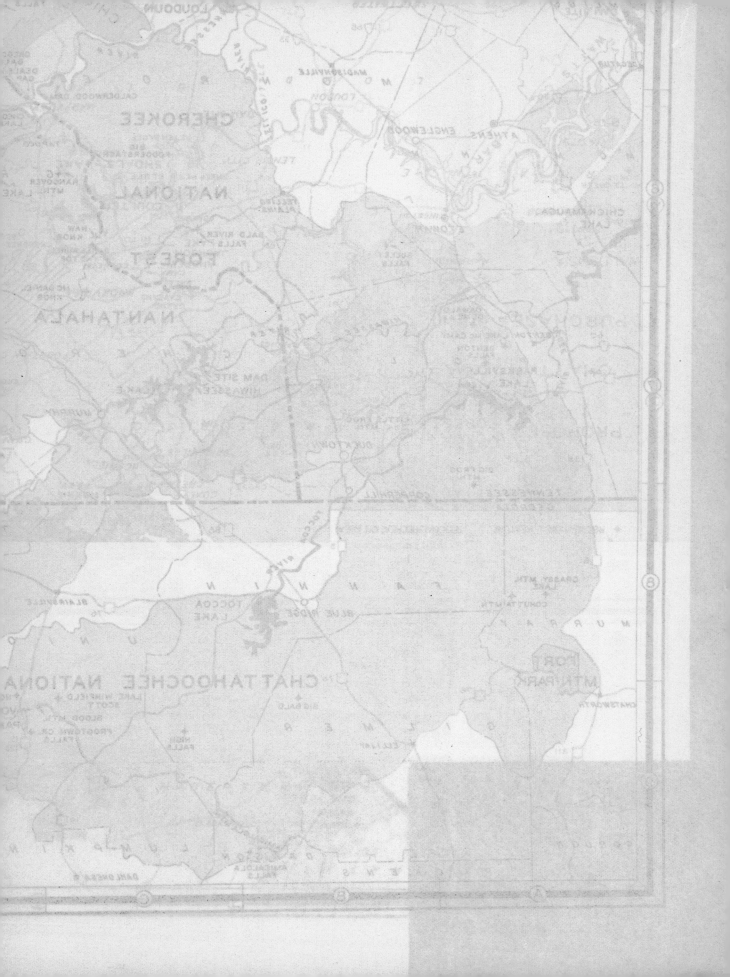

The Chattanooga Area

GENERAL DESCRIPTION OF THE AREA

THE Chattanooga area centers around the city of Chattanooga, its only large city, which lies slightly south of the geographical center of the area. In 1930 Chattanooga had an official population of 119,798, approximately one-fourth of the population of the entire area. Estimates of Chattanooga's 1936 population range as high as 170,000.

The area is cut diagonally in a northeast-southwest direction by the Tennessee River and its adjoining valley land, part of the Great Appalachian Valley. Above Chattanooga, the valley divides the Appalachian Plateaus of the northwest half of the area from the Blue Ridge Province which makes up the southeast half. Below Chattanooga, the river cuts through the Sand Mountain and the Walden Ridge Plateaus, is joined by the Sequatchie River, and then flows between Sand Mountain and the main Cumberland Plateau into the valley of north Alabama.

Peneplains with an average elevation of 1,600 to 2,000 feet, 800 to 1,500 feet above adjacent territory, rise to occasional points 3,000 feet in elevation. They are generally made up of sedimentary sandstone, shales, and conglomerate, underlain with coal measures. Their boundaries are, for the most part, clearly defined by escarpments of various heights, capped by rimrock with talus slopes beneath. Frequently the palisade-like cliffs follow narrow gorges and coves far into the interior of the plateau. For the most part continuous, they form the headwalls of the coves. Stream courses are steep; usually there is a waterfall at the escarpment with rapids and

cascades bow. Flood plains and flats are unusual.

The Highland Rim, which constitutes the extreme northwest corner of the area, has a general elevation of 1,000 feet. The Blue Ridge Province, in the southeast, has none of the plateau character but is dissected into individual ridges and peaks by steep, narrow valleys. These peaks have no uniformity of height and reach elevations up to 4,200 feet.

The area has a mean annual rainfall of from 50 to 55 inches. It has mean annual temperatures of 55° to 60° and mean summer temperatures between 70° and 80°. Temperatures, in general, vary inversely with the altitude; the plateaus and mountainous sections are markedly cooler than the lowlands.

Description of the Chattanooga area shows that it embraces three distinctly different physiographical areas—the mountainous Blue Ridge Province, almost all of which is included in Cherokee and Chattahoochee National Forests; the Great Valley; and the Appalachian Plateaus. Within the national forests, recreational facilities have been developed as an integral part of the land use program for the area. Because many of the factors which affect the recreational use of either the Valley or the Plateau also affect other problems of land use and because, in many cases, these factors are general conditions not limited or controllable within a specific territory, it would seem that, in order to achieve an adequate system of recreational areas, the Chattanooga area, perhaps more than any other portion of the Tennessee Valley, depends on a comprehensive regional plan rather than on a recreational plan for specific localities.

The Great Valley has neither spectacular scenic interest nor wilderness character, but in it there should be areas primarily for intensive recreation. The development by the TVA of the Chickamauga and Watts Bar Lakes will provide large bodies of water which will offer opportunities for recreational development, subject, of course, to the factors of drawdown, malaria, and pollution. The shore lines of these reservoirs will be studied carefully for the location of outing areas. There should be several potential sites on inlets kept fresh by tributary streams, provided these streams have adqeuate watershed protection. Additional sites will become available on other streams when a terracing and erosion control program for the valley is complete, and when sewage treatment plants are provided by the larger towns.

No less important from a recreational standpoint than the carrying out of the reservoir program, is the establishment of a coordinated control of land use on the plateaus. Because the plateau land, except in the coves, is too generally flat to have topographical interest, it is dependent for recreational value upon a healthy condition of forest and stream. Past exploitation of the land has seriously impaired the scenic and recreational value of both. Forests have been "mined" of salable timber and subject to heavy grazing and frequent burning. Remaining forest stands, except in the coves, are often of inferior second growth, unhealthy and fire-scarred. In spite of a high annual rainfall, streams of the plateaus are almost universally dry in summer because water-holding humus has been destroyed by fire. As a result, fish and game have few places to breed, scant food, and limited cover in which to live. Planning for fire control,

watershed protection, and forest stand improvement cannot be carried out with fullest effectiveness on a limited area. Such planning must be comprehensive.

With the restoration of a vigorous forest stand and the accompanying regulation of stream flow, restocking of fish and game, and improvement of existing scenic values, it may be expected that the plateaus will assume considerable importance for recreation. Large wilderness areas would have varying scenic interest. The climatic advantage over adjacent valleys and basins would attract vacation camp uses of various sorts. Hunting and fishing could be carried on to a considerable extent under proper restrictions. Thus a variety of recreational activities would be assured.

Inspection of the map of the Chattanooga area will show that it has extensive scenic recreational potentialities. A large portion of the area is included in existing or proposed national forests. No town of a population greater than 1,000 is more than 25 miles from potential wilderness recreation in these forests. The reservoir program of the TVA will provide large water areas with sites for outing recreation along attractive shore lines. Many features of outstanding scenic interest compare favorably with the best available elsewhere in the Tennessee Valley.

At present, recreational facilities concentrate in the Blue Ridge Province or in the vicinity of Chattanooga. Notable exceptions, however, include Bledsoe State Forest, Cumberland Homesteads Park, Falls Creek Falls Park, and developments at Tracy City and Monteagle. A growing consciousness of the need for developed recreation areas is indicated by the increasing use of Cherokee National Forest, by the efforts of Chattanooga people to establish a park at Montlake, and by the recent development at Falls Creek Falls.

EXISTING REGIONAL RECREATION AREAS

CHICKAMAUGA AND CHATTANOOGA NATIONAL MILITARY PARK

[E–6]

THE Chickamauga and Chattanooga National Military Park consists of several scattered areas in and about Chattanooga. These embrace points of importance in the "Campaign for Chattanooga" in 1863. In addition to a small area on Signal Mountain, Point Park on Lookout Mountain, and four small cemeteries; the reservation includes Chickamauga Park of 5,000 acres and Lookout Mountain Park of 2,700 acres. Of these, the latter is the area of principal significance for active recreation. It consists of forested land on the slope of Lookout Mountain. The area is traversed by bridle and foot trails leading to observation points and other places of interest.

Chickamauga Park, several miles south of the Tennessee-Georgia boundary, has been dedicated entirely to perpetuating memories of the battle. Numerous monuments, tablets, and markers outline the story, details of which are filled in by guides. A large stone building, of Georgian architecture, serves as headquarters for the park. As a museum, it houses exhibits which are the result of research by the Historical Division of the park management. There are bridle trails in the park and horses are available nearby at Fort Oglethorpe. There is also some incidental use of the area for picnicking but such use is not encouraged and no facilities are provided.

Cline, Chattanooga

Towering 1,000 feet above the valley, Lookout Mountain contemplates the Tennessee River and the level sweep of the Cumberlands.

149

Chickamauga Bluff, on the east front of Lookout Mountain, overlooks Missionary Ridge and Chattanooga.

LOOKOUT MOUNTAIN PURCHASE UNIT
[D-7]

The Lookout Mountain Purchase Unit, consisting of 204,000 acres of forest land, is located on Lookout Mountain in northeast Alabama and northwest Georgia. The unit includes a total of 143,000 acres in Chattooga, Dade, and Walker Counties, Ga., and 61,000 acres in DeKalb and Cherokee Counties, Ala. It was approved by the National Forest Reservation Commission in the fall of 1936.

The purchase unit includes the slopes and summit of Lookout Mountain, a high narrow plateau which is part of the Appalachian Plateaus. The slopes, for the most part, consist of an escarpment capped by rimrock, vertical outcroppings of sandstone 30 to 100 feet high. The plateau surface is gently rolling, and occasionally cut by narrow gorges which penetrate the general line of the escarpment. Its elevation varies from 1,800 to 2,300 feet and is 800 to 1,000 feet above the surrounding land. The northern portion of the unit drains into the Tennessee River, but the southern or major portion drains into the Coosa River.

A forest of mixed hardwoods and shortleaf pine originally covered the area, but is has been entirely cut over and the present growth consists of pure pine stands, most frequent on the east slopes, and mixed stands of pine and hardwood. Of particular recreational interest are the many flowering trees and shrubs, including dogwood, redbud, laurel, rhododendron, azalea, service berry, and hydrangea. The area was the natural home of upland game such as deer and turkey, although these are now almost nonexistent.

Natural advantages of climate, spectacular views, interesting rock formations and other scenic features, and a rich flora have attracted considerable recreational development to the area. Present resort developments center about Cloudland, Ga., and Mentone, Ala., and include several resort hotels, several boys' and girls' camps and numerous private cottages. Two scenic highways extend along the length of the mountain.

Lake Lahoosage, on the East Fork of the Little River near Cloudland, is a recreational lake created by a 50-foot dam. The narrow arms of the lake extend between well-wooded shores for a distance of several miles along the river. Together with several smaller lakes at other points on the river, it represents the principal effort to exploit the water resources of Lookout Mountain.

Cattails and waterlilies fringe the glassy surface of the Little River on Lookout Mountain.

Cline, Chattanooga

The huge rock at the brink seems to lessen the 100-foot drop of Lula Falls.

Lula Falls
[E-6]

Lula Falls is one of the few outstanding scenic features of Lookout Mountain that has not received intensive commercial development. It is located in McCallie Gap on Rock Creek, a tributary to Chattanooga Creek. The falls, 100 feet high, drop from the headwall of a pine-wooded gorge. Above the falls an attractive pool, some 300 feet long and 75 feet wide, is too small to justify the term "lake." The waters of the creek flow into the pool over a cascade some 20 feet high. One side of the pool is formed by an overhanging cliff and the opposite side by the steep slope of the hillside. The waters of the creek are clear and in the depths of the pool have a bluish tinge.

Although surrounding woodland has a poor quality, its natural beauty could be restored under a program of conservation. The altitude of the place affords it a scenic and climatic advantage. Excellent views extend from many vantage points across intervening lowland to the mountains of the Blue Ridge Province in the distance.

A spur railroad line to the mines of the Durham Coal Co. has a right-of-way through the gap close to the falls. Though it is unfortunate, from a recreational standpoint, the railroad is not a serious drawback because traffic over it is not heavy. It is likely that the railroad will outlive its usefulness in the near future; either it will be displaced by trucks, or the limited coal supply on Lookout Mountain will be exhausted.

DeSoto Falls
[D-7]

DeSoto Falls is a scenic feature of note near Mentone, Ala. The Little River, rising on the summit of Lookout Mountain, here takes its initial plunge into the gorge through which it flows for 25 miles before emerging from the mountain. Historically, the falls are associated with the Cherokee Indians, who supposedly used a large cave in the east wall of the basin as a council house, and with DeSoto. The ruins of the Spanish explorer's fortified camp remain in the gorge below. The gorge, with its large poplars, hemlocks, and profusion of rhododendron, still retains a primitive appearance.

In formation, the falls are geologically similar to many others on the plateaus. After a series of preliminary cascades, they drop from the overhanging side of the basin directly into a large pool; about the pool, sandstone walls rise from the water's edge to points varying from 100 to 200 feet above the water's surface. Opposite the falls, the river flows out and into the gorge.

The vicinity of the falls has been considerably developed. A summer home occupies a site overlooking both falls and basin; paths have been built to other vantage points. In the recent past, an effort was made to generate power from the falls. The dam, powerhouse, and penstock remain to disturb the naturalness of the feature.

Trenton Gulf
[D-6]

Trenton Gulf, also known as Sitton's Gulch, is a deep, forked cove in the west side of Lookout Mountain. Its sides are 800 feet high, sheer for half the distance, and devoid of growth save for shrubs and scrub pine which cling to crevices and thrust their roots into the softer layers of sedimentary rock that make up the mountain. Harder layers are exposed and have weathered to various shades of soft greys and tans. The floor of the cove has a stand of virgin hemlock, birches, and other species which like shade and moisture at their roots.

152

Precipitous walls of Trenton Gulf contrast sharply with the soft texture of foliage and flowering mountain laurel.

The view from the point between the two forks of the gulf is equalled by few in the Tennessee Valley. The geologic structure of the vicinity is illustrated both in distance and foreground. Little or no evidence of human occupation is visible, for a low hill cuts off a view of cultivated lands in the valley. From far below come the sounds of the forest and of the stream as it makes a 75-foot plunge into a deep pool.

The Lookout Mountain Scenic Highway passes close to the edge of the gulf.

ARMUCHEE PURCHASE UNIT
[E–7]

The Armuchee Purchase Unit [1] is in northwestern Georgia on the Armuchee Ridges in Catoosa, Chattooga, Floyd, Gordon, Walker, and Whitfield Counties. It consists of 250,000 acres and was approved by the National Forest Reservation Commission in the fall of 1936.

The Armuchee Ridges are composed of a series of long, narrow linear ridges separated by wide agricultural valleys, running in a general northeast-southwest direction. The ridges rise to almost uniform elevations of 1,600 feet, 800 feet above the floors of the intervening valleys. The northern part of the purchase unit lies within the Tennessee Valley and the southern part drains into the Coosa River.

The original forest stand consisted of Appalachian hardwoods with a mixture of pine. It has been depleted by years of cutting until now nearly all the merchantable timber has been cut. Because of the depleted forest stand, run-off is rapid and the convergence of creeks creates serious floods at Rome.

While watershed protection is the primary consideration in establishing this purchase unit, the area has some recreational merit. Restoration of a healthy forest cover will make the area available for extensive recreation, such as hiking and riding. The presence of several mineral springs within the tract suggests localized intensive-use facilities about the springs.

GUNTERSVILLE LAKE
[A–8]

Two dams in the TVA program for the development of the Tennessee River lie within the Chattanooga area. These are Guntersville and Chickamauga, both now under construction.

The site of Guntersville Dam is 9 miles down-river

from the town of Guntersville, Ala. The lake created will have a normal surface area of slightly less than 100 square miles, backing the river upstream 82 miles to the existing, privately owned Hales Bar Dam, near Jasper, Tenn. Normal fluctuation of the reservoir should have a negligible effect on its recreational use, for it seldom exceeds 1 foot.

Guntersville Lake lies between dissected portions of the Appalachian Plateaus, Sand Mountain on the southeast and the Cumberland Plateau on the northwest. These plateaus rise 1,000 feet above the level of the reservoir.

Sand Mountain and the Cumberland Plateau contrast sharply in spite of their similar formation. Sand Mountain is less broken; between Hales Bar Dam and the bridge on Alabama Highway 35, its escarpment presents an almost continuous straight line. Below this bridge, coves increase in number and size as far as Browns Creek Valley below Guntersville, which extends southwest for 25 miles. The Sand Mountain escarpment is completely wooded and rises abruptly from the lake shores so that it constitutes an outstanding scenic attraction of the lake.

The Cumberland Plateau has been severely dissected and isolated monadnocks stand separated from the valley lands by steep escarpments. Above Scottsboro the plateau escarpments lie 5 miles or more from the lake. Below Scottsboro, Gunter Mountain parallels the lake 1 or 2 miles from its shore, and at Lewis Mountain the escarpment drops directly into the lake.

The lower portion of Guntersville Lake will be bordered at several points by fine bluffs. The largest expanse of water in the lake will occur immediately below the town of Guntersville. Since the town will be relatively accessible to the larger water areas, it will be a logical center for recreational activities.

One of the main routes from Chattanooga to the west parallels the reservoir along its west side. That whole side of the lake is generally accessible, but on the opposite side access is limited and sometimes very difficult, especially in wet weather. However, recreational development in connection with the lake may involve sites on Sand Mountain, which is a part of the proposed Scottsboro Purchase Unit.

Guntersville Lake should attract the population in northeastern Alabama and tourists from beyond the area. The setting is perhaps as beautiful as any of the TVA reservoirs on the Tennessee River. Fishing, boating, and swimming will be popular on its waters. Cabin and camping facilities will be needed. Fortunately several sites along the shores seem suited to

---

[1] Information is based on U. S. Forest Service studies.

Outposts of the Cumberland Plateau flank the Tennessee River in this view from Lewis Mountain toward the Guntersville dam site.

various types of recreational development. The potential Short Creek Falls Park, described elsewhere in this chapter, is adjacent to an arm of the lake southeast of the town of Guntersville.

CHICKAMAUGA LAKE
[F-4]

Chickamauga Dam is now under construction at a site on the Tennessee River 7 miles above Chattanooga. The reservoir will extend 59 miles upstream to the site of the proposed Watts Bar Dam. Its area at normal pool elevation will be approximately 50 square miles. Its average width will be less than a mile, but its lower half will average more than a mile across.

The main body of Chickamauga Lake parallels the southern ridge of the Cumberland Escarpment. The lower part is relatively straight as far as its confluence with the Hiwassee River, but upstream from this point the lake winds and twists through wooded ridge country. The longest arm of the reservoir reaches up to Charleston on the Hiwassee River. Other sizable arms extend up Ooltewah Creek, Soddy Creek, Sale Creek, Opossum Creek, and Richland Creek.

Ridges and valleys are less pronounced along the lake than in the northeastern part of the Great Valley. In general, the country bordering the reservoir is half forested land and half agricultural land on the lower section, and predominantly forested ridges above the Hiwassee River arm. The main reservoir is within 4 to 8 miles of the Cumberland Escarpment, with four arms reaching nearly up to its base.

Because of the proximity of the lake to Chattanooga, its relation to the Cumberland Escarpment, and its own comparatively large proportions, Chickamauga Lake may become an important one for recreation. The reservoir will be generally accessible on both sides by State and Federal highways and county roads.

United States Highway 27, the direct route from Chattanooga to Cincinnati, passes between the reservoir and the foot of the escarpment along the west side. Tennessee Highway 58, along the east side, will afford good views of the reservoir and access to possible outing areas close to Chattanooga.

The Hiwassee River arm of the reservoir, reaching to Charleston, traverses relatively flat country and is believed unimportant for recreational development in view of other opportunities nearer Chattanooga. Possibilities of recreational development on the upper half of Chickamauga Lake also exist.

Sun and shadow pattern the slopes of Georgia's Grassy Mountain, in the Cohuttas, as seen from Fort Mountain State Park.

FORT MOUNTAIN STATE PARK
[G-6]

Fort Mountain State Park is on Fort Mountain, 16 miles airline east of Dalton, Ga. The mountain, rising to a point 2,832 feet above sea level, is one of the peaks of the Cohutta range and derives its name from ruins which are to be found near the highest point. The ruins are in the form of a stone wall 855 feet long, made up of small, flat rocks—now scattered but believed to have been once piled to the height of a man's head. The location suggests that the rocks were thrown up as breastwork to prevent access to the top of the mountain from its only scalable side, the southwest. The origin of the fort is unknown; various historians have ascribed it to DeSoto, deVelasco, or the Cherokee Indians. By the Cherokees themselves, the work is attributed to a white-skinned race called moon-eyed people because they could see only at night. This race, possibly kin to the mound-builders, was driven out by the Cherokees, according to Indian legend. Whatever their origin, the ruins are an interesting relic in a beautiful setting—worthy of preservation as a State park.

At present, only a limited area of 700 acres, including the ruins on the top of the mountain and two other unrelated tracts on the side, is owned by the State. Park authorities hope to acquire a total of 5,200 acres as a logical unit for development. Views from the peak extend over cultivated farm land to the west, into the Cohuttas at north and south, and over the mountains of the Blue Ridge to the east. It is essential that more land be obtained on the slopes in order to preserve the foreground of the view and to allow space for such intensive-use features as are needed.

A new highway, United States Highway 76, has been built over the southern shoulder of the mountain from Chatsworth to Ellijay. This road commands superb views to the southwest. From it a stone-surfaced drive has been built for a distance of 2½ miles north along the main ridge of the mountain to a parking space a short distance from the fort. Trails and paths lead up past the fort to a stone observation tower on the summit. Aside from trail building, forest stand improvement, and clearing, development of the area is being held up pending acquisition of more land.

Development plans include the building of a 50-acre lake in the northeast corner of the property. There will be a combined boat and bathhouse to permit swimming and boating. It is also planned to build a small inn near the top of the mountain with a group of ten vacation cabins about it. A water supply and sewage disposal system will serve the inn, cabins, and also a public camp ground and three picnic areas. The whole park will be quite intensively developed by trails, roads, and additional planting.

DESOTO STATE PARK
[D–8]

DeSoto State Park consists of two separate tracts some distance apart, located along the Little River in northeastern Alabama. The older of the two units, comprising 934 acres at the junction of the west and east forks of the river, has been developed as a typical outing area during the ECW program. The area has a rich, natural endowment of rugged topography and a desirable summer climate. The major part of the park area is covered with a second-growth forest and a rich understory of laurel, azalea, and rhododendron. Developments include vacation cabins, a lodge and recreation building, a dam to impound water for fishing, swimming, and boating, as well as the necessary trails, paths, and roads. It may be reached by a road leading across Lookout Mountain from United States Highway 11 W at Fort Payne, Ala.

The second unit, known as the Little River Gulf, or Mays Gulf, includes 1,650 acres which have recently been acquired by the State from the United States Public Domain. It ranges for 10 miles along the lower gorge of the Little River, 250 to 600 feet deep, by far the deepest gorge in Alabama.

The steep course of the stream cascades frequently, presenting many attractive vistas between the steep or sheer walls of the gulf. These walls are broken by an occasional tributary, but for the most part they form palisades of uniform appearance.

At the present time, adequate development of this unit is hampered because the State holds title to very little land outside the gorge itself. However, some roads and trails, leading along the rim to various vantage points, have been constructed. Desiring to make the entire area available for the public, the State has tentative plans to carry a road through the bottom of the gorge. Such a plan is open to question. It would seem better for additional lands to be acquired along the rim so that roads and trails could be constructed without disturbing the rugged natural beauty within the gorge itself.

FALLS CREEK FALLS PARK
[E–2]

On the Cumberland Plateau, between Spencer and Pikeville, Tenn., the National Park Service is developing a recreational demonstration park on a 20,000-acre tract. It may be reached from Tennessee Highway 30, which borders it on the north.

Within this area are four waterfalls outstanding among those on the Cumberland Plateau. In addition, there is a cascade 40 feet high immediately above one of the falls. The four are at the head of three arms of a great gorge carved out of the plateau by the waters of Cane Creek and its tributaries. The combination of features makes the area one of outstanding significance.

Falls Creek Falls, 257 feet high, are the most noteworthy of the falls. A spectacle of sheer height, their slender column of water drops a distance 100 feet greater than the height of Niagara, from the side of a basin 400 feet in diameter with walls that, for most of their circumference, are overhanging. A small stream, at one side of the larger Falls Creek, goes over the edge of the basin as a small, independent fall and, reduced to a fine spray, disappears from sight.

Cane Creek Falls have a very different character from Falls Creek. They are much lower, only 85 feet, nearly as broad as their height, and having a

157

flow considerably greater than that at Falls Creek. Their crest has worn down to a point 100 feet below the sidewalls of the gorge into which it flows. Copper-colored, lichen-covered walls stand out in a marked contrast to the whiteness of the water. The pool is large, shallow, and always turbulent.

Rock House, or Bridal Veil, Falls enter the same pool from a height 110 feet above it. Rock House Creek is a small stream, but has a swift flow which projects the water of the falls in a single jet a considerable distance out from the base of the cliff. If falls have personalities, that of Rock House is one of direct simplicity in contrast to the dignity of Cane Creek and the spectacular quality of Falls Creek.

Cane Creek above the falls is an attractive stream with steep, rocky shores. Its bed is made up of the surfaces of the same rock strata whose edges are exposed in the walls of the gorge. Some distance above the falls is Old Mill Cascade, 40 feet high. On the steeply sloping, fractured surface of this cascade the water is churned into a foaming whiteness or, when the flow is small, is divided into many tiny streams.

The gorge of Cane Creek and its tributary, Falls Creek, approaches canyonlike proportions. Its walls, 300 feet high, are sheer or overhanging and are cut into angular blocks which, in many cases, are almost free-standing. Seen in succession they seem to be great buttresses flung against the wall to resist lateral pressure. At the lower end of the gorge soft sandstone and coal measures have been worn away to form several caves. In periods of high water, streams of intermittant flow create other falls at various points along the gorge.

Plant growth in the gorge consists of giant hemlocks, beeches, and sycamores with an undergrowth of holly, laurel, and rhododendron. Together with large sandstone and conglomerate boulders they form

In old Mill Cascade, on Cane Creek, fractured rock divides the water into myriad rivulets.

an almost impenetrable wilderness. On the plateau land above, the forest cover is inferior second growth, chiefly of hardwoods. Along stream courses there is a good deal of laurel, holly, and rhododendron. All upland growth shows evidence of damage by frequent fires and too close grazing.

Falls Creek Falls is potentially one of the outstanding scenic areas of the Eastern United States; potentially, because, like the rest of the plateau country, its scenic values have been impaired by the use of the surrounding land. The nature of this use, however, is not one which has resulted in permanent injury of the area itself. It is chiefly evident in the inferior quality of shrub and tree growth on the plateau and in the diminished flow of the streams during summer months. An adequate conservation program on the watersheds would restore the area's natural beauty more nearly to its natural state.

National Park Service plans for development include such a conservation program. Afforestation and forest culture will be practiced and fire-control methods adopted. Plans for recreational development include parking spaces, picnic and camping areas, trails, shelters, and overlooks. A low dam on one of the streams will deepen it to provide a swimming pool.

In the expected use of the camping facilities primary emphasis will be placed on a program of group camping for underprivileged children, sponsored by various civic and service clubs and similar organizations.

CUMBERLAND HOMESTEADS PARK
[F–1]

In connection with and within the boundaries of the Cumberland Homesteads, Farm Security Administration project 2 miles south of Crossville, Tenn., a park of some 1,500 acres is being developed by CCC labor under the direction of the National Park Service. The park area utilizes the steep, wooded slopes of stream valleys and other areas unsuited to cultivation and homesteading. A 300-foot dam 45 feet high will create a 30-acre lake. Around the lake will be grouped boathouse, bathhouse, museum, picnic areas, shelters, and vacation cabins. Bridle paths and foot trails will lead from this area through woodland of mixed hardwoods and evergreens with an undergrowth of rhododendron, azalea, dogwood, and other flowering shrubs. The project is intended to fulfill the functions of regional as well as strictly local recreation, and to utilize land unsuited to the primary purpose of the homesteads project.

The falls of Cane Creek, one of several spectacular waterfalls in Falls Creek Falls Park. Copper-colored walls, softened by lichen, enhance its beauty.

GRUNDY LAKES
[D-4]

One mile northeast of Tracy City, Tenn., is a tract of 149 acres which has been donated to the State by the Tennessee Coal & Iron Co. Under the name Grundy Lakes, it is being developed as a fish hatchery and outing area camp. Two existing dams already create ponds covering several acres; the largest dam of clay with a creosoted plank core is now under construction; a total of six dams is contemplated. Picnic grounds, a tent campground, and a club house are also planned. Although many coal waste piles (the product of coke ovens) along the sides of the lower valley detract from its appearance, local officials expect that the presence of moisture from the ponds, and perhaps some provision of topsoil, will facilitate ground cover growth. This expectation seems to be justified by an excellent meadow turf growing on similar coal waste material in the lower valley. Further extension of the contemplated developments to include provision for swimming, boating, and general aesthetic improvement of the tract appear logical in view of the general lack of water features on the Cumberland Plateau.

One of the several tree-bordered lakes in Grundy Lakes park near Tracy City, Tenn.

GRUNDY FOREST
[C-4]

A wooded tract of 200 acres lying along the upper reaches of Big Fiery Gizzard Creek within a half mile of Tracy City has been purchased by local subscription and donated to the State of Tennessee as a State park. It is hoped eventually to increase the size of the area to 10,000 acres. The area is of more than average scenic interest and contains two features of note,

Sycamore Falls and Blue Hole.

Sycamore Falls, near the south boundary of the park, is 15 to 20 feet high and lies in the bottom of a gorge several hundred feet deep. Near it are three tall "Chimney Rocks", one containing Indian carvings, which rise above the top of the dense hemlock growth in the gorge. It is planned to develop the falls with a minimum of hiking trails.

Blue Hole is a natural swimming pool immediately below a 10-foot waterfall a mile above Sycamore Falls. The steeply sloping side walls of the creek are densely clothed with a tangled laurel growth.

Sycamore Falls, in Grundy Forest, is dwarfed by the depth of the enframing canyon.

BLEDSOE STATE FOREST
[E-2]

Bledsoe State Forest is a tract of 10,925 acres of plateau woodland. It is located chiefly in Bledsoe County with a small acreage in Cumberland, White, and Van Buren Counties. It was purchased in 1907, as coal land, the mines to be operated by convict labor. At present the property is managed as a State forest although 1,500 acres are cleared in the vicinity of Seals, a village within the tract. The Negro department of the State Training and Agricultural School for Boys is located in this portion of the forest. Labor from the school is used to cultivate the cleared acreage. The rest of the tract is wooded with the mixed hardwood and pine growth typical of second-growth plateau forest.

The southern part of the forest is flat or rolling with the streams close to the general level of the land. The northern half is deeply dissected by several streams. Bee Creek, largest on the property, leaves it at the bottom of a deep gorge reached by an irregular series

Tenn. Dept. of Conservation

Copperas Cliff along the gorge of Bee Creek, Bledsoe State Forest.

of small cascades and waterfalls. Dead Timber Branch plunges into this gorge over a 30-foot sandstone bluff. Glade Creek, forming the western boundary of the property, flows for a while on the ground surface and then cuts into the plateau to enter the Bee Creek Gorge at its bottom. Above the creek at this point rises Copperas Cliff, 300 feet high, a contorted and precipitous outcrop of picturesque character.

There are a few springs on the area. One of these is Saratoga Springs, whose chalybeate waters have attained a considerable local reputation; a small summer resort has sprung up in its vicinity.

The State forest service, in addition to conducting extensive reforestation work, is developing the recreational features of the tract by means of CCC labor. Bridle and foot trails, picnic and camping areas, small fish-breeding pools, and low dams in the various creeks are included in the plans for development. A fire tower has been built and has proved to be a popular objective of hikers.

Adequate development of the area, however, is hampered by lack of control over nearby areas. Cultivation of land at the headwaters of streams which flow across the tract causes rapid runoff and severe silting with subsequent drying up in seasons of little rainfall. As a result, flow stops in all but the larger streams during the summer months. Fish-rearing pools become stagnant so that many fish are lost. Fires on adjacent territory are a menace to game.

CROSS CREEK STATE FOREST

[C-5]

Cross Creek, or Franklin, State Forest consists of 7,000 acres of cut-over forest land on the Cumberland Plateau in Marion and Franklin Counties, Tenn. The property has only recently been acquired by the State and remains largely undeveloped except for an access road to Tennessee Highway 56. The forest straddles a narrow plateau headland from whose level surface the land slopes precipitously east and west into the coves of Sweden and Crow Creeks. Cross Creek, draining down the west slope into Crow Creek, gives the forest its name.

Extensive views from the rim rock capping the steep slopes are typical of cove and plateau scenery. The second-growth forest cover of mixed pines and hardwood provides shelter for game. The recreational significance of the forest will apparently depend to a large extent on the type of development which is provided by State authorities.

Tenn. Dept. of Conservation

Cascades and pools vary the course of Bee Creek in the Bledsoe State Forest.

BLACK MOUNTAIN WILDLIFE PRESERVE

[F-1]

The Black Mountain Wild Life Preserve consists of 560 acres of land on Black Mountain, southeast of Crossville, Tenn. The area includes the top of the mountain, which has an elevation of 2,900 feet, and a considerable area down on all sides, the greater portion lying on the northern slope. The preserve is wooded and rugged except for a relatively level tract of 20 acres on the summit. This tract is cleared and contains two cabins, one occupied by a caretaker. The only other improvement on the property is a heavy wire fence enclosing 300 acres.

The property was donated to the trustees of the Cumberland Mountain School, Crossville, who administer it. The policy of the school allows public use of the area for hiking, picnicking, and camping when special written permission is obtained from the local trustee.

UNIVERSITY OF THE SOUTH DOMAIN
[B-4]

The Domain of the University of the South contains 9,500 acres, chiefly flat plateau land with a small acreage on the slope of the escarpment. The town of Sewanee, Tenn., containing the campuses of the university and of Sewanee Military Academy, is slightly east of the center of the domain. The area is largely wooded and is open to the public for recreational use. Its value as a recreation area, however, is slight for it has in general no more than average scenic interest. The domain has been designated as a game preserve by university authorities, who have also made hitherto unsuccessful attempts to have the State manage the area as a State forest.

Included in the domain is a natural bridge, a feature of considerable interest. It lies 3½ miles out from Sewanee and less than a mile southeast of Tennessee Highway 56. The approach road from the highway is unsurfaced but in good condition and ends in a turn-around space 100 yards from the bridge, which is located just over the edge of the escarpment out of sight of the turn-around.

The bridge has an arch 20 feet high with a span of 25 feet, pierced through a wall some 6 to 8 feet thick, set out approximately 30 feet from the cliff. The flow of a very slight spring, at the back of a small cave in the cliff, has apparently carved the bridge. The view through the arch extends across the wooded cove. Near at hand the growth of large tulip trees is especially fine.

A trail, leading from the turn-around, down the slope to the east end of the bridge, across it and down to the cave behind, comprises the principal development of the area except for hundreds of initials chiseled into the soft rock. The place is popular as a picnic and outing spot for students of the university and local residents. Waste disposal cans have apparently provided the incentive to the public for keeping the place unlittered by papers and other rubbish.

On the grounds of the University of the South, the natural bridge is a popular spot for picnics and outings.

LAKE WINNEPESAUKAH
[E-5]

The outstanding developed water resource in the vicinity of Chattanooga, Lake Winnepesaukah, includes a 5-acre lake and adjacent swimming pool. The development is a private enterprise located in Georgia immediately south of the Tennessee State line between United States Highways 27 and 41. The lake is available for boating and for other water sports associated with amusement parks. The pool is large, concreted, and provided with bathing and safety equipment. A limited shallow area is reserved for children. Amusement park attractions and areas for field games, picnicking, and camping, efficiently operated, are available to the public at a reasonable cost.

GREAT FALLS LAKE
[D-2]

The Great Falls Lake of the Tennessee Electric Power Co. is located on the Caney Fork immediately above Horseshoe Falls north of McMinnville. The reservoir extends for approximately 6 miles up Caney Fork and two of its main tributaries, the Collins and Rocky Rivers. The result is a lake of three narrow arms, in no case going very far out of the original banks of the streams. The effect of draw-down, thus, is not serious.

Considerable recreational use is made of the Reservoir, but the development is such as to illustrate the need for suitable restrictions and general rural zoning. Dance and amusement halls, filling stations, and similar structures are intermingled with many private cabins. This type of development is chiefly centered about the Collins River. A private boys' camp is located on Caney Fork 4 miles above the dam. Around and below the dam, the power company has developed its property with paths, ornamental shrubs, and picnicking facilities. Observation points have been developed from which the public may view the falls, now dry except in flood seasons.

LOOKOUT MOUNTAIN CAVERNS
[E-5]

The Lookout Mountain Caverns, penetrating the north end of Lookout Mountain, form one of the principal objectives of the Chattanooga tourist traffic. They have been highly commercialized, the manage-ment offering such services as complete electric lighting, regular guide service, and an elaborate entrance building, containing facilities for dining and dancing. This building stands over an artificially pierced elevator shaft which provides the only present entrance.

The caverns lie on two levels with interconnecting passageways. On the lower level are the historic Twin Caves, which have interest as a home of the Chickamauga Indians and the resort of both Confederate and Union soldiers during the Civil War. Names, initials, and other marks are evidence of these early occupants. The chief natural interest in the lower level is the fluting and etching of the solid rock and the winding passages. The natural entrance to this level was closed with the building of the railroad around Lookout Mountain, and the caverns were not reopened until 1923 when the present elevator shaft was drilled. The Ruby Falls route and the upper level were discovered at that time, unmarred by previous entrance. The upper level is charcaterized by delicate and brilliantly colored onyx formations in numerous forms. Also noteworthy is the translucent quality of even the large columns and heavy drapes.

Ruby Falls, however, is the outstanding feature of the caverns. This natural phenomenon, a 145-foot waterfall 1,120 feet underground, drops through a large, circular chamber which is reached by a corridor extending one-half mile into the mountain from the elevator shaft. The straight fluted sides of the room rise nearly 200 feet above the floor and have the appearance of gigantic stone curtains drawn back to reveal the spectacle. The falls have a considerable volume of flow which is seemingly magnified by the echo of the sound beneath the domed ceiling and the concentration of spray in the room.

NICKAJACK CAVE
[D-5]

Nickajack Cave lies at the foot of Sand Mountain in Marion County, Tenn., one-half mile south of the Tennessee River at Shell Mound. A creek of considerable flow issues from the large and impressive entrance, 175 feet in width and 60 feet in height. By means of this stream, a boat may enter the lower of the cave's two known levels, which has been penetrated for nearly 2 miles. This lower level consists of three immense rooms or domes joined by a nearly straight passageway, averaging 100 feet in width and 25 feet in height. The domes themselves may reach 700 feet in length, 200 to 500 feet in width, and nearly 100 feet in height. The upper level has never been fully explored, and its entrance was closed by a slide prior to 1930.

Although the cave has the curious and colorful formations typical of water-worn limestone caverns, geologic interest centers chiefly on the size of the rooms and connecting corridor. In addition, its historical tradition is rare among Tennessee caves. Nickajack, largest town of the Chickamauga Indians, occupied a position at the mouth of the cave, and the first dome bears evidence of continuous occupation by the Indians. Destruction of the town in 1794 by white invaders ended in a single bloody battle the warfare which had devastated settlements in the vicinity for 20 years.

WONDER CAVE
[C-4]

Wonder Cave is located 3½ miles north of Monteagle, Tenn., in Burrow Cove. Cultivated land extends up a stream valley to the mouth of the cave which forms the source of the stream, but woodland extends above and at the sides of the cave along the plateau escarpment. Although arrowheads and fragments of pottery, found in profusion about the mouth of the cave, indicate that this was an Indian camping ground, they apparently did not enter the cave, for no such artifacts have been found in chambers beyond its mouth.

The cave has two natural entrances, one completely filled by the stream, and a second which was enlarged at the time the cave was opened to visitors just before 1900. It has been explored for a distance of 3,200 feet, the first quarter mile being easily traversed. For the most part, a long narrow corridor closely following the stream, the cave has two major chambers at the stream level and two above. Onyx formations—multi-colored stalactites and stalagmites, columns, draperies, and grotesque forms—fill the rooms to which the visitor ordinarily penetrates. Another room, more difficult of access has none of these formations, but is nearly completely filled by a pyramid of limestone 120 feet high and 250 feet in diameter at its base.

MONTEAGLE ASSEMBLY
[C-4]

The Monteagle Assembly, located in Monteagle, Tenn., at the junction of United States Highways 41 and 64, may be regarded as the present recreational center of the Cumberland Plateau. The assembly, managed by a nonprofit organization now more than 50 years old, conducts an ambitious chautauqua program during the summer months on a parklike assembly ground of several hundred acres. Numerous cottages available for rent, an auditorium, concert hall, library, studio buildings, and golf club are grouped about the grounds. The buildings are used for varied recreational and amusement programs including concerts, movies, and lectures. Facilities are provided for swimming, tennis, golf, horseback riding, and other outdoor sports as well as for indoor sports in a large gymnasium.

The town is a center from which numerous trips by foot, horse, or motor into country of outstanding scenic interest may be made. In this chapter detailed accounts of several nearby features are discussed in connection with the proposed Scottsboro Purchase Unit. In spite of these opportunities and of the extensive facilities provided by the assembly, sedentary "front porch" types of recreation seem to prevail at Monteagle.

BEERSHEBA SPRINGS
[C-3]

An ante-bellum resort hotel, Beersheba Springs, occupies a site on the western escarpment above the Collins River Valley. The rim rock on which the hotel is built is exceptionally high, allowing unobstructed vistas over the valley below. Upstream from this vantage point, views extend over forested head waters, and are limited by glimpses of other rim-rock at the eye level. Downstream, views lead down the narrow valley and out onto the agricultural land of the Highland Rim.

The hotel has considerable architectural character and most of the private cottages surrounding it are of a superior type. At a relatively higher altitude than Nashville, Beersheba has been popular with residents of that city since before the Civil War.

PROPOSED REGIONAL RECREATION AREAS

PROPOSED SCOTTSBORO PURCHASE UNIT
[B-6]

Location: Northeast Alabama, northwest Georgia, and south-central Tennessee.
Size: 975,400 acres.
Type: Wilderness with occasional outing areas.
Characteristics: Dissected plateau land; mixed second growth; cove and valley views.

THE proposed Scottsboro Purchase Unit includes the extreme southern portion of the Cumberland Plateau in Alabama and Tennessee and the northern extremity of Sand Mountain in Georgia, Alabama, and Tennessee. It is divided into two unequal parts by the Tennessee River, which drains the entire forest.

Within the forest boundary, the Cumberland Plateau is severely dissected by coves and gorges which leave many portions completely separated into isolated monadnocks. Pines in variety and cedar constitute the only evergreen species; a larger proportion of the forest stand includes such hardwoods as the oaks, poplar, hickory, ash, bass wood, cucumber, buckeye, and maple. Trout and bass, originally abundant throughout the area, are still found in those streams which do not go dry. A few quail, rabbit, squirrel, and turkey still persist, remnants of the once-abundant game resources of the area. Both fish and game might become plentiful under an adequate game-management program, provided that the necessity for subsistence hunting and fishing is removed.

The water courses in this part of the plateau show extreme seasonal variation and, especially in the northeast half, contain great numbers of falls and cascades. A sizeable artificial lake at Lakeview, 11½ miles airline southeast of Winchester, Tenn., illustrates a recreational opportunity which lies in other similar coves. A small dam could, in most

The pastoral loveliness of fertile Sequatchie Valley separates Walden Ridge from the main Cumberland Plateau.

165

locations, store a considerable body of water behind it. Such lakes would be useful both for recreation and for fire protection.

The Sand Mountain portion of the unit differs radically in topographic form from the northern portion. It has less interest, for it has not been as severely dissected by coves. Stream courses are short and the volume of flow small, frequently disappearing altogether during the summer months. For this reason, several small waterfalls have little scenic significance because they are completely dry at times when they may be visited. These falls include Laurel Falls, which flow directly into the Tennessee River above Hales Bar Dam, Little Falls, and High Falls, on two arms of Long Island Creek in Alabama. Cover and wildlife conditions similar to those in the northern half of the unit prevail on the slopes and level surface of Sand Mountain.

Recreational significance of Sand Mountain, very limited at the present time, will depend on a forest-management program which may restore to the area considerable opportunity for hunting, fishing, hiking, and other extensive forms of recreation.

The Palisades
[C-4]

Location: Four miles east of Monteagle, Tenn.
Types: Outing area combining developed scenic and intensive-use areas.
Characteristics: Rolling plateau land; second-growth cover; excellent views.

The Palisades include a particularly high and sheer portion of rim rock on the Cumberland Escarpment. They afford, southward down Cave Cove to Battle Creek, an excellent view, typical of the beautiful plateau scenery. In the cove, densely and completely wooded, no evidence of man is visible. The characteristic flat horizon determines for the eye the general level of the plateau. Color gradients show five successive headlands of lesser coves, all with identical contouring of their side slopes. Upstream the view is cut off by the headwall of the cove.

The rolling plateau land in the vicinity of the Palisades, forested with an open timber growth and an undergrowth of laurel, azalea, dogwood, and rhododendron, has a parklike character which would be enhanced by judicious treatment. Occasional open fields are moderately cultivated. The area is suited to treatment as a developed scenic area with provision for some intensive use. A parkway loop road of 5 miles would permit access from Tennessee Highway

So nearly identical are the contours of these plateau headlands on Cave Cove that they appear to have been cast from the same mold.

56 at Summerfield and pass by two waterfalls, Monteagle and Bridal Veil. The area would serve as a logical nucleus about which outdoor recreational activities of the vicinity would be centered. Hiking and bridle trails would lead from it to various other points of interest.

A Bridal Veil Falls that truly deserves its name, near Monteagle, Tenn.

166

Bridal Veil and Monteagle Falls
[C-4]

Location: 3 miles east of Monteagle, Tenn.
Type: Developed scenic area.
Characteristics: 60-foot waterfall; 20-foot waterfall.

Bridal Veil Falls is in reality a cascade formed when the waters of the stream rush down a steeply inclined face of the escarpment. Profusely jointed and fractured, the rock face keeps the water agitated or divided into many smaller streams according to the flow and season of the year. Although at present the flow is irregular and disappears in the dry summer months, a few years of proper forest management would tend to regulate the flow and to minimize, if not entirely eliminate the dry period.

The falls have a natural setting of mixed evergreen and hardwoods. At present hiking over uninteresting topography through inferior second growth permits the only access. Intensive forest management would restore some of the natural scenic beauty of the place by enriching foliage and floral displays.

Monteagle Falls, a small 20-foot falls of considerable beauty, drops from a cliff with a wide overhang. At present they, too, are a wet-weather fall only, but the flow may become permanent in the event of adequate forest management.

Raven Point hangs high over the rough gorge of Big Fiery Gizzard Creek.

Raven Point
[C-4]

Location: 4 miles south of Tracy City, Tenn.
Type: Wilderness.
Characteristics: Superb view of Gizzard Cove.

Raven Point, a plateau headland rising above Big Fiery Gizzard Creek at the junction of Anderson Creek, falls away in a sheer drop some 200 feet to the floor of the cove. Its cliffs are clothed with pitch pine, picturesquely contorted by exposure to the wind. In the cove below, a single clearing breaks the otherwise complete forest cover of dense mixed hardwoods and evergreens. The sound of Anderson Falls below on the creek of the same name is clearly audible. Views lead in three directions, up and down Big Fiery Gizzard, and up Anderson Creek.

An objective for hiking, the point has considerable recreational interest.

A woods road which may be negotiated by car in dry weather leads from Tracy City to a farmyard, one-half mile away, from which it is necessary to hike. An ancient ox-cart road allows hiking between the point and the gorge below.

Foster Falls
[C-4]

Location: 8 miles southeast of Tracy City, Tenn.
Type: Wilderness.
Characteristics: 60-foot waterfall; gorge and large pool; outstanding hemlock growth.

Foster Falls, from the standpoint of water volume, is probably the largest in the Chattanooga Area. On Gizzard Creek, 4 miles above its junction with Big Fiery Gizzard, it has a considerable watershed above so that the flow of the stream diminishes but little during the summer months. The creek has carved from the sandstone a circular basin, at the bottom of which is a large pool. It extends back of the falls under the overhanging cliff, its walls varying in height from 6 to 120 feet. The basin forms the head of a gorge which is contiguous with the larger gorge of Big Fiery Gizzard. Both basin and gorge are filled with superlative hemlocks in great numbers, and an excellent second growth of pine is found on the plateau in the vicinity. Many square miles of forest are broken by only a few clearings and no main highways.

Unfortunately, the wilderness character of the falls is destroyed by the presence of a power line in a 100-foot swath which passes close by the eastern brink of the basin. A main highway between Tracy City and Sequatchie is being constructed, along a telephone line and old woods road, passing within 2 miles of the falls and gorge.

In view of the general wilderness character of the vicinity, it would be desirable that further study be made to determine the feasibility of relocating the power line at some distance from the falls. Such relocation is extremely desirable; but if it is not possible, control of cutting in the immediate vicinity of the falls would have a beneficial effect.

In dry seasons, one may drive from Tracy City nearly to the falls over 8 miles of unimproved dirt roads. At other times, a 6½-mile hike from Tracy City along the power line permits the most direct access.

Fullerton Bluff
[C–5]

Location: East escarpment of Cumberland Plateau above Jasper, Tenn.
Type: Developed scenic area.
Characteristics: Valley views, plateau woodland.

Fullerton Bluff as a vantage point, affords a magnificent view. In addition, it offers an excellent opportunity to study the geology of the section. The view glimpses the patterned lowlands of the valley, through which the Tennessee River winds in long curves, and extends to the wooded plateaus of Walden Ridge and Sand Mountain. In the distance Lookout Mountain Hotel caps the mountain's highest point. Picturesque pines frame many different vistas.

Trails leading to the bluff from points on United States Highways 64 and 41 might well serve as nature trails as they are so located as to afford opportunity for the study of geology, botany, biology, and other natural sciences close at hand. They might lead to a shelter in which could be located permanent charts and exhibits which would point out features of geologic interest illustrated both near at hand and in the distant view. Such a technique would be simple and inexpensive and should arouse considerable popular interest in a study of nature and general interest in the out-of-doors.

In a deep cove of the Cumberland Plateau the powerful waters of Gizzard Creek have carved a cavernous basin below Foster Falls.

PROPOSED CHATTANOOGA PURCHASE UNIT

[E-3]

Location: East-central Tennessee.
Size: 1,078,400 acres.
Type: Wilderness with occasional outing area.
Characteristics: Plateau land; second growth, cove and valley views.

The proposed Chattanooga Purchase Unit consists of 1,078,400 acres (1,685 square miles) of which 73 percent or 784,000 acres are estimated to be purchasable. It is located entirely within the Tennessee River basin in nine counties of Tennessee; Marion, Hamilton, Sequatchie, Bledsoe, Rhea, Cumberland, Fentress, Morgan, and Roane Counties. The area is drained in the north by the Emory River, and at the south by the Sequatchie River; between the two, many short tributary streams of the Tennessee lead from Walden Ridge. The purchase unit includes the slopes and surface of Walden Ridge and part of the Cumberland Plateau. It adjoins the northern boundary of the Scottsboro Purchase Unit.

The forest area within the unit is nearly 100 percent cut over except in the most inaccessible coves. Lumbering has been carried on extensively within the past 30 years by methods which have given little consideration to future forest growth. This purchase unit, together with others on the Cumberland Plateau, is considered by the United States Forest Service to be especially suited to public ownership because the possibilities of early financial returns from timber are too remote to enable private individuals or companies to hold the lands until the next forest crop may be cut. The area has been severely burned and a State program of fire control has proved inadequate to cope with the prevalent practice of burning forest lands for pasturage. The present second growth consists of 41 per-

Lookout Mountain lies like a watchdog over the narrows of Moccasin Bend, in the Tennessee River at Chattanooga. This view of the familiar profile is from Signal Mountain.

169

cent made up of various oaks, 22 percent in pines and the remainder in hickory, gum, yellow poplar, hemlock, beech, birch, maple, bass wood, cedar, sycamore, black walnut, elm, and cherry. Originally a favorite hunting ground of the Indians and the home of abundant upland game, the plateau has been depleted of most wildlife except for the smaller species such as rabbit, squirrel, grouse, and quail. It is believed, however, that turkeys, deer, and other larger species would become plentiful under a forest and game management program.

The interior of the forest lacks general scenic interest in either topography or forest cover. The edges, however, permit extensive views across adjacent valley land. A few coves indent the prevalent straight line of the escarpment and lend additional interest. The small water courses within these coves are usually steep and frequently cascading. Their interest will increase with the restoration of a healthy forest cover on the plateau and the resultant regulation of the clarity and volume of their flow.

Ozone Falls
[G–1]

Location: At the village of Ozone, 12 miles west of Rockwood on United States Highway 70.
Type: Developed scenic area.
Characteristics: Waterfall at head of deep gorge.

Ozone Falls, a spot of exceptional natural beauty as yet largely unspoiled by the presence of a village and highway at its very crest, makes a fall 100 feet in height into a considerable pool from whence it passes down through a gorge some 150 to 200 feet deep. United States Highway 70 winds down the northern wall of the gorge.

The south wall of the gorge has been cut over but is now completely clothed by a dense growth of laurel among second-growth timber. Given protection from frequent burning, the natural character of the gorge would be restored. Public acquisition or scenic easements over the gorge should be obtained and would insure such protection.

An overnight camp might be located on a tract of

Cline, Chattanooga

The Tennessee River, cutting its way through the Cumberlands, shaped this broad gorge between Walden Ridge and Sand Mountain.

170

land back from, and southeast of, the brink of the gorge. Entrance to this area may be obtained from a road leading south from the highway, 100 feet east of the bridge above the falls. In anticipation of the popularity it will achieve, this wayside should be intensively developed.

From a point 3 miles east of Ozone westward to the village, the highway borders Mammy Creek, and crosses its tributaries. The deep valley, through which the stream and highway run, approaches the character of a gorge, its steep walls being clothed with an excellent tree growth and luxuriant undergrowth of rhododendron. The resultant visual effect is that of a deep forest. Unless there is immediate forest acquisition, to prevent discordant encroachments and to preserve the natural beauty of the valley, scenic easements should be secured to the top of the slopes on both sides along the entire distance. Such strips would range from 100 to 600 feet up the slopes on either side of the highway.

Like a shaft of light penetrating forest depths, Crystal Falls plummets from the escarpment.

Travelers on United States Highway 70 know Ozone Falls, on the Cumberland Plateau west of Rockwood.

Crystal Falls
[E–3]

Location: At the headwaters of Crystal Creek, on the west slope of Walden Ridge, 5 miles airline south of Pikeville.
Type: Wilderness.
Characteristics: Wooded plateau land; escarpment; unspoiled gorge; 100-foot waterfall; views of Sequatchie Valley.

Crystal Falls are the only falls on the west slope of Walden Ridge. Dropping 100 feet over the escarpment into a deep, narrow cove, they are a typical headwater falls of the plateau country. The cove is a tangle of virgin growth, traversed by the stream which makes its way over and around large boulders.

The rim rock at this point is severely dissected into fragments of varying sizes—many large masses being almost detached and seemingly precariously balanced. These crags are the homes of buzzards, which often may be seen flying over the cove. From various vantage points superb views extend over the cove and the Sequatchie Valley to the main plateau beyond. The forest above the escarpment has been cut over and the land subsequently subjected to grazing and frequent burning, with resultant damage to tree and shrub growth.

One may drive within a mile of Crystal Falls by turning south from Tennessee Highway 30 at Morgan Springs, and driving 6½ miles on dirt road. The falls should be preserved in its natural state as an objective for hikers. The cove, particularly, still has a primitive character unusual in this section.

Little Piney Creek Falls
[G–2]

Location: On Walden Ridge, 1 mile southwest of Grandview.
Type: Wilderness.
Characteristics: Two waterfalls, each 75 feet high; cascading stream; gorge with rich growth.

The falls on Little Piney Creek are two of the numerous falls at the escarpment of Walden Ridge and the Cumberland Plateau. Like many of the others their beauty is impaired by forest depletion of their watersheds, for the creek is dry during the summer months. The upper falls are 75 feet high and have a slight overhang. The rock beneath is pitted with numerous pot holes. A pool, surrounded with a dense undergrowth of rhododendron, is a popular swimming hole for the locality. The lower falls, one-half mile below, are just as high and have a greater overhang. The gorge between the two, and for some distance below, has great natural beauty. It should be reserved in its natural state as an objective for hikers and fishermen. The falls are reached by hiking south from Grandview or west from the point where Tennessee Highway 68 crosses the creek.

Montlake
[E-4]

Location: On Walden Ridge immediately west of United States Highway 27 at Daisy, Tenn.
Type: Wilderness; outing area combining intensive-use areas and developed scenic areas.
Characteristics: Narrow, gorgelike valley; sinkhole; valley views.

Montlake is a very deep pond in a sinkhole on the Cumberland Plateau above the gulch of North Chickamauga Creek. Its name has been given to a 6,000-acre tract of land which has been considered as a public park and game preserve. The Durham Coal Co., owners of the tract, once offered to donate the surface rights of the land to the State on condition that a right-of-way be built for a distance of 1 mile through the tract to a coal prospect which the company desired to open. The project has backing in Chattanooga sportsmen's and garden club groups, but funds are lacking for its development. Federal funds are not available because the title is not free of restrictions.

Development plans include the construction of fish-rearing pools on North Chickamauga Creek, and the restocking of its upper reaches. Most of the area would be subjected to a rigid fire-control and game-management program which would restore the forest growth, provide food and cover plants, and restock the area with game. The area would be patrolled, and both hunting and fishing would be allowed only with proper restrictions.

About Montlake itself, it is proposed to develop a "Dogwood Garden" by suitable cultivation of existing groups and additional plantations. This project would be carried out with the idea of creating a spring floral display about a natural feature of great interest. The lake is a pool of reported depths ranging from 90 to several hundred feet. It lies at the bottom of a circular sink some 600 feet in diameter, with sheer sandstone walls. At two points one may descend to the water's edge to obtain a closer view of the clear but lifeless water. Improvement of existing truck trails, and removal of numerous renters and squatters will be necessary if the proposed development is to have its fullest effectiveness.

In case the property is developed as a regional park, plans might provide for swimming, picnicking, camping, and other features of an intensive-use area along the lower part of North Chickamauga Creek.

Falling Waters
[E-4]

Location: On the east slope of Walden Ridge, 10 miles airline north of Chattanooga.
Type: Wilderness.
Characteristics: Steep mountain valley stream with enormous boulders; several waterfalls.

Falling Waters is a mountain stream on the east slope of Walden Ridge. Its precipitous course makes a vertical drop of 900 feet in a horizontal distance of 2 miles. The initial plunge over the main escarpment is 100 feet high on the south fork of the stream, and half that height on the north fork. The descent,

This 40-foot cataract halts those who would essay the difficult gorge of Falling Waters.

Falling Waters, a tumbling mountain stream, drops 900 feet down the east face of Walden Ridge. The torrent, dodging gigantic boulders, occasionally rests in crystal pools to reflect its beauty.

below the escarpment, embraces numerous cascades over boulders of gigantic proportions, which have, in ages past, broken off the escarpment above. They are now strewn the length of the stream, some apparently balanced, others firmly wedged by smaller rocks. Still others rest solidly on the bedrock, appearing as stratified outcroppings over which the water tumbles to form many of the more beautiful cascades. Occasionally large pools are created back of a fallen log or boulder. These reflect the nearby boulders, cliffs, and overhanging branches.

The valley today looks much as it must have appeared when first seen by white men. Most of the forest growth is virgin, the whole atmosphere redolent of the primitive.

Falling Waters Valley might well be preserved in its natural condition, for it affords an admirable opportunity to study processes of nature unchanged by contact with man. An outdoor laboratory for the nature student, it illustrates geologic processes both in the flow of the stream itself and in the structure of the ridge, as it is exposed in the stream bed. A natural trail of unusual interest could be developed along the stream.

The area is reached by turning west from United States Highway 27 where it crosses Falling Waters Creek, 12 miles north of Chattanooga.

Laurel Creek Falls
[F–3]

Location: On Walden Ridge, 3½ miles north of Dayton, Tenn.

Laurel Creek Falls, on the side wall of Richland Creek Gorge, is more than 100 feet high. The great wooded area surrounding it includes the spectacular gorges of Richland and Morgan Creeks, but the wilderness character of the area is partially destroyed by the presence of the swath cut for a transmission line, which passes within 1,400 feet of the falls.

The falls may be reached by a 4-mile hike up Richland Creek from Dayton. A mountain road leads up onto Walden Ridge above the falls from Evensville, a village on United States Highway 27, 6 miles north of Dayton. A 4-mile drive up this road brings one to the crossing of the transmission line, and a 2-mile hike will then allow access to the falls.

Mount Roosevelt
[G–1]

Location: On Cumberland Escarpment, 1 mile west of Rockwood.
Type: Developed scenic area.
Characteristics: Vantage point of unusual interest.

Mount Roosevelt, an eminence on the eastern escarpment of Walden Ridge above Rockwood, has an elevation of 1,900 feet, 400 feet above the general level of the escarpment. The name was officially adopted by Congress in honor of President Franklin D. Roosevelt. The place commands an outstanding view to the east over the Tennessee Valley to the Blue Ridge Province as well as over the northern part of the Cumberland Plateau. A fire tower has been built there by the State.

A one-lane gravel road, 2 miles long, leads to Mount Roosevelt from United States Highway 70 immediately west of the cut through the escarpment. A group of cabins belonging to Rockwood people has been built about the tower.

White Creek Gorge
[G–1]

Location: In Roane and Cumberland Counties on the Cumberland Plateau 6 miles west of Rockwood.
Type: Wilderness with some developed scenic area.
Characteristics: Spectacular gorges 400 to 700 feet deep carved from sandstone; unusual rock forms, waterfalls, cascades, and "blue holes"; unusual plant life.

White Creek and its tributary streams, Piney, Fall, and Laurel Creeks, have carved deep gorges from the heart of the Cumberland Plateau west of Rockwood. Their combined scenic quality lacks the spectacular character of the Caney and Falls Creek Gorges in Bledsoe and Van Buren Counties, but their intimate charm is considerable. Unusual rock forms, pools, cascades, and small waterfalls become softened beneath a luxuriant mantle of various trees and shrubs. An ancient inn and stage road lend interest of historical association with early travel.

At the point where it breaks through the escarp-

In dry summer months the flow of White Creek may be reduced to "Blue Holes", translucent pools of great depth.

ment, White Creek lies at the bottom of a 700-foot gorge. The side walls are not sheer but steep, displaying occasional outcrops of vertically faced sandstone. Flowing in a rocky channel, the creek recedes in dry weather into a series of clear pools, 200 to 300 feet long and 50 to 100 feet wide. A variety of shrub and plant growth adds increased charm.

White Creek rapidly spreads, fanlike, into its several tributaries, each of which displays similar characteristics resulting from common geologic origins. Laurel Creek presents erosion on a less heroic but correspondingly more delicate scale. It has two small waterfalls. Piney Creek, perhaps, is the most rugged of these gorges, for its walls rise precipitously more than 600 feet to Willet Mountain, an eminence on the plateau back of the escarpment. Low cascades and large "blue holes" interrupt its stream course. Fall Creek maintains its gorge character as far as Ozone Falls and United States Highway 70. Basin, Mammy, Otter, and upper White Creeks invite further exploration by hikers and fishermen.

An ancient stage road, at one time a principal route across the plateau, ran along the north bank of White Creek, forded Piney Creek shortly above its mouth, and led up Nigger Jumpoff Branch to the plateau surface. Thence it joins the old Walton Road at the present village of Crab Orchard. Traces of the old road still exist and may be used as a foot trail. The hiker may see channels worn deep in the sandstone by innumerable carriage wheels.

Rest for the traveler over this early road was provided at Gibson Inn, on Nigger Jumpoff Branch, one-fourth mile from its mouth and 2½ miles back from the escarpment. A 2-story frame structure, with porches along the front of both stories, it was famous for "the fine table which Aunt Rachel used to set." The table attracted the younger set from Chattanooga and other nearby towns, and for many years the inn occupied a prominent place in the social life of the locality. Built 116 years ago, it is now in ruins with one end caved in, but sufficient character remains to enable a restoration.

Shadows follow the wake of retreating sunlight up the walls of White Creek Gorge.

PROPOSED PLATEAU PURCHASE UNIT
[D–2]

Location: Central Tennessee on Cumberland Plateau.
Size: 1,916,850 acres.
Type: Wilderness with occasional outing areas.
Characteristics: Plateau land; second growth; cove and valley views.

The proposed Plateau Purchase Unit, lying entirely outside the Tennessee River Basin, includes approximately 2,000,000 acres north and west of the proposed Scottsboro and Chattanooga purchase units. It is bounded on the north by the Kentucky line and on the west by the agricultural land of the Highland Rim. Its southern and western portions have characteristics of topography and forest cover similar to those of other purchase units on the plateau. Its northern and eastern portion, however, differs radically as to topography. The general level character of the plateau becomes one of a mountainous nature nearly approaching that of the Blue Ridge Province, although maximum elevations rarely exceed 3,500 feet.

The unit is drained by tributaries of the Cumberland River, whose gorges have become deeply incised into the surface of the plateau. Those of the Collins River, Rocky River, Caney Creek, Caney Fork, Calfkiller River, and South Fork of the Cumberland rank among the most spectacular of the Appalachian Plateaus. The western escarpment is extremely irregular and capped for most of its distance by sheer palisades of rim rock. Frequent vantage points along the top of the escarpment afford views of great interest across the gorges themselves or beyond into the Highland Rim.

Because of the depleted forest cover, however, the stream flow of even the larger tributaries is irregular, frequently ceasing altogether during the summer months. Such intermittent stream flow detracts from the scenic values of many waterfalls and reduces the number of game fish within the streams. As is the case in other portions of the plateau, both fish and game would benefit from a game and forest-management program which would insure natural conditions of food and shelter in addition to protection from subsistence hunting. Three small lakes within the purchase unit, together with the large lake created by the Great Falls Dam, on Caney Fork, indicate the potentialities for water recreation which might be developed on other streams by building small dams to create recreational lakes. These lakes would be useful for fire protection and in the conservation of wild life as well as for such water sports as swimming, fishing, and boating.

Ravenscroft Lakes
[E–1]

Location: In White County near Ravenscroft, just off United States Highway 70 Alternate.
Type: Intensive-use area.
Characteristics: Small artificial lakes with wooded shores.

Near Ravenscroft are two small artificial lakes used by the Tennessee Products Co. in connection with their mines in the locality. Situated near the headwaters of small streams, they have wooded watersheds. Both are clear.

The smaller, some 5 acres in extent, is backed up by means of a plank and clay-fill dam. The shores are generally attractive although somewhat littered with stumps of dead timber; below the dam, iron waste from the mines is ugly. Recreational use of the lake at present is out of the question, for it is often pumped dry. If it were not for this complete draw-down, however, considerable use for swimming, boating, and fishing could be made.

The large lake, some 10 acres in extent, is created by a long railroad embankment. Except for the presence of the railroad, this is the more attractive of the two. It is much used at the present time for swimming, boating, and fishing. Should the mines be closed, its recreational value would be improved by removal of the railroad and noninterference with the water level.

The two lakes are chiefly significant as examples of potential water areas at numerous other available sites. Such lakes would be comparatively inexpensive to construct, would be clear and permanent if adequate protection were given the watersheds, and would, in turn, furnish additional protection, for they are themselves reservoirs for fire-protection purposes. They would afford opportunity for the breeding and rearing of fish and would be havens for waterfowl.

Deerlick Falls
[C–4]

Location: 4 miles northeast of Monteagle.
Type: Wilderness.
Characteristics: Gorge 200 feet deep; 100-foot waterfall; rich laurel growth.

Deerlick Falls, a water feature little known even in its own locality, is reached by turning north from Tennessee Highway 56 at Summerfield, 2 miles east of Monteagle. One and one-half miles of driving over good, unsurfaced road brings one to a farm gateway on the west side of the road. A half-mile hike over woods roads and trails leads to the brink of the gorge

Deerlick Falls, a transparent spray 100 feet in height, is hidden deep in a primitive setting near Monteagle, Tenn.

immediately above the falls. The level plateau land of the vicinity has been cut over and is clothed at present with good second growth and a dense undergrowth of laurel.

The gorge, 200 feet deep, is narrow and winding, with precipitous walls which overhang in many places. Within a distance of one-quarter mile the stream, describing a huge S, reverses its direction twice. Two types of rock formation are visible in the side walls of the gorge and an equally distinct line of demarcation is discernible at the level of the top of the falls. Above the falls only the soft, cross-veined upper layers have been cut through. Below it the harder, stratified layers have also been worn away.

The falls itself, approximately 100 feet high, has, according to local report, a year-round flow. In addition to the geologic interest in the gorge and falls, there is the appeal of the primitive appearance of plant growth in the gorge.

Pilot Falls
[E-1]

Location: On Caney Fork at Clifty.
Type: Intensive-use area.
Characteristics: Low waterfall and cascades; picturesque rock outcrops in river bed.

Pilot Falls is hardly worthy of the name, for it is scarcely 6 feet high. Nevertheless, it is beautiful as a cascade and is, traditionally, a scenic feature of the neighborhood. The river at this point is wide and flows over successive, irregular shelves of rock. In most places it is shallow with an occasional pool or pothole. Fifty acres about the falls might logically be developed as a vacation camp. Relatively isolated, the place may be reached by fair roads and would be a center from which other recreational activities might be carried on.

In all probability, the water is at present polluted by waste from the nearby village of Clifty, now a stranded community with its mines shut down and their entrances blasted in. The village cannot long exist under present conditions. It is possible that upon materialization of proposed reforestation plans for the area, Clifty may find new life as a community of forest workers. Should this be the case, the town should be provided with sanitary facilities which would not pollute the river.

Pilot Falls is best reached by turning south from United States Highway 70 Alternate, 13 miles east of Sparta, and following a red cinder road, 3½ miles to Clifty, then a half-mile farther to the falls.

The Gulf
[E-1]

Location: On Caney Fork, in White and Van Buren Counties, 8–10 miles above crossing of Tennessee Highway 111.
Type: Wilderness.
Characteristics: Narrow river valley with steep, wooded slopes; cave.

Below Pilot Falls the Caney Fork descends rapidly into a steep, narrow valley, one which does not, however, have the precipitous walls and gorgelike character of many of the plateau streams. The deepest portion of the valley is known locally as the Gulf. Its sides, sloping steeply, rise 900 feet above the stream and are densely wooded with pines and mixed hardwoods. On the south slope, Rose Cave has been explored for 3 miles, and its terminus not then reached. Several good springs issue from either slope.

A local favorite for fishing and hunting, the Gulf might become a game preserve and wilderness area under a comprehensive recreation program, for it lies in the center of what is probably the wildest portion of the plateau and has no superlative scenic interest. Access to it is difficult. Usually a hike of 10 or 15 miles is necessary although truck trails and woods roads, negotiable by auto in dry weather, lead from Clifty and Eastland to the brink. Access roads from below, cross and recross the bed of the stream, dry during the summer but impassable in spring.

Cline, Chattanooga

An outlook over the Highland Rim on United States Highway 70 between Crossville and Sparta.

POTENTIAL REGIONAL RECREATION AREAS

DUCK RIVER FALLS
[B–3]

Location: Coffee County, Tenn., 1 mile northwest of Manchester.

Communities served: Manchester, 1 mile; Tullahoma, 13 miles; McMinnville, 23 miles; Winchester, 25 miles; Murfreesboro, 30 miles; Cowan, 31 miles; Palmer, 31 miles; Tracy City, 32 miles; Shelbyville, 34 miles; Fayetteville, 41 miles; Nashville, 63 miles; Chattanooga, 75 miles.

Size: 3,000 acres.

Type: Outing park, combining developed scenic and intensive-use areas; wilderness.

Characteristics: Gorges of Duck and Little Duck Rivers, their confluence within the tract; evidence of prehistoric fortifications within the angle formed by the two rivers; rolling, partly wooded submarginal land which should be reforested; existing 45-acre artificial lake.

THE suggested tract is severed by United States Highway 41 (the principal road from Chattanooga to Nashville, and a main highway from Chicago to Florida). The area north of the highway would lend itself well to intensive use. Lake Manchester, an existing artificial lake of about 45 acres, formed by damming the Duck River, would be usable for boating, swimming, and fishing, and its shores for vacation cabins and other suitable features. The much larger tract across the highway is eminently suited to becoming a developed scenic area. The largest part of it, however, though it now contains a large proportion of cleared submarginal land, should be reforested, and designated as a wilderness.

A great deal of interest would be added to such a park by the historical and archeological significance of the "Old Stone Fort." Evidence of this creation still remains in the form of low earthworks and a shallow ditch which apparently was once a deep moat.

This tract is located in a fairly populous section which is not served by any public recreation area, and in which there are very few tracts that are especially suited to recreational use. Steps are being taken to acquire it for public ownership, and the project has the hearty backing of the local population.

Cline, Chattanooga

Duck River Falls—a confusion of tumbling waters in a proposed recreation area on United States Highway 41.

Lake Manchester would provide space for water sports in the Duck River Falls recreation park.

WALDENSIA
[G–1]

Location: On Cumberland Plateau, northeast of Ozone, 5 miles off
  United States Highway 70.
Communities served: Rockwood, 13 miles; Crossville, 21 miles;
  Harriman, 27 miles; Chattanooga, 80 miles; Knoxville, 64 miles;
  Sparta, 46 miles.
Size: 300 acres.
Type: Intensive-use area.
Characteristics: Dam site; plateau second growth; rolling topog-
  raphy; existing lake of 7 acres.

Lake Waldensia is an existing recreational site under
private ownership. It is part of a tract of 8,000 acres
that has been offered for sale to various Government
agencies for recreational purposes. The tract is that
of a mining company, which has ceased operations and
sold the land, including mineral rights. Several
miners' cottages have been remodeled by the present
owner for vacation cabins, and others on the property
are suitable for remodeling. Other buildings of
recreational importance include a small hotel, two
large modern houses, running water supplied from
artesian wells on the property, a bathhouse, and small
store. The existing 7-acre lake is created by a stone
dam some 70 feet long and 20 feet high. A dam 150
feet long and 40 feet high at a natural site some distance downstream would create a lake of 50 acres.
There are a number of coke ovens which could be dis-
mantled to furnish stone suitable for the construction
of such a dam. The watershed of the stream is well
wooded; thus a regular flow of clear water is assured.

Existing cabins are attractively situated with
regard to the present lake—others could be as advan-
tageously grouped about it or the suggested larger
lake. There are opportunities for playfields, picnic
and camping areas, and parking space nearby. Portions of the rest of the property which are unadaptable
for cultivation should be kept in woodland. These
areas are stream valleys, steep slopes, and ridge tops
where the soil is shallow. A system of bridle trails
might well be constructed through these woods, and
a stable maintained in the central recreation area.

SHORT CREEK FALLS
[A–8]

Location: Marshall County, 7 miles airline southwest of Guntersville, Ala.

Communities served: Guntersville, 7 miles: Albertville, 4 miles; Scottsboro, 36 miles; Huntsville, 50 miles; Cullman, 42 miles; Gadsden, 31 miles; Alabama City, 29 miles; Attalla, 26 miles.

Size: Minimum, 500 acres.

Type: Outing area, combining developed scenic and intensive-use areas.

Characteristics: Falls; gorge; variety of plant growth, future embayment of Guntersville Reservoir.

Short Creek Falls is about 15 feet high and 75 feet across. Interest lies in its power and size rather than in delicacy or spectacular height. The stream channel above the falls is a smooth, gently sloping face of rock so that the creek moves swiftly but quietly. Below the falls it becomes turbulent, and cascades along in an irregular and boulder-filled course. The steep, wooded side slopes of the stream vary from 150 feet to 200 feet high. The result is a narrow steep-walled valley of a gorgelike character.

About a mile below the falls the valley widens and the slopes become less steep. Flat bottom land will be covered by an embayment of Guntersville Lake. The resultant effect would be that of a narrow lake kept clear and fresh by the waters of Short Creek.

The cover of excellent first- and second-growth timber which clothes the slopes of the Short Creek Valley wall extends to the northeast along Sand Mountain, comprising a wooded tract of several hundred acres, with comparatively little cleared land, which borders Guntersville Lake.

The Short Creek tract is so situated as to serve a very considerable urban population, in addition to a large farm population. The falls are now best reached from Albertville over 4 miles of gravel road to Hustleville, then 2 miles westward, and finally a quarter-mile walk to the edge of the gorge.

The swift-flowing waters of Short Creek plunge into seething rapids below the falls.

Centuries of carving by the gently flowing stream have cut two natural bridges from the soft sandstone near Waynesboro.

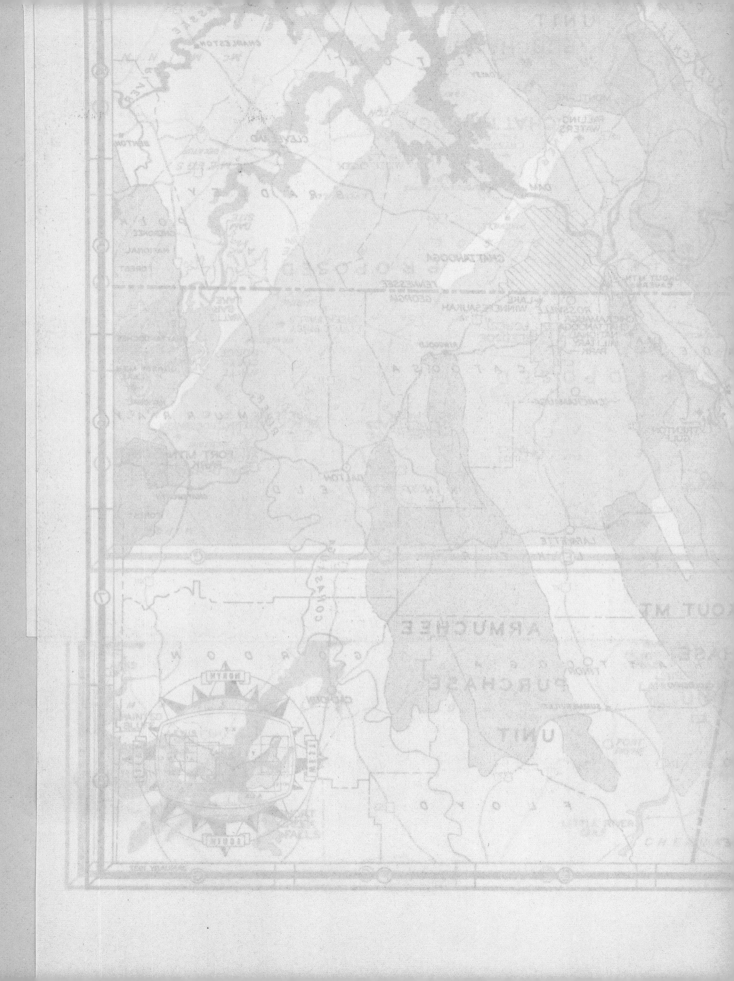

The Wheeler Basin Area

GENERAL DESCRIPTION OF THE AREA

THE Wheeler Basin area includes most of northern Alabama, a large part of south-central Tennessee, and a corner of northeast Mississippi. Somewhat south of the center of the area the Tennessee River cuts across it, comprising the entire Wheeler, Wilson, and Pickwick Reservoirs. Major tributary water-courses include those of the Elk River, which lies in the northeast quarter of the area, flowing southwest into the Wheeler Reservoir; and the Duck and the Buffalo Rivers, which flow west and north in the northwest quarter.

In general, this section of the Tennessee Valley contains good farm land. The eastern part contains the southern end of the Cumberland Plateau. Wooded ridges and hills are scattered throughout the area, but the clearly defined northeast-southwest ridges and valleys that characterize the Valley of East Tennessee are not found here. The central portion, near Athens and Decatur, is decidedly flat, nearly completely cleared, and the tributary streams in this section are frequently sluggish and marshy.

of the region and is also a railroad center. Decatur, and the Tri-Cities (Florence, Sheffield, and Tuscumbia), in Alabama, and Columbia and Shelbyville, in Tennessee. Huntsville, though the trading point for a fertile farming area, is essentially an industrial center. It is the focus of cotton-milling industries of the region and is also a railroad center. Decatur, with a 1930 population of 15,593, is the largest city on the Tennessee River between Paducah and Chattanooga and is the principal industrial city of this section. It is also important as a railroad center and as

a terminal for river navigation. The Tri-Cities are primarily local trading and railroad centers. Florence also has significance, second to Decatur, as a navigation terminal. Columbia and Shelbyville, Tenn., are trading centers for several agricultural counties, and the former is also the center of important phosphate deposits now being commercially exploited.

Reference to the accompanying map of the Wheeler Basin area will demonstrate that all parts of it lie within easy driving distance of present or potential forest wilderness areas, which will afford opportunities for such extensive forms of recreation as hunting, fishing, hiking, and camping although they lack the superlative scenic quality of the eastern half of the Tennessee Valley. The agricultural character of the land which lies between these forested highlands accounts for the lack of potential scenic areas in the fertile Duck River drainage basin.

In a territory such as that comprised within Wheeler Basin area, which includes few outstanding mountains, scenic areas of recreational significance tend to be based either on the existence of forests or water features. Thus, outside of the national or State forests, every potential regional recreation area noted has water as its nucleus of interest, either in the form of purely scenic features such as Welcome Falls, Marcella Falls, and Grin Creek; or areas adjacent to usable waterways like those on the Wheeler Reservoir, and Wilhoite Mills, Shoal Creek, Limestone Creek, and Ravens Bluff; or a combination of the two, as at Short Creek, Duck River Falls, and Bear Creek Falls.

183

EXISTING REGIONAL RECREATION AREAS

BLACK WARRIOR NATIONAL FOREST
[E-8]

THE Black Warrior National Forest, an enlargement of the old Alabama National Forest created in 1918, has a gross area of 560,604 acres. It was set aside mainly to protect the headwaters of the Black Warrior River, which has considerable significance for the production of waterpower and for navigation in its lower reaches.

This area was formerly inhabited by Cherokee and Chickasaw Indian tribes. In Lawrence County, near the north boundary there remains a large number of Indian mounds.

Within the forest, 16,000 acres have been set aside as the Sipsey River Game Refuge, which has been stocked with deer. The rivers are stocked with bass and bream. Kinlock Forest Camp is open to tent campers. As in other national forests, increased emphasis on suitable development for recreation, as one of the recognized forest uses, is to be expected.

Although the elevation above sea level of this forest is negligible as compared with such national forests as those in the Blue Ridge Province, even the few hundred feet greater height above the neighboring country, together with the forest shade, have a mitigating effect on summer temperatures. The terrain is rough and is cut by picturesque gorges. On one of its score of streams is found an attractive waterfall and, in another location, a natural bridge.

Three Alabama State highways, 5, 31, and 36, meeting near the center of the forest, at Double Springs, divide it roughly into quadrants and assure ready access to points of special interest.

MERIWETHER LEWIS NATIONAL MONUMENT
[D-1]

This tract of 300 acres, which lies in Lewis County a few miles east of Hohenwald on Tennessee Highway 20, was set aside as a memorial to Gen. Meriwether Lewis, co-leader of the Lewis and Clark Expedition to the West Coast. Lewis died in this place, in the Grinder Inn, on the site of which a two-room cabin is now being built, typical of that period, but not intended to be a replica of the original. Lewis's grave is here, marked by a monument.

Some development of the tract has been accomplished recently. A new entrance road has been built, as well as a loop road around the monument, and one to a new superintendent's lodge. In addition to the Grinder house previously mentioned, a lodge with public rest rooms is being erected. One loop path leads back into the more remote part of the area. A large part of the wooded tract is not being disturbed.

Apart from historical interest the recreational significance of this monument area appears to be quite limited in its possibilities.

WILSON LAKE
[D-5]

Wilson Dam is on the Tennessee River about 3 miles above Florence, Ala. Started during wartime to supply power for the manufacture of nitrates, the project was completed in 1925, thus creating a navigable pool over the historic rapids at Muscle Shoals, in addition to fulfilling its primary purpose. The reservoir extends 15½ miles to Wheeler Dam. Its normal surface area is 16,000 acres and it has an average width of more than 1½ miles.

Unlike all other reservoirs in the present TVA program, the shores of Wilson Lake are almost entirely in private ownership and are not controlled by TVA. The country surrounding the lake is rolling agricultural land with many small wooded tracts. There are only a few low bluffs along the lake, but most of the shoreline is wooded and views across the broad waters are attractive.

Boating and fishing are popular. There is swimming at several points, although malarial conditions prevail along the shores. There are many summer cottages around the lake and some use of the shores for picnics and outings.

WHEELER LAKE
[F-6]

Wheeler Dam is located on the upper end of Muscle Shoals, about 16 miles east of Florence. Wheeler Lake extends for a distance of 74 miles east-southeast to Guntersville Dam. At normal pool elevation its area is slightly more than 100 square miles, ranking second among TVA reservoirs to the proposed Gilbertsville Lake in point of area. It has a general lowland setting, but physiographic differences separate it into two distinct divisions, upper and lower. Downstream from a point due south of Huntsville,

From this overlook in Wheeler Park the upper face of Wheeler Dam attracts the observer.

adjacent land is flat except for an occasional small bluff, and the lake varies from one-half mile to 3 miles in width. Above this point it remains mostly in the original river channel, winding between steep wooded bluffs with occasional arms extending up tributary stream valleys.

Wheeler Lake has a normal pool elevation of 555 feet, but variations from this level will affect various recreational uses of the lake. From May to October the level will probably be fluctuated within a 1-foot range. However, the most desirable sites for swimming and boating facilities occur where the shores are relatively steep and hence the draw-down involves no great difficulties.

Except for the bluff areas described elsewhere in this chapter in detail, the land surrounding Wheeler Lake has little recreational attractiveness. Interest largely centers on the lake itself. Sporting appeal will increase as the opportunities for fishing and waterfowl-

shooting become better known. Boating will become more popular. Picnicking and swimming at various points will command at least a local patronage. There may be a demand for cottage sites, trailer camps, and tourist cabins at certain points.

Malarial conditions prevail along certain sections of the lake, making them unfit for development involving the use of water. However, a large portion of the local population is in the habit of swimming, fishing, and boating here in spite of this danger, and it has been recommended that these activities be restricted to areas where control methods can be applied with reasonable effectiveness.

PICKWICK LAKE
[B–5]

Pickwick Dam is now under construction at a point in Hardin County, Tenn., 53 miles downstream from Wilson Dam. The normal surface area of the reservoir will be 41,600 acres, or 65 square miles, and its 413-foot normal level subject to a maximum downward fluctuation of 10 feet.

The upper third of Pickwick Lake has a general lowland setting, and the surrounding land is largely in agricultural use. Low limestone cliffs border the flood plains of the Tennessee River and wooded bluffs occur along some of the tributary streams.

The lower two-thirds of Pickwick Lake lie in table land that is highly dissected by tributary streams. The shores of the lake rise abruptly to this highland country, which has a thin forest of pine and deciduous trees. All of this section along the north side of the reservoir and the Alabama portion on the south side fall within the boundaries of the proposed Duck River Purchase Unit.

A long arm of the lake extends south into the Bear Creek valley for a distance of almost 15 miles. This embayment is about a mile in width. Smaller embayments occur on Second Creek, near Waterloo, and on Indian Creek and Yellow Creek.

Potentialities for recreation on Pickwick Lake and its shores have not yet been studied in detail. Two areas within the proposed Duck River Forest, namely, Waterloo Bluffs and Bear Creek Peninsula, are briefly described in this chapter in the description of that forest unit. There are undoubtedly other areas worthy of development for recreational use. The scenic values on most of the lake and its surroundings are outstanding by comparison with their immediate locality although they are not comparable with the eastern half of the Tennessee Valley.

TENNESSEE VALLEY AUTHORITY RESERVATIONS

Five TVA reservations in the Wheeler Basin possess recreational significance. Three of them—Nitrate Plant No. 2 Reservation, Wilson Dam Park, and Wheeler Dam Park—already have been provided with intensive-use facilities; another—Pickwick Dam Reservation—is being developed; and the fifth—Nitrate Plant No. 1 Reservation—remains a potential site.

Nitrate Plant No. 2 Reservation
[D–5]

Nearly 400 acres of the Nitrate Plant No. 2 Reservation have been designated as Muscle Shoals Park. This area, lying on the south side of the Tennessee River (soon to be the upper reaches of Pickwick Lake) and in the northwest corner of the reservation, is rugged and heavily timbered, with a precipitous bluff bordering the water. Among the features now provided are picnic grounds, parking spaces, a nature study museum, a boat house, toilet facilities, cabins, and trails. A number of tennis courts have recently been laid. At the northeast end of this reservation is Wilson Dam and the powerhouse, which attract great numbers of visitors.

At the southeast corner of Nitrate Plant No. 2 Reservation an area of about 70 acres, two-thirds covered with timber, has been established as a park for Negroes. Picnic and parking facilities, among other attractions, are provided.

An auto parking space permits the motorist to obtain broad views over Wilson Lake.

Wilson Dam Park
[D–5]

On the north side of the Tennessee River at Wilson Dam about 50 acres of Government land abutting Wilson Lake are available for picnicking and similar activities. This land, practically the only publicly owned waterfront property on the north side of the lake, is partly timbered and slopes gradually toward the water. Wilson Dam Park, accessible from United States Highway 72, has proved a popular site for obtaining views of the dam and powerhouse.

An overlook along the shoreline trail in Wheeler Park.

Wheeler Dam Park
[E–5]

The Wheeler Reservation on the south side of the river contains 1,100 acres; present recreational facilities include picnic grounds, tent campground, parking space, overlook and other shelters, and trails. The dam and powerhouse are, of course, features of interest. The bridge across Wheeler Dam (unlike that at Wilson Dam where the height of the side walls obscures vision from passing cars) permits unobstructed views of Wheeler and Wilson Lakes. At the north abutment of the dam the navigation lock is a source of considerable attraction.

Pickwick Dam Reservation
[B–4]

The TVA has established a reservation of 1,725 acres around Pickwick Dam. About 100 acres of this tract, adjacent to the south end of the dam and the reservoir, are particularly adapted to intensive recreational use to serve the many visitors to the dam and the residents of communities in the vicinity. Picnic and camp facilities have been developed, with the necessary park roads, bridges, foot trails, shelters, water supply, sewage disposal facilities, and ornamental planting, besides extensive work in reforestation and other methods of soil erosion control.

Beyond this area and across a bay of the lake is an extensive timber area suitable for a game preserve.

This trailside shelter of native limestone and timber permits views in three directions over Pickwick Lake.

This area is isolated from outlying points, and the plans now call for making it accessible only by foot or bridle paths.

Nitrate Plant No. 1 Reservation
[C-5]

At present there are no public recreation facilities in this tract, which lies due west of and is adjacent to Tuscumbia. However, nearly two-thirds of its 1,500 acres are suitable for park purposes and have been suggested for development as a park. The land is rolling, partially wooded, and has an attractive stream flowing through it. The reservation has frontage on the upper reaches of Pickwick Lake.

WAYNESBORO NATURAL BRIDGES
[D-2]

Eight miles northeast of Waynesboro, Tenn., two natural bridges of sandstone span the gorge of a small creek tributary to the Buffalo River. The bridges, located but a short distance apart, have arches approximately 25 feet in length and 15 feet in height. Picturesque bluffs of stratified sandstone in the vicinity of the bridges have considerable interest in themselves. The gorge and bridges lie in a heavily wooded tract, within the boundaries of the proposed Duck River Purchase Unit.

The owner of the 80-acre tract surrounding the bridges has developed them as a commercial recreational feature. A dam beneath the upper bridge impounds a small lake, fed by the stream and several springs, which supplies facilities for swimming and boating. A lodge, equipped for dining, and several vacation cabins serve as a seasonal resort. Paths lead to the bridges and to several small caves in the side walls of the gorge.

A drive to the place leads from United States Highway 64, 3½ miles east of Waynesboro, 4 miles over Tennessee Highway 48, and 2½ miles over a good county road.

Wiles, Nashville

A fisherman's fly ripples the small lake above Waynesboro Natural Bridges.

MONTE SANO STATE PARK
[H-5]

Rising 1,000 feet above the surrounding lowlands, Monte Sano, a fragment of the Cumberland Plateau lying 5 miles east of Huntsville, Ala., attains a height of more than 1,600 feet above sea level. On its summit and slopes has been established Monte Sano State Park, noteworthy as an example of successful cooperation among government bodies for the advancement of a unified regional recreational program.

Developments within the 1,900-acre park include a lodge, several cabins for overnight use, parking spaces, two picnic grounds, many miles of trails, a stable for saddle horses, a commissary, and several overlooks, some with shelters, which permit panoramic views over the valley below and the Cumberland Plateau proper to the east. A swimming pool has been proposed as a future project.

A most unusual feature of Monte Sano Park is its interesting natural well and cave. This weird phenomenon consists of a winding corridor, 200 to 300 feet below the surface of the earth, whose only entrance is through a 180-foot vertical well. The cave is 250 feet long and, in places, more than 200 feet high. The floor at its lowest point is 320 feet underground. Its sheer perpendicular walls are fluted. The well, dropping vertically to the floor of the cave,

187

pierces numerous rock strata, affording one a living picture of the geologic formation of the area.

Several rare insects have been found in the cavern although no evidence of prehistoric man or beast has as yet been discovered. Geologists who have visited the cave marvel at its formations. All propose that it be developed, with lighting and safe access being provided, for public enjoyment.

Monte Sano served as a summer resort for the residents of Huntsville, which has a metropolitan population of around 25,000. Its name, of Spanish origin, means "Health Mountain" and it was, in the latter nineteenth century, the location of an extravagant resort hotel. Monte Sano Park is reached by a loop road, one end joining United States Highway 241, which skirts the area on the southwest, and the other running east from Huntsville.

Federal, State, and county governments united efforts toward the establishment and development of Monte Sano Park. The land was acquired by Madison County and turned over to the State of Alabama for management under its State park system. TVA and National Park Service furnished the park plans, while the CCC executed them.

TISHOMINGO STATE PARK
[B-6]

One of Mississippi's newly developed parks is Tishomingo State Park, 4½ miles southeast of the town of Tishomingo, near Mississippi Highway 25. The tract includes 700 acres. It is traversed by Bear Creek, a meandering stream with bordering sandstone cliffs about 100 feet high, and is heavily timbered with oak, other hardwoods, and some pine. Plans for its development call for an intensive-use area on a peninsular ridge overlooking the stream, where an administration building and a group of cabins are proposed, together with the necessary access road and utilities. The remainder of the area will be accessible by trails, some of which will lead to overlooks on points commanding good views of the surrounding country.

Observation points along the escarpment of Monte Sano embrace views leading over cultivated low land into the depths of the Cumberland Plateau.

PROPOSED REGIONAL RECREATION AREAS

PROPOSED DUCK RIVER PURCHASE UNIT
[C–1, B–6]

Location: In northwest Alabama, northeast Mississippi, and south-central Tennessee immediately east of the lower Tennessee River.
Size: 1,724,390 acres.
Type: Wilderness with occasional outing areas.
Characteristics: Extensively wooded rolling highlands with occasional cleared valleys; high rock cliffs in certain sections; extensive frontage on Pickwick and proposed Gilbertsville Reservoirs.

THE proposed Duck River Purchase Unit embraces the largest unified forest area in the western Tennessee Valley. Originally proposed by the TVA, it now awaits final approval by the National Forest Reservation Commission. It lies entirely within the drainage of the Tennessee River and its main tributaries, the Buffalo and the Duck.

In general, its topography is high, rolling country with long, steep slopes to the principal streams. The red-clay loam, forming the predominant soil type in the northern part of the unit, has little agricultural value, which is demonstrated by the fact that only 15 percent of the land has been cleared. This small fraction occupies the limestone and gravelly soils in the valleys of the larger streams. Shale and sandstone soils, predominant at the higher elevations in the southern portion, support a forest cover of two principal types: The hardwoods and pine-hardwoods. Both soils and climatic conditions suit the area more for forest growth of these types than for agriculture. The growing season averages 7 months, and rainfall aggregates nearly 50 inches annually.

The proposed Duck River Purchase Unit has a frontage on a large portion of Pickwick Lake, and will border several miles of the eastern shore of the proposed Gilbertsville Lake. In many places along the lake shores, low limestone cliffs rise directly from water, commanding extensive views over the lakes. Similar bluffs border the Buffalo River. These features give to the forest a scenic interest which is unusual to the general vicinity, and may merit recreational developments, such as camp and picnicking grounds. Additional recreational interest will come with the replenishing of upland game species, such as deer and turkey. Restocking of game should follow closely an adequate program of protection and management, for they were formerly abundant throughout the area. With the opportunities for fishing and waterfowl-shooting on the nearby lakes, the Duck River Forest should have much sporting appeal.

Bear Creek Peninsula
[B–5]

Location: On the south shore of Pickwick Lake immediately east of the Bear Creek embayment, 27 miles west of Tuscumbia, Ala.
Type: Intensive-use.
Characteristics: Dissected upland, heavily forested, and watered by clear streams and numerous springs.

The northern and western portions of the Bear Creek Peninsula rank among the highest and roughest sections of the south shore of Pickwick Lake. The immediate shore rises as a forested wall 300 feet above the lake. The once level surface of the upland back of this wall is now cut by three main valleys with many tributary ravines and coves deeply incised into the prevailing level. Streams in the coves drain rapidly and directly into the reservoir, in steep cascading courses. Many springs and a heavy forest cover, predominantly of pine, insure a fair degree of permanence to the stream flow. A general forest program with regulation of grazing would soon insure a healthy forest stand and abundant bird life.

While no single feature of specific scenic significance is noted, the area has a general attractiveness which marks its suitability for recreational use. The area is readily accessible from United States Highway 72 at Cherokee, 15 miles west of Tuscumbia, where a good county road leads 12 miles north to the reservoir. A narrow taking-line extends along the 15-mile shore front of the peninsula, but optimum recreational development must follow acquisition by the United States Forest Service.

Waterloo Bluffs
[B–5]

Location: On the north shore of Pickwick Reservoir near the town of Waterloo, 24 miles west of Florence, Ala.
Type: Intensive-use.
Characteristics: Wooded bluffs, rising to steep, narrow ridges 200 feet above the lake.

The most outstanding bluffs along the north shore of Pickwick Lake lie east of the mouth of Second Creek opposite the town of Waterloo. Their vertical faces of limestone rise from the water's edge and taper off to steep wooded slopes which reach elevations 200 feet above the lake. These slopes are seldom less than 60 percent in gradient, and support a dense growth of pine. The bluffs command extensive views over the main body of the lake and southward down the Bear Creek inlet.

Only the narrow bottoms of the Second Creek valley have been cleared and many of these will be flooded by the reservoir. The clarity of the stream and the protection afforded by its heavily wooded watershed suggest good fishing, which, combined with the possibilities of hunting both waterfowl on the lake and upland game in the forest, should lend considerable significance to the bluffs as the center of sporting activities in the Duck River Purchase Unit. The bluffs would offer suitable sites for cabin or tent camping as well as picnicking.

Such use, however, will depend on final road relocations incidental to Pickwick Lake and on the acquisition program of the purchase unit. Although the bluffs themselves and a small portion of the land behind them are included in the reservoir taking line, optimum development of the site is dependent on the purchase of additional land by the Forest Service. Hunting and, to a considerable degree, fishing will depend on an adequate game management program for adjacent land.

Tenn. Dept. of Conservation

Rattlesnake Falls, despite its ominous name, has long been popular as a local picnic ground.

La Grange Mountain
[D–6]

Location: 3 miles airline southwest of Leighton, Colbert County, Ala.

Communities served: Florence, 19 miles; Sheffield, 15 miles; Tuscumbia, 13 miles.

Type: Developed scenic area.

Characteristics: Low eminence rising 300 feet above surrounding countryside; sweeping views; historical associations.

La Grange Mountain, a wooded ridge of several thousand acres, lies near the southern portion of the proposed Duck River Purchase Unit, 3 miles airline southwest of Leighton, Ala. On top of the mountain, in 1833, was founded La Grange College, which in 1863 was burned by Union troops and not rebuilt. A marker on the site outlines a brief history of the institution. Descendants of various alumni have maintained a keen interest in the history of the college and are eager to see some form of government reservation created there.

In addition to these historical associations, the mountain possesses natural advantages inherent in its elevation, 250 to 300 feet above the flat plain around Muscle Shoals. Comparatively cool summer temperatures and sweeping views over adjacent lowland indicate that the tract may have some potential value for recreation if suitably developed.

PROPOSED MAURY STATE FOREST PURCHASE UNIT
[E–2]

Location: Maury and Lewis Counties, Tenn.

Communities served: Columbia, 20 miles; Lawrenceburg, 14 miles; Pulaski, 33 miles; Hohenwald, 21 miles; Mount Pleasant, 9 miles.

Size: 18,900 acres.

Type: Outing area combining developed scenic and intensive-use areas.

Characteristics: Steep, broken topography drained by small headwater streams; 79 percent forest land; two waterfalls.

The proposed Maury State Forest lies in western Maury County and eastern Lewis County in south-central Tennessee, overlapping the border of the proposed Duck River Purchase Unit. Topographically, a series of steep, narrow ridges of low elevation, the forest is drained by many small headwater streams. The soil is a deep sandy clay loam, fertile but too steep for cultivation. Erosion is rampant on cleared lands. An excellent hardwood growth has been heavily cut over and needs forest management, which is essential to protect the watershed of the Mount Pleasant municipal water supply.

The forest has distinct and useful recreational

Spray from Stillhouse Hollow Falls provides moisture for lush herb growth on the cliff over which it drops.

possibilities, for it might supply needed camp and picnic facilities for several nearby towns. As a game refuge it would serve to replenish the wildlife on adjacent property. Two waterfalls within the tract are outstanding. Rattlesnake Falls, 60 feet high, have served as a picnic and outing spot for several generations of local people. Such use is recognized by the present owner who asks public cooperation in maintaining the attractiveness of the area in return for freedom of access. Several artificial ponds below the falls have been stocked with fish, but fishing in them is prohibited. Stillhouse Hollow Falls is an unusually attractive semicascading waterfall located in a cove of the same name less than one-half mile away; 75 feet in height, they combine the character of cascade and sheer drop, and have a pleasant setting on a rocky hillside covered with profuse growth.

The Maury Forest is proposed for acquisition under the Fulmer Act. The tract would be managed by the Tennessee Department of Conservation with the cooperation of the United States Forest Service, with the provision that part of the earnings from the forest would go to repay the Federal funds invested. Plans for the development of the forest include recognition of its recreational possibilities.

NATCHEZ TRACE
[A-6, E-1]

The old Natchez Trace, leading 500 miles from Nashville on the Cumberland River to Natchez on the Mississippi, became in 1780 a principal highroad of the South. Travelers and traders journeyed over it by foot, horseback, or coach; troops marched its length for military conquest. Previous to this time, it had served as a trail and warpath for the Natchez, Chickasaw, and Choctaw Indians. Some historians date the trail even earlier, to wandering tribes of Aztecs who established a capital below Natchez and blazed a trail for trade and intercourse with eastern tribes. The trail is rich in historical incidents relating to the cotton empire of the South.

For a number of years, increasing public interest has been directed toward the construction of a national parkway along the route of the old Trace. The National Park Service has made preliminary plans and construction has been started on two 12½ mile lengths between Natchez and Jackson, Miss. The parkway will include an automobile drive through a strip of park land averaging 100 acres to the mile; bridle trails and paths will parallel the

roadway. Markers will designate those remains of the old Trace which still persist; picnic and camp facilities will be developed at intervals. Existing forest growth within the right-of-way will be improved and ornamental shrubs planted.

The route of the proposed parkway enters the Wheeler Basin Area northwest of Columbia, Tenn., and crosses in a southwest direction through Tennessee, northwest Alabama, and Mississippi. It will pass through the proposed Duck River Purchase Unit, and it will lead close to Meriwether Lewis National Monument and Tishomingo State Park. Its crossing of Pickwick Lake, whether by bridge or ferry, may prove an interesting feature of the Trace.

MONTE SANO FOREST
[H-6]

Location: Madison County, Ala., east and south of Huntsville.
Size: 32,000 acres.
Type: Predominantly wilderness; possible limited outing areas.
Characteristics: Elongated, flat-topped ridge, elevation 1,100 to 1,300, 800–1,000 feet above the adjacent valleys.

The Monte Sano forest tract has been suggested by the TVA Division of Forestry as a State forest. It extends from a few miles northeast of Huntsville south to the Tennessee River, where its ultimate point is called Rowe Mountain. Most of this tract is rocky, and ill-suited for land use other than forestry. It would also make an excellent game preserve.

Within its boundaries is located Monte Sano State Park, described elsewhere. A limited development of foot and bridle trails through the forest would supplement the more intensive types of recreation which will be provided in the State park.

MORGAN-MARSHALL FOREST
[H-7]

Location: Morgan and Marshall Counties, Ala.
Size: 43,500 acres.
Type: Wilderness, broken by possible resettlement communities; limited outing areas.
Characteristics: Partly wooded mountain and plateau land, several bluffs along Wheeler Lake.

This area of rugged wooded slopes and cleared rolling uplands has been suggested by the TVA Division of Forestry as a combination State forest and rural resettlement area. The possibilities for recreation lie chiefly in the use of wooded bluffs along Wheeler Lake. These include Bean Rock, across from the mouth of the Paint Rock River; Blue Rock, 4 miles up river; and Georgia Mountain, below Guntersville Dam.

POTENTIAL REGIONAL RECREATION AREAS

BEAR CREEK FALLS
[C–8]

Location: Marion County, Ala., 15½ miles south of Russellville.

Communities served: Haleyville, 12 miles; Russellville, 21 miles; Tuscumbia, 41 miles; Sheffield, 42 miles.

Size: 1,250 acres.

Types: Outing park, combining developed scenic and intensive-use areas.

Characteristics: Waterfall and gorge.

BEAR CREEK FALLS, at one time, was much more impressive than it is now. Before its watershed was cleared, water went over the 11-foot main drop in a sheet 150 feet or more in width. Now, except after long rains, most of the rock fall is dry, and the creek drops through a sharp cut at the south end. The creek is impressive under any condition. Even in dry weather there is a fairly good flow. Below the falls a fine gorge is characterized by large tumbled rocks and steep bluffs. Some of the flat-topped monoliths above United States Highway 43 are reputed to have been favorite pow-wow places for the Tishomingo Indians. Just below the falls is a fair-sized pool which is now used considerably for swimming.

At present the falls is approached by a county road, which leaves United States Highway 43 five miles south of Phil Campbell. At one-quarter of a mile east of this highway, a dirt road runs southward for a mile, and stops at the edge of the bluff on Bear Creek. From there one must walk a quarter mile to the falls.

This tract appears to be of such caliber as to justify its being acquired and developed for an outing park.

Tumbled rocks enclose this natural swimming hole just below Bear Creek Falls.

WELCOME FALLS
[G–7]

Location: Morgan County, Ala., 14 miles northeast of Cullman, on the South Fork of Cotaco Creek.

Communities served: Cullman, 18 miles; Hartselle, 26 miles; Guntersville, 27 miles; Decatur, 35 miles; Huntsville, 46 miles; Athens, 50 miles.

Size: 1,800 acres.

Type: Wilderness park.

Characteristics: Waterfall; cascades; gorge, with outstanding rock formations; variety of plant growth.

Sand Mountain in Alabama, like the Cumberland Plateau of Tennessee, is a great peneplain built up of sedimentary rock. The edges of this plateau are cut by gorges and deep narrow coves which often extend for many miles in toward the center of the plateau. At the headwall of one of these gorges are Welcome Falls, 40 feet high. Below the falls the stream follows a steep, cascading course to a point where it joins another branch. The two, merged, become the South Fork of Cotaco Creek. The valley and gorge are well timbered with mixed hardwoods, and there is a considerable pine growth on the plateau above.

The headwall of the gorge is in the form of an arc, with a chord length of some 300 feet. The wall is vertical, in many cases overhanging, and is from 20 to 40 feet high. Ascent may be made at only one point. The exposed vertical faces of the side walls are less high and the talus slopes in a great many cases reach nearly to their top. Those which are exposed are picturesquely eroded, resulting, in many cases, in shallow caves or free-standing monoliths. The slopes are made up of huge boulders, the exposed faces of which show fossils. A wide variety of shrub and herb growth is found among the boulders.

The stream flows over and around similar large boulders. Consequently a number of small cascades in an infinite variety of form and size alternate with many pools of varying mood and color. The spot is almost idyllic in the intimate charm of its character. It would appear that the gorge had been cut by a much larger stream than now exists. Although much of the beauty of the falls is lost in dry weather, the beauty of the stream remains even with a much diminished flow.

The area should be reserved as a wilderness park. It would have an aesthetic, primitive and scientific appeal to large numbers of people. In addition to the gorge and wooded slopes of the lower valley, sufficient acreage of the cleared land above the falls should be purchased in order to provide for reforestation so that a more even stream flow may be assured. Development plans should include only access road, service area, and a limited number of trails.

The falls are reached over 6½ miles of gravel and mud road from Baileyton, which is 8 miles west of the intersection of Alabama Highways 31 and 38. Inquiry about the route should be made at Baileyton.

GRIN CREEK GORGE
[G-7]

Location: Morgan County, Ala., at Valhermoso Springs.
Communities served: Hartselle, 15 miles; Huntsville, 19 miles; Decatur, 26 miles.
Size: 837 acres.
Type: Outing park, combining developed scenic and intensive-use areas.
Characteristics: Interesting gorge and stream valley, unusual plant growth; historic house.

In the early part of the nineteenth century, the present Alabama Highway 35 was a part of the main travel route between New Orleans and the northeast coast. At that time a tavern was built at Valhermoso Springs on the east brink of Grin Creek Gorge. The inn was a two-story structure with a large gable above, which faced the road. The building was approximately 50 feet wide and 100 feet in length, and a two-decked porch ran across its entire front. In the front yard was a herb and bulb garden of geometric pattern surrounded by rich shrub and tree growth. An open passageway or "dogtrot" ran the entire length of the house, below the ridge line, and connected this garden to a formal allée of crepe myrtle which in turn led to a large open lawn in the rear. This lawn was flanked by an imposing array of service buildings, slave quarters, and stables. A series of springs containing seven kinds of mineral waters flowed in the gorge below the inn.

Today only half the house remains, the rear part having been torn away. The geometric form of the front garden is still visible and many of its plants have become naturalized. The symmetry of the allée has gone with many of the plants, but age has lent picturesqueness to those individuals that remain. A few

The waters of Welcome Falls drop sharply from an overhanging ledge into a gorge of intimate charm.

cabins in the slave quarters still exist and, together with the house, remain structurally sound but badly in need of repairs. The natural beauty of the creek valley is still unimpaired.

The gorge is small, averaging 200 to 300 feet across and having side walls 50 to 75 feet high. The stream forms large pools of clear water among huge boulders which have dropped down from the side. In the gorge an artificial basin of concrete encloses the outlets of seven different types of mineral springs, the Valhermoso Springs known to early travelers. Several hundreds yards downstream from the house, the gorge widens into a glade some 3 acres in extent. The side walls become hillsides of a less steep slope with a cover of deciduous trees and a uniform undergrowth of dwarf rose buckeye. The dispersion of shrub and tree growth, contrasts between deciduous and evergreen foliage, and the relation of the plants to the open space, have a pleasing parklike character.

A vacation camp of unusual character could be built about these features as a nucleus. The inn might be restored to its original purpose and serve as a lodge with dining and assembly-hall facilities. Existing slave quarters and more of the same pattern would serve for vacation cabins. Adjoining fields could be developed as playfields with various facilities, and the gorge explored by means of a series of walks of intimate charm. The nearby Morgan-Marshall State Forest, if established, would be available for longer hikes and horseback rides. It is possible that the boundary of the forest might be extended sufficiently to include this area.

The streaked sides of Painted Bluff drop abruptly 500 feet into the waters of Wheeler Lake.

PAINTED BLUFF
[H–7]

Location: Madison County, Ala. On Wheeler Lake, east of the mouth of Paint Rock River.

Communities served: Huntsville, 30 miles; Guntersville, 24 miles; Athens, 53 miles.

Size: 3,000 acres.

Type: Outing park, combining developed scenic and intensive-use areas.

Characteristics: Spectacular river views; high bluff above river.

Painted Bluff, or Paint Rock, is a flat-topped monadnock above Wheeler Lake near the mouth of Paint Rock River. It has an elevation of 1,100 feet, 550 feet above the level of the reservoir. The southwestern corner of the bluff rises vertically from the shore of the reservoir as a bare rock face whose marked color variations furnish its name. From the point of the bluff superlative views over the river and lowland are cut off only by the wooded slopes of the various ridges which make up the north Alabama plateau.

The top of the bluff has been cleared, and supports an isolated community of submarginal farms. The land is gently rolling, and cleared sections are pleasantly interspersed with scattered trees, individually and in groups. A few surface-water streams and

Slanting shelves of broken rock form clear pools in Grin Creek Gorge, near Valhermoso Springs.

several springs furnish water supply. The sides of the bluff are steep and, for the most part, wooded.

Several factors tend to make the area suitable for recreational use. The altitude, in addition to allowing excellent views, affords a decided climatic advantage over adjacent territory. The flat top is suitable for play and picnic areas, and for a series of bridle trails and park drives. The side slopes are available for hiking trails and footpaths. A boat landing on Wheeler Lake would enable the recreation activities of bluff and reservoir to be coordinated in a recreation area of unusual interest.

The tract may be reached as follows: From New Hope on United States Highway 241, drive south 3¾ miles on that highway, then three-fourths of a mile southwest to the foot of the bluff, and take the left turn. A poor road then winds up and across the bluff for about 5 miles to a clearing about one-third of a mile walk from the edge of the cliff.

CLARK BLUFF
[H-7]

Location: Madison County, Ala., on Wheeler Lake, west of the mouth of Paint Rock River.
Communities served: Huntsville, 28 miles; Guntersville, 26 miles; Athens, 51 miles.
Size: 5,000 acres.
Type: Wilderness (State forest).
Characteristics: Wooded bluff and river views.

Clark Bluff fronts on Wheeler Lake directly across Paint Rock River from Painted Bluff. Its river aspect is only slightly less spectacular than that of Painted Bluff and, as a whole, it has greater natural charm. The monadnock of which it is a part is more irregular, has no flat top and is almost completely wooded. The area should be preserved in its natural state for those who prefer the more rugged type of recreation. Intensive recreation facilities at Painted Bluff would serve as a base for activities at Clark Bluff.

The narrow upper reaches of Wheeler Lake extend between tree-fringed shores below Painted Bluff.

TIMMONS BLUFF
[G–6]

Location: Madison County, Ala., 10 miles southwest of Huntsville.
Communities served: Huntsville, 13½ miles; Decatur, 26 miles (by water).
Size: 16½ acres in TVA ownership.
Type: No development contemplated.
Characteristics: Wooded bluff with rock face, flat bottomland adjacent.

Timmons Bluff lies 2½ miles upstream from Bell Bluff and is somewhat similar topographically, though not over 50 to 75 feet high. The view up the river is perhaps equally good. This bluff is part of a crescent-shaped ridge at the other end of which is a less outstanding elevation called Leeman Bluff. This ridge is separated from Bell Bluff and its narrow ridge by a largely cleared valley.

As in the case of Bell Bluff, no present development is recommended for Timmons Bluff. Conditions of ownership and possible recreational use are practically identical.

BELL BLUFF
[G–6]

Location: Madison County, Ala., 12½ miles southwest of Huntsville.
Communities served: Huntsville, 16½ miles; Decatur, 24 miles (by water).
Size: 28 acres in TVA ownership.
Type: No present development contemplated.
Characteristics: Wooded bluff with sheer rock face; fairly flat land adjacent.

Bell Bluff is one of the few rock cliffs on Wheeler Lake. It rises 100 feet or more, slightly back from the river's edge, and offers an excellent view up the river. It forms the south end of a narrow ridge, a few hundred feet across, which extends inland for 1½ miles at a 45-degree angle from the river. Back of the bluff the ridge broadens into a higher wooded knob. The bluff may be approached from the south where a mile of fair field road comes in from a good north and south county road. This, in turn, meets the Triana-Farley road 3½ miles from the bluff.

The actual bluff, together with adjacent flat river bottoms which will not be flooded, comes within the TVA reservoir taking-line. No recommendation for development or increasing the area of the tract is made because there seems to be no occasion for either in the near future. TVA ownership will assure protection of the chief scenic values, and the wooded ridge shows so much rock outcrop that there is little likelihood of its being further cleared for agriculture.

LEWIS BLUFF
[G–6]

Location: Morgan County, Ala., 4½ miles north of Valhermoso Springs.
Communities served: Decatur, 32 miles (20 miles by water); Huntsville, 26 miles; Hartselle, 22½ miles.
Size: 50 to 60 acres.
Type: Outing park for intensive-use.
Characteristics: Rock bluff, wooded, jutting out into Wheeler Lake.

Lewis Bluff is an arc-shaped sheer cliff about 100 feet high, which projects 500 feet into Wheeler Lake. It commands a particularly good view of the reservoir below Laceys Spring bridge. At the north end of the bluff (the direction from which it is approached by road) the land slopes gradually, affording adequate space for a boat landing, parking space, and a bathing beach. Picnic areas and sites for vacation cabins are available on the bluff itself, and there is sufficient flat land for a playfield. At present the bluff is considerably used as a picnic ground and day outing area by the people of that vicinity.

Wheeler Lake spreads its rippling surface beneath Lewis Bluff.

197

The bluff is now reached from Valhermoso Springs by 3 miles of good gravel road and 2 miles of dirt road which is in satisfactory shape during dry weather.

This tract undoubtedly offers excellent opportunities for active recreation, and would be much used by persons from Decatur and the surrounding territory. All the land necessary for its development has been included within the reservoir taking-line.

FINLEY ISLAND BLUFF
[F-6]

Location: Morgan County, Ala., on Wheeler Lake, 4½ miles airline northwest of Decatur.
Communities served: Decatur, 6½ miles; Athens, 22 miles; Hartselle, 19 miles; Cullman, 37 miles; Huntsville, 43 miles.
Size: 80 acres.
Type: Outing park for intensive use.
Characteristics: Wooded knoll adjacent to Wheeler Lake.

Finley Island Bluff is one of the few waterside areas along lower Wheeler Lake that stands well up above the water. Its proximity to Decatur gives it particular significance as a potential outing area, and its topography is favorable for such facilities as picnic grounds, boathouse and landing, playfield, and perhaps eventually a bathing beach and bathhouse. Most of the tract is fairly well wooded. Access is over 2 miles of fair straight county road which runs north from the Decatur-Tuscumbia Highway, half a mile west of the Decatur airport. All of this tract lies within the TVA taking-line for the reservoir.

LIMESTONE CREEK
[F-6]

Location: Limestone County, 8 miles airline northeast of Decatur.
Communities served: Decatur, 10 miles; Athens, 10 miles; Huntsville, 22 miles; Hartselle, 22 miles.
Size: 750 acres.
Type: Outing park, combining developed scenic and intensive-use areas.
Characteristics: Excellent woodland; streams; potential play areas.

Limestone County, north of Wheeler Lake, is mostly flat. Drainage is for the most part by sluggish, meandering streams. Most of the available land has been cleared for cotton, and woodland is confined mainly to low, swampy areas with the result that it is largely unfit for recreational use. An exception is a 550-acre grove on Limestone Creek, 3 miles north of the village of Mooresville.

The wood is predominantly of a variety of deciduous growth, large oaks, maples, willows, and sycamores. There is an undergrowth of red cedar, horn-

beam, scattered holly, dogwood, and other lesser trees. Light pasturing has kept a number of openings and trails cleared and covered with a good turf. The creek flows along the eastern margin where it is overhung by magnificent, large trees.

Limestone Creek has a large, sparsely settled watershed, its origin being near the Alabama-Tennessee line. The flow through the grove is adequate even in dry seasons. The nature of the watershed would indicate that the stream has little pollution.

Because of its position near the center of a large Negro population, this site is a possible location for a Negro outing area. The woods might be fairly intensively developed with paths and walks; a small dam in the stream would create a swimming pool; adjacent fields could be converted into playfields.

MILTONS BLUFF
[E-5]

Location: Lawrence County, Ala., south side of Wheeler Lake directly north of the town of Wheeler.
Communities served: Sheffield-Tuscumbia, 30 miles; Decatur, 25 miles.
Size: 100 acres.
Type: Outing park for intensive use.
Characteristics: Wooded bluff; reservoir views.

Miltons Bluff is now a much-frequented picnic spot on the south shore of Wheeler Lake. Preservation of the area for future use of the same sort is guaranteed by the inclusion of an easily administered unit within the TVA reservoir taking-line. The bluff is wooded, and stands high above the reservoir, offering interesting views over the water. Development plans might include provision of parking space, sanitary facilities and waste receptacles, boathouse and landing, shelter, picnic tables and ovens.

It is reached by 8 miles of fair county road leaving Alabama Highway 20 at Wheeler.

POPLAR SPRINGS BRANCH
[E-5]

Location: Lauderdale County, near Elk River, 7 miles east of Wheeler Dam.
Communities served: Athens, 20 miles; Florence, 24 miles; Decatur, 36 miles.
Size: 350 acres.
Type: Outing park for intensive use.
Characteristics: Suitable sites for playfields; minor dam to create lake for swimming; picnic grounds; reservoir views; several springs.

This tract has promise for local recreational use, and might well attain considerable popularity among persons from more distant cities, for it holds favorable natural advantages for swimming purposes. A clear stream flows through attractive woods into an open valley before entering the Elk River. A dam 200 feet long and 20 or 30 feet high across this valley would cut off a small arm of the reservoir and would create a 15- to 25-acre constant-level lake. The clarity of the water at the present time in spite of fairly intensive agricultural use of the vicinity, together with two large springs in the basin, indicate that the water will remain clear and fresh. The wooded bluffs will guarantee future attractive shores for the small lake and along the reservoir. These woods afford many picnicground sites, and present agricultural land that can be converted into playfields or be reforested.

The area may be reached over 1½ miles of fair county road, which leaves United States Highway 72 at Oliver, 1¼ miles west of the Elk River bridge.

SHOAL CREEK
[D–5]

Location: Lauderdale County, two alternate sites, facing on Shoal Creek arm of Wilson Lake; one (A) near the United States Highway 72 bridge, the other (B) near United States Highway 43.

Communities served: Florence, 8 miles; Sheffield, 13 miles; Tuscumbia, 14 miles; Russellville, 33 miles; Lawrenceburg, 33 miles; Athens, 35 miles.

Size: Site A, 250 acres; Site B, 350–450 acres.

Type: Outing park, combining developed scenic and intensive-use areas.

Characteristics: Site A, wooded ridges dropping fairly abruptly to water's edge; several small inlets. Site B, wooded slopes; largest spring; Shoal Creek frontage.

Site A.—This tract is best reached from United States Highway 72, over a fair gravel road that runs northwest from the highway a quarter-mile west of the Shoal Creek bridge. The area consists of some fairly flat land, together with wooded ridges which slope rather steeply to the water's edge. There are several small fingers of Wilson Lake which would be suitable for boat landings, but none contains any stream or spring. The north water frontage faces an embayment of the lake which is fed by three fair-sized streams. The rest of the frontage, somewhat over half, borders Shoal Creek proper.

Site B.—This tract has frontage on United States Highway 43 and may also be reached from United States 72 by the same gravel road which passes site A. The area is more predominantly wooded than site A. Though it has somewhat less frontage on Shoal Creek than the other tract, it contains Poplar Spring, the largest spring in this section of Lauderdale County.

This spring appears in the midst of the wooded tract, and flows half a mile into a small inlet of the reservoir which may offer excellent possibilities for developing water-sport facilities. On the whole, this tract appears to be more desirable than site A, but either one could be developed into a waterside park which should be greatly used by people of the Tri-Cities and their environs.

RAVENS BLUFF
[E–3]

Location: Lawrence County, Tenn., 2½ miles southwest of Lawrenceburg.

Communities served: Lawrenceburg, 4 miles; Pulaski, 22 miles; Mount Pleasant, 26 miles; Columbia, 36 miles; Florence, 39 miles; Sheffield, 44 miles; Tuscumbia, 45 miles.

Size: 1,500 acres minimum.

Type: Outing park, combining developed scenic and intensive-use areas.

Characteristics: Usable artificial lake a mile long and from 300 to 700 feet wide, rock bluffs, numerous caves, wooded slopes.

South of Lawrenceburg on Shoal Creek are two dams of the Lawrenceburg municipal power plant. The lower dam creates a lake of 60 acres or more, which is used now to a considerable extent for boating and swimming, and its shores for picnicking. Suitably developed and without interfering in the use of the reservoir for creating electric power, the tract would make a very satisfactory State park in an area not otherwise served by such facilities. There is an occasional draw-down of 4 feet or so, but that does not appreciably affect the appearance of the lake, although under such conditions mud flats may be created in the upper reaches of the reservoir.

The fact that the lakes have been created by the city of Lawrenceburg suggests the opportunity for multiple public use of the present investment by provision of recreational facilities which might be added at a comparatively small additional cost.

The sheer rock cliffs along the north and east sides of the reservoir give the area its name. Numerous caves honeycomb these bluffs.

The land adjacent to the reservoir is predominantly wooded; cleared areas are largely submarginal, requiring reforestation. Acquisition of a tract of between 1,500 and 2,000 acres, including both reservoirs (but not purchase of the dams or powerhouses) is suggested to serve as an outing park. The proposed Duck River Purchase Unit, which would come within 10 miles of Lawrenceburg, on the north and west, would offer more extensive forms of recreation.

The powerhouse, at the lower end of the main

reservoir, may now be reached by a good gravel road 1½ miles long, which runs west from United States Highway 43, 2¾ miles south of Lawrenceburg Square.

MARCELLA FALLS
[E-2]

Location: Lawrence County, Tenn., 11½ miles northeast of Lawrenceburg.

Communities served: Lawrenceburg, 13½ miles; Mount Pleasant, 19 miles; Columbia, 29 miles; Pulaski, 25 miles.

Size: 100 acres minimum, 800 acres maximum.

Type: Outing park, combining developed scenic and intensive-use areas.

Characteristics: Beautiful small waterfall and cascades, rolling country, largely wooded.

Marcella Falls, an unusually attractive small waterfall 20 feet high, forms a nucleus for a local outing area. It lies in a small wooded valley immediately above the fork of two headwater streams. Below the fork is a small cascade. The immediate vicinity of the falls is suited to development of paths and picnic spots; intensive-use facilities might be located some distance away. A little-used existing road which passes below the falls would then be abandoned and a path substituted which would lead from the intensive-use area.

The falls are reached by a 4½-mile road from Tennessee Highway 6, nine miles north of Lawrenceburg.

WILHOITE MILLS
[G-1]

Location: Marshall County, Tenn., on west side of Tennessee Highway 11 at the Wilhoite Mills crossing of Duck River.

Communities served: Columbia, 23 miles; Lewisburg, 12 miles; Murfreesboro, 32 miles; Franklin, 35 miles; Shelbyville, 23 miles; Nashville, 43 miles.

Size: 300 to 500 acres.

Types: Outing park for intensive use.

Characteristics: River scenery, pastoral scenery; interesting plant growth.

A swimming hole in the Duck River and the river terraces on the north shore form the nucleus of the suggested Wilhoite Mills tract. The river at this point has long been a favorite swimming place for residents of Lewisburg, although no development has been carried out. The general character, topography, and disposition of plant growth seem so pleasing as to warrant treatment as a public park in order that the river may be made more generally available to a wider territory. Around the river facilities as a nucleus, other features of a regional park could be grouped and the whole given a rather intensive development.

The river at this point varies from 75 to 100 feet in width and averages 8 feet in depth. The south bank of the stream is approximately 20 feet high and wooded so as to screen effectively the land beyond.

Sloping, wooded shores border this spot on the Duck River below Wilhoite Mills—a favorable site for recreational development.

The Lower Tennessee Valley Area

GENERAL DESCRIPTION OF THE AREA

THE LOWER Tennessee Valley area centers around that section of the Tennessee River which includes the proposed Gilbertsville Lake, the largest reservoir in the TVA program. The river enters the area from the south and flows north across Tennessee and Kentucky to its confluence with the Ohio River at Paducah. The lower portions of the Duck and Buffalo River Basins lie within the area east of the Tennessee River, but to the west no streams of consequence occur. Big Sandy River, a comparatively small stream flowing through undulating territory, is the chief tributary of the Tennessee River from the west. The Cumberland River flows through the northeastern part of the area to join the Ohio River a few miles above Paducah.

Within the lower Tennessee Valley area, the Tennessee River forms the boundary between two characteristic types of land, to the east a rugged, hilly country, mostly wooded, and offering few agricultural advantages; to the west an undulating country mostly cleared, and in general well suited for agriculture.

East of the Tennessee River, farming is largely confined to the bottom lands along the Tennessee, Buffalo, Duck, and Cumberland Rivers and attenuated strips along minor stream valleys. Agriculture is relatively a minor land use. The 80 percent of the land that is forested lacks virgin timber areas, but contains good marketable timber. The cutting of rough lumber and ties and to a lesser extent the fabrication of dimensional stock furnish occupation for a considerable part of the resident population. There is very little manufacturing in this area.

West of the river the soil is, on the whole, more fertile, and some land is highly productive. Crops are diversified, but tobacco and cotton predominate as cash crops. A considerable amount of timber cutting is done along the Tennessee River. West of the river, in the larger towns, there are manufacturing plants.

Principal urban centers in the area are Jackson and Paris, Tenn.; Paducah and Mayfield, Ky. Paducah, with a population of about 33,000, located at the junction of the Ohio and Tennessee Rivers, is primarily an industrial center. Jackson, Paris, and Mayfield, lying in the undulating agricultural section of the area, are trading and industrial cities.

The lower Tennessee Valley area lacks exceptional scenic features. Several existing and potential recreation areas, however, have scenic value. It will be wise to preserve these areas for the use of local people, since every town lacks recreation facilities.

The scenic Tennessee serves as a broad avenue of water commerce.

201

EXISTING REGIONAL RECREATION AREAS

SHILOH NATIONAL MILITARY PARK

[C–10]

ON THE west side of the Tennessee River, about 6 miles upstream from Savannah, Tenn., Shiloh National Military Park commemorates the site of the Battle of Shiloh—one of the major engagements of the Civil War.

The park comprises 3,583 acres of undulating wooded land, overlooking the river and possessing considerable natural beauty. Recently placed under the control of the National Park Service, the tract is undergoing intelligent, effective development. Maintenance of the area has been exceptionally good under both the United States Army and the National Park Service. Paved roads traverse the area and numerous monuments mark the events of the 2-day battle.

No recreational developments other than picnic areas are at present contemplated, but some thought is being given to introduction of camping grounds and

Wiles, Nashville

A ferry plies its peaceful course where gunboats took positions during the Battle of Shiloh in 1862.

horseback trails. An existing boat landing is used by excursionists to visit the park, which is a point of considerable interest for tourists.

Wiles, Nashville

A canopy of oaks shades the scene of intense fighting around the Bloody Pool at Shiloh.

FORT DONELSON NATIONAL MILITARY CEMETERY AND PARK
[E-3]

Overlooking the Cumberland River just west of Dover, Tenn., an area of great historical interest, Fort Donelson National Military Cemetery and Park includes 103 acres (92 acres of park and 11 acres in the cemetery). Here in February 1862 Gen. Ulysses S. Grant broke the Confederate line of defense.

The area includes superb examples of Civil War methods of defense—the old fort, earthworks, rifle pits, and water batteries—all of which are in good state of preservation. The park is a long, narrow, irregular strip of land following the general outline of the defense position. It is a unit in the system of national parks administered by the Department of the Interior through the National Park Service. Roads and trails lead to all points of interest, following the earthworks; and here, as at Shiloh, the United Daughters of the Confederacy have erected an impressive monumental memorial to the Southern soldiers.

NATHAN BEDFORD FORREST MEMORIAL STATE PARK
[E-5]

This park, better known as Pilot Knob, is about 8 miles northeast of Camden, Tenn. The park includes only 87 acres. It was used as an observation point by Gen. Nathan Bedford Forrest of the Confederate Army before the Battle of Johnsonville Ferry and commands splendid views of the surrounding terrain and the Tennessee River.

On the elevated area have been constructed a picnic and overlook shelter, ovens, tables, and an overlook trail and cabins. A road has been built giving access to the knob and another picnic shelter has been erected near the base of the slope. This work was accomplished by the CCC.

At the point of observation used by General Forrest, an obelisk has been erected commemorating the historic event in which Federal gunboats were captured by the Confederate forces.

MONTGOMERY BELL PARK
[G-5]

This is one of three National Park Service recreational demonstration areas in Tennessee, the others being Falls Creek Falls and Shelby County Forest.

This park lies in Dickson County on the north side of United States Highway 70, about 30 miles west of Nashville and 8 miles east of Dickson. It contains over 4,000 acres of undulating picturesque land, 75 percent wooded with good second-growth timber. It is drained by several attractive streams that have added beauty in the cascades over many rocky shelves. A 50-acre lake is now under construction. There will be a beach, bathhouse, boating facilities, and a picnic area in a fine grove of large trees. Fishing will be permitted as soon as practicable. One, or possibly two, organized camp areas, with a central mess hall, administration building, and group cabins, will be located near the lake.

Within the park area are the remains of the old Montgomery Bell iron furnace, where cannon balls were forged for the Battle of New Orleans in the War of 1812. Several of the original buildings are still in a good state of preservation.

STEWART STATE FOREST
[E-4]

In Stewart County on either side of Tennessee Highway 49 between Dover and Erin, the Stewart State Forest includes 4,500 acres of land recently acquired by the State. The tract is rugged and hilly, heavily forested with a hardwood stand predominantly of oak and hickory. It has received no recreational development as yet, nor have plans indicated that any is contemplated. The area may be expended in the near future under provisions of the Fulmer Act.

CHICKASAW FOREST
[B-9]

Chickasaw Forest is a Farm Security Administration land utilization project which contains 11,292 acres of mostly submarginal, eroded land 14 to 21 miles south of Jackson, Tenn. Its primary purpose is reforestation, but its recreational areas are being developed. Projected Tennessee Highway 100, a new short-line road from Nashville to Memphis, runs through the north part of the forest, connecting at the western end with Tennessee Highway 18 to Jackson and Bolivar. Tennessee Highway 105 runs across the area in a northeast-southwest line.

Two intensive recreational developments are planned, and are under construction at the present time. Each is centered around an artificial lake approximately 60 acres in extent. On one lake will be constructed a public lodge, bathhouse, 10 vacation cabins, picnic area, baseball field, and a landing field. The other lake will be used primarily for private cabin development. Six cabins are under construction at the present time on one side of the lake in a beautiful pine grove. The far side of the lake is to be reserved for future recreational demands. These areas will be fully equipped with utilities: Running water, sewer, and electric power.

NATCHEZ TRACE FOREST
[D-7]

Like Chickasaw Forest, this is a resettlement land utilization project undertaken primarily for reforestation of badly eroding land. It is an area containing 40,497 acres, lying 6 miles northeast of Lexington, and extending to within 10 miles of Camden, Tenn. A road 25 miles long is now being built from one end of the project to the other, and two cross roads are contemplated in the present plans.

Three recreational areas are planned. At Cub Creek a 60-acre lake has been built, with a development including a public lodge, bathhouse, bathing beach, and 20 brick cabins. An athletic field and a natural amphitheater are to follow. Brown's Creek area, centering around a 157-acre lake, will be used by organized groups, such as Boy Scouts, Girl Scouts, 4–H groups, and others with responsible sponsors. The development will include the construction of an assembly hall, a dining hall and kitchen, 10 cabins, 2 wash houses, and a bathing beach. A third area, on Maple Creek, will be developed last. At this 100-acre lake, there will be only two small bathhouses and a picnic area with a shelter. When stocked with fish, this lake will be used primarily for fishing. All three areas will have drinking water, electric lights, and sanitary facilities.

This picnic spot in Kentucky's Coalins Forest overlooks the slumbering Cumberland River.

204

COALINS FOREST
[D-2]

Coalins Forest is a resettlement land utilization project. It is a tract of about 50,000 acres lying between the Cumberland and Tennessee Rivers, and between United States Highway 68 and Kentucky Highway 58. At one inaccessible point it has frontage on the proposed Gilbertsville Lake. A forest road nearby—built along the top of the watershed—will afford opportunity for good views of both rivers. The land is rugged and heavily wooded. The timber is second-growth, mostly of scrub oak, but with a considerable number of fair-sized trees. Picnic areas along the road have been planned.

JEWEL AND RUSKIN CAVES
[F-5]

In Dickson County, Tenn., west of the town of Dickson and about 7 miles north of the United States Highway 70 are Jewel and Ruskin Caves—about one-half mile apart. Jewel Cave, having interesting colored stalactite formations, has been lighted and is commercially operated. Ruskin Cave is void of the usual cave formations, but it has galleries 100 feet wide and possibly 300 feet long with a height of 40 feet. At the opening to this cave is a sheer rock bluff over 100 feet high. Both caves are close to the Yellow River. The surrounding territory is agricultural land of considerable fertility.

Stern-wheelers nose their freight-laden barges on the Cumberland River opposite Coalins Forest.

PROPOSED REGIONAL RECREATION AREAS

GILBERTSVILLE LAKE
[D-1, E-9]

Location: From the dam site near Gilbertsville, Ky., to Pickwick Dam.

Size: 148,000 acres, or 230 square miles.

Type: A reservoir created primarily to maintain a navigable channel on the Tennessee River.

Characteristics: A long, wide lake with more than 1,500 miles of shore line in a setting of predominantly hilly, wooded country.

GILBERTSVILLE LAKE, lowest TVA reservoir on the Tennessee River, will extend south from the dam near Gilbertsville, Ky., through Kentucky and Tennessee to Pickwick Dam. It will occupy a setting of hilly or undulating country, predominantly forested on the east shore, and also on the Tennessee portion of the west shore as far south as Tennessee Highway 114. The eastern shore line is indented by many small inlets and one large embayment, that of the Duck River. On the western shore of Gilbertsville Lake there are five large embayments; namely, those of Jonathan Creek, Blood River, Big Sandy River, Beech River, and White Oak Creek.

Gilbertsville Lake will be almost 185 miles in total length, more than twice as long as Guntersville Lake, the next longest on the Tennessee River. Between Gilbertsville Dam and the confluence of Duck River, the reservoir will vary from 1 to 3 miles in width; above this point it will be much narrower, ranging from a quarter mile to 1 mile in width. At normal pool elevation, the lake will have a surface area of 148,000 acres or approximately 230 square miles.

Along the east side of the lake the land is rugged, hilly, and very largely wooded, but with numerous cleared, narrow valleys and the broader bottom lands of the Tennessee and its tributaries, the Buffalo and the Duck. South of Tennessee Highway 114, cleared land extends back 2 or 3 miles from the Tennessee River bottoms. Tributary streams with watersheds limited by the Cumberland River and the Duck and the Buffalo Rivers are dry except after rain; between Tennessee Highway 76 and United States Highway 70, and also south of United States Highway 64, streams

At the base of Coffee Landing Bluffs, the Tennessee describes a broad arc, visible from Tennessee Highway 22.

generally have sustained flow and are usually clear.

West of the river, except for a 2- to 5-mile strip of rough, wooded land, extending along the reservoir throughout most of Tennessee, the land is undulating and predominantly cleared. Tributary streams are characteristically muddy and sluggish.

The land near Gilbertsville Lake possesses no exceptional inherent advantages for recreation, but the reservoir itself and its immediate shores should provide a recreational medium of more than local interest. The lake is expected to be exceptional for fishing and waterfowl shooting. Its large expanse of still water should be ideal for sailing and motor boats. Wooded shores and inlets would be inviting for canoes and rowboats. Pleasing, if not outstanding, scenery and relatively cool nights should make river excursion trips popular. The expected maximum draw-down of 5 feet will not eliminate the possibility of bathing beaches. In spite of the probable warm temperature of the water in summer, it is likely that there will be a considerable demand for swimming facilities.

Picnicking will probably be the most popular use of the shores; followed by hiking, camping, group sports, use of overnight or vacation cabins. Considerable overnight and day patronage may be expected from tourists; camping grounds, cabins, and boating and swimming facilities will be needed.

PROPOSED DECATUR STATE FOREST PURCHASE UNIT
[D–8]

Location: In Decatur County, Tenn., bordering the west shore of the Tennessee River.
Communities served: Lexington, 35 miles; Savannah, 30 miles; Henderson, 45 miles.
Size: 24,600 acres.
Type: Wilderness with occasional intensive-use areas.
Characteristics: Rolling land broken by numerous gulleys, forested with mixed hardwoods, pine, and cedar; extensive river views from low bluffs bordering the Tennessee River.

The Decatur State Forest, tentatively proposed for purchase under the provisions of the Fulmer Act, lies in southeastern Decatur County along the western shore of the Tennessee River. Topographically, the area is rolling and broken by the gulleys of small streams tributary to the Tennessee. River banks are high and steep with little intervening lowland between bluff and the water. Such lowland would be flooded by the proposed Gilbertsville Lake. A good stand of second-growth forest covers the area which was cut over many years ago. Important species

A wooded ridge through the Coalings furnishes excellent views over river knobs bordering the Tennessee.

include oak, beech, hickory, shortleaf pine, and cedar. Timber is thrifty and growth rapid.

Within the forest the river makes a 180-degree bend around a point of land 5 miles long and 1 to 1½ miles wide. Locally known as "The Coalings," this bend offers a most favorable site for recreation. Years ago it was mined for coal, but operations proved unprofit-

Tenn. Dept. of Conservation

A shallow creek bed provides a primitive thoroughfare in the proposed Decatur Forest.

able. A high ridge, almost completely forested, bisects the point along its length. It furnishes excellent views over the river and the surrounding countryside. For summer home sites, it combines the advantages of elevation, good forest land, and ready accessibility to the river or future reservoir. Other excellent sites for summer homes and for campgrounds and picnic areas adjoin the river at frequent intervals along the tops of the bluffs. Some small game within the unit indicates that strict law enforcement and game management would help to restock the area with upland game species such as deer and turkey.

PROPOSED BENTON STATE FOREST PURCHASE UNIT
[E–5]

Location: In eastern Benton County, Tenn., along the western shore of the Tennessee River.
Communities served: Paris, 22 miles; Waverly, 30 miles; Huntingdon, 31 miles.
Size: 32,600 acres.
Type: Wilderness with occasional intensive-use areas.
Characteristics: Rough, broken topography with steep slopes; second-growth hardwood forest; river views.

The proposed Benton Forest lies in the eastern part of Benton County bordering the Tennessee River on the west. It has an extremely rough and broken topography consisting of narrow, sharp ridges with steep slopes unsuited to anything but forests and wildlife. Soils are mostly of sandstone and shale derivation, and excessive erosion is evident where steep hillsides have been cleared. The forest cover consists of mixed hardwoods: Oak, hickory, river birch, beech, and maple. Some deer and turkey persist within the area and small game remains abundant, but it appears that the area would support a much richer variety of wildlife under an adequate protective and management program.

The Nathan Bedford Forrest State Park of 87 acres is enclosed within the boundaries at the southern end of the proposed forest. Pilot Knob, on which the park is situated, commands extensive river views which probably constitute the outstanding scenic feature of the forest. Limited recreational development might also take place along Harmon and Sulphur Creeks where some excellent sites for camp grounds and picnic areas border the streams.

The forest is proposed for acquisition under the Fulmer Act. In the opinion of both State and Federal foresters, the area will benefit by public acquisition. It would afford a measure of watershed protection for the proposed Gilbertsville Lake, would tend to replenish the game within its borders and in the vicinity, and would form the basis for reviving forest industry within the county.

POTENTIAL REGIONAL RECREATION AREAS

PAINT ROCK FOREST
[E–5]

Location: Humphreys County, Tenn., between United States Highway 70 and the Duck River.
Communities served: Waverly, 1 mile; Camden, 13 miles; Bruceton, 22 miles; Huntingdon, 22 miles; Paris, 42 miles; Nashville, 58 miles.
Size: 5,000–10,000 acres.
Type: Wilderness with developed scenic and intensive-use areas.
Characteristics: Rugged forest land; river bluffs; potential lake views.

FROM a point 3½ miles east of the Tennessee River on United States Highway 70 a good gravel road runs southeast to the Duck River embayment of the proposed Gilbertsville Lake, which at this point will be from 1 to 2 miles wide. This road then runs northeastward in view of the future embayment for about 2 miles to Paint Rock, a towering cliff 150 feet high, through a part of which the road is cut. For another mile, the road skirts the Duck River with vertically cut cliffs on the land side. It then leaves the embayment and joins United States Highway 70 a mile or so west of Waverly. This road covers a distance of 10 miles as against 6½ on United States Highway 70 between the same two points. Lying between the two roads and extending beyond the ends of the local road, are more than 10,000 acres of rugged, forested land, suitable for wilderness forms of recreation.

This tract might be developed as a State forest with recreation areas within it. Recreational possibilities are largely predicated on the creation of Gilbertsville Lake. If this lake is created, an outing park might be developed on the waterfront which would include a campground, cabins, and provision of facilities for swimming and boating.

BRELSFORD CAVES
[E-2]

Location: Trigg County, Ky., near United States Highway 68.

Communities served: Hopkinsville, 16 miles; Cadiz, 3 miles; Princeton, 23 miles; Eddyville, 25 miles; Murray, 37 miles.

Size: 150 acres.

Type: Intensive-use area.

Characteristics: Caves; wooded bluffs.

About 3 miles east of Cadiz are five unexploited and undeveloped caves located in a timbered area surrounded by agricultural land. A large spring and a stream, known as Little River, are in the immediate vicinity, and a portion of the area has interesting rock bluffs affording good distant views. When this area is considered for recreational use, it should include Roaring Springs, a deep pool 60 feet wide and a cave with an underground river. The temperature of this area is noticeably much lower than in the surrounding territory. This spot has decided scenic and recreational value which is as yet unspoiled.

Tenn. Dept. of Conservation

Wind and rain have carved grotesque forms from the sandstone bluffs of Paint Rock Forest.

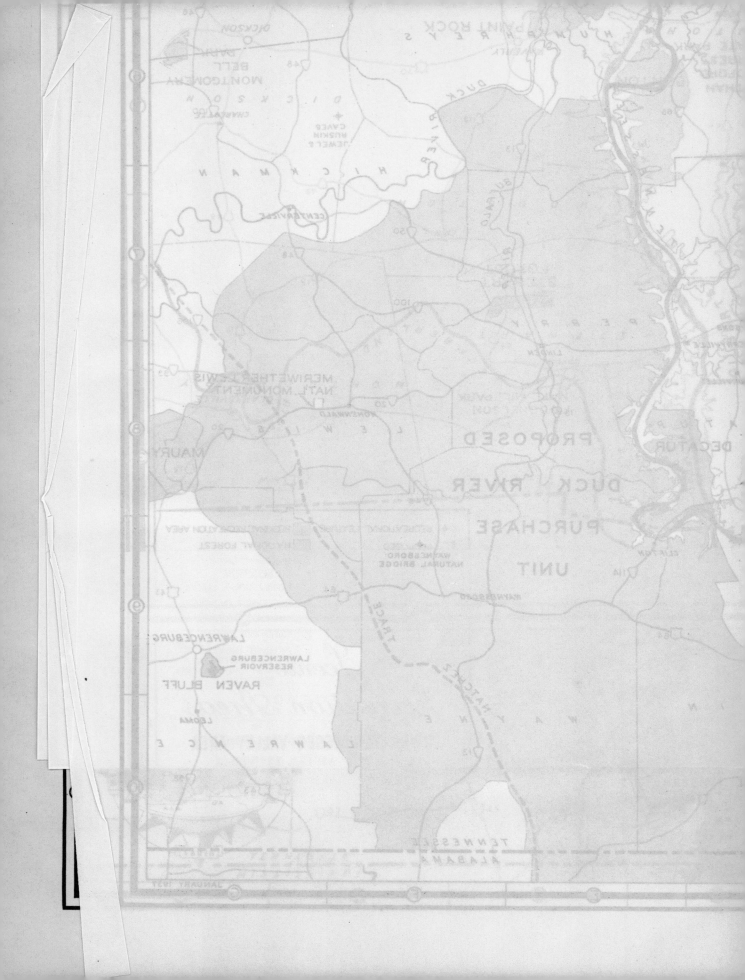

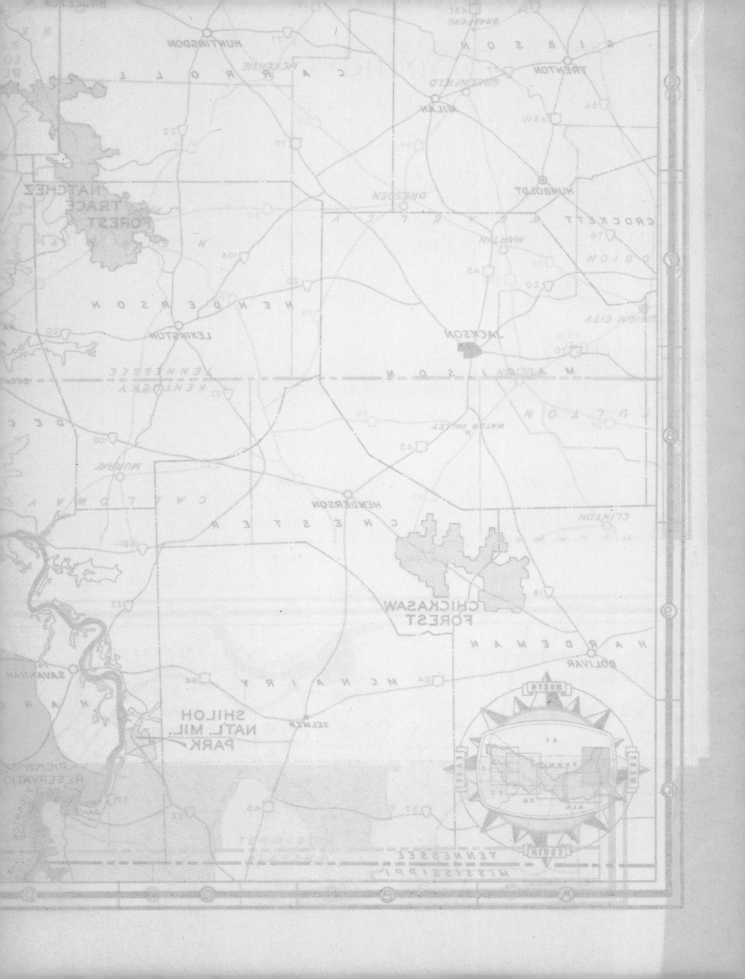

Appendix

NONURBAN OUTDOOR RECREATION

AN ANALYSIS OF ITS FUNCTIONS, FORMS, AND TYPES OF AREAS

IN VIEW of the increasing activity in the field of nonurban outdoor recreation by the Federal and State Governments, and because there has been much diversity of opinion as to appropriate types of recreational development, it seems advisable to seek a definition of recreation and its functions, and to analyze its forms and the types of areas through which it finds expression. It would seem that such an analysis, to be valid, must be based on the functions of recreation areas, rather than on their jurisdictional status, such as Federal, State, county, or local.

FUNCTIONS OF NONURBAN OUTDOOR RECREATION

Recreation is constructive relaxation. It is the reanimation of the body, mind, and spirit after toil; the turning from something one *must* do to something one *wants* to do. Recreation in its true sense implies personal and profitable participation, as contrasted with amusement, which is an uncreative use of leisure time. In this sense, recreation obviously needs no defense, but merely clarification and classification.

Recreation has two phases: The form or act, and the means. An example of the first is a game of baseball; of the second, the ballfield. The first involves group organization or social planning; the second, land planning, with which this paper deals. With respect to recreation, land planning is concerned with providing areas for outdoor recreation.

Outdoor recreation may be broadly classified as urban and nonurban. While a well-rounded system of urban recreational areas will supply close at hand certain opportunities, the range of these opportunities is limited by the very nature of the city, and use is localized in the community. Nonurban areas not only complete the range of recreational opportunities, but when well located, they become regional centers, serving many communities and large areas. If their attraction is extraordinary (as in the case of National Parks and National Forests) there is no definite geographic limit to their recreational influence.

FORMS OF NONURBAN OUTDOOR RECREATION

Before noting the various *types* of nonurban recreational areas, it is advisable to consider what various *forms* of recreation may be sought in rural and wilderness environments. They form a background for two types of recreational activity; physical or athletic; and nonphysical or nonathletic. The first gives to the body, its muscles, nerves, and lungs, relief from the routine tasks and movements of everyday life; the second revitalizes mind and spirit, wearied by daily contact with urban sounds and sights.

There are two major types of physical recreation: group and solitary. The first is participated in by large groups, clubs, or teams, for which the gregarious and competitive aspects of recreation furnish the principal satisfaction. Solitary recreation may include not only an individual, but also a family or other intimate group; its satisfaction comes from physical effort rather than from company.

Nonphysical recreation likewise involves two phases: diversion and inspiration. The first appeals to those who ask merely some variation from the accustomed urban environment; inspiration pertains to those who crave stimulations completely different from those which are possible in a metropolitan environment.

Each of the four types of recreation calls for a distinct kind of area.

Areas for *group* recreation involve provision of facilities for more or less intensive use by numbers of people. Provision should be made for organized picnics, group-outings, games and sports, and similar social activities. Such items as shelters, water supply, sanitary facilities, waste receptacles, parking spaces, roads, and surfaced paths should be provided for the convenience of the users, and to protect the area from misuse. Tracts intended for such intensive use must be carefully defined so that there may be no encroachment on areas reserved for solitary recreation.

Solitary recreation demands a sense of privacy. Contacts with crowds, which are unavoidable in community life, should be absent when an individual seeks recreation in its fullest sense. This fact necessitates provision of large areas in which an individual or small group may move freely, unaware of the presence of other persons. Thus the area provided for solitary use should be far greater per capita than that for group recreation.

For the person who seeks nonphysical recreation as casual *diversion* from accustomed surroundings, there is seldom the time or the desire for more than brief rural excursions. A motor trip through a pleasing or unusual countryside is the customary form of such diversion. As adjuncts to the trip may be included a picnic, part of the day spent idling about, a night in a tent or cabin and brief stops for views of more than passing interest along the highway. In no case is the range of activity very far from the means of conveyance.

The *inspirational* aspect of nonphysical recreation involves seeking in the out-of-doors a complete release from contacts with civilization. Any metropolitan intrusion into a wilderness area will destroy, for the individual who is seeking inspirational recreation, the very values he desires. He who wants solitude under completely natural surroundings does not need to have access made easy by roads and wide paths.

It is, of course, impossible to draw a definite line between *solitary physical* recreation and *inspirational nonphysical* recreation; true recreation of any type involves body, mind, and spirit. Nevertheless there is a clear distinction between the objectives of the two types which appears to justify considering them as distinct from each other.

TYPES OF NONURBAN OUTDOOR RECREATION AREAS

Having noted these *forms* of nonurban outdoor recreation, it remains to consider *types of areas* which are or should be provided to serve such recreational needs. Such areas are tracts of land or water, or both, suitable for recreation and dedicated, wholly or in part, to recreational use. Such use may be very intensive, involving thousands of persons daily, or it may bring only a few visitors during a year. Recreation may be the only use to which an area is put, or, as in the case of national forests, it may be only one of several concurrent uses. Recreation areas may vary in size from a fraction of an acre to hundreds of square miles. Their scenic value may range from the nominal to the superlative. They may be under the jurisdiction of public agencies (Federal, regional, State, county, or municipal), or under private control. They may be known as parks, forests, playgrounds, camps, or by various other names.

Broadly speaking, these areas are of two kinds: Regional areas and travelways.

I. Regional Areas

Regional areas for recreation are tracts, of an essentially rural or primitive character, with sufficient inherent interest to attract more than local patronage. According to the functional character of a regional area, its location should be determined either because of its relation to the population pattern of the region, or because of its intrinsic merit. In order to give recognition to various types of regional areas, they are herein enumerated with general recommendations as to size, character of natural features, and suitable development.

Regional areas may be classified under two major headings: Outing Areas and Conservation Areas.

A. OUTING AREAS.—In order to provide opportunities for physical recreation in nonurban environments a number of outing areas should be established as parts of any regional system. The outing area is a public recreation area to which one may go, usually as one of a group, for physical recreation or for diversion. An outing area should be of attractive but not of superlative scenic character. Its location should be determined by its availability to centers of population. It will, of necessity, receive more or less intensive development.

There are two types of outing areas: Intensive-use areas and developed scenic areas.

1. *Intensive-Use Areas.*—As its name implies, the intensive-use area is designed to receive the brunt of concentrated, active recreation. Because its development will often depreciate most of the natural beauty, only a tract of average scenic interest should be chosen for this type of area. Special care must be taken to avoid encroachment on other types of recreational areas.

212

The intensive-use area must be approached by a good access road and must contain adequate parking space, conveniently but inconspicuously located. A simple design may include a playfield; picnic area with tables, benches, and ovens; overnight camping area; safe water supply; toilets; waste receptacles; and shelters. The design may be elaborated through varying degrees to include a lodge, swimming and wading pools, stable, riding field, playground equipment, tennis courts, golf course, and amusement-park attractions. The number and kind of features should be determined by the size and location of the area, and by the use to which its environs are to be put. A minimum of 50 acres and a maximum of 300 acres should be sufficient to provide space for development of features and accompanying service buildings.

A particular type of intensive-use area is the vacation camp, which includes all forms of resident vacation use of regional recreation areas. The type may include individual vacation cabins, Boy or Girl Scout camps, simple or elaborate health camps, and resort hotels. With a minimum of discomfort and a maximum of convenience, such facilities afford close contacts with the out of doors. They serve the need for pleasant living in places from which industrial and commercial noise, dirt, and odors are absent. Buildings and their grouping should be simple, dignified, and in harmony with natural surroundings. The scenic value of vacation camp areas may well be considerably higher than for other forms of intensive use.

Other special forms of intensive-use areas are such semi-educational types, as zoos, arboretums, and botanic gardens. These usually appear as parts of various city park systems, but study should be given to the possibilities of adapting their design to regional locations.

2. *Developed Scenic Areas.*—The developed scenic area is intended to provide for extensive recreational use in relatively natural surroundings. It should be recognized as being, in effect, a transition type between intensive-use areas and wilderness areas. It should be of attractive natural character which will not suffer from moderate development in the form of trails and roads. The design of such an area should include measures designed to prevent impairment of its scenic values, and risk of injury to those using it. Access road, adequate parking space, paths, drinking water, sanitary facilities, and shelters are suitable features.

In order to restrict picnicking to certain definite localities, picnic grounds with tables, benches, and ovens should be provided. Pleasure drives and bridle trails may be, in some cases, appropriate items in the design. In developed scenic areas will logically occur such semi-educational features as demonstration forests and trailside museums.

B. CONSERVATION AREAS.—Conservation areas constitute the second type of regional area. They are so designated because their primary purpose is *conservation* of the tracts involved, as contrasted with outing areas where *recreational use* is the primary consideration. Conservation areas comprise wilderness areas and monuments.

1. *Wilderness Areas.*—Wilderness areas are tracts of land containing no permanent inhabitants, and possessing no means of mechanical conveyance or any other perceptible evidence of civilization. Their foremost value is an environmental one, that of permitting complete solitude in entirely natural surroundings.

In order to secure this character, wilderness areas will usually, though not invariably, be of considerable size. They may or may not at present exist in a primeval condition and they do not necessarily possess superlative scenic quality. It is important to note, however, that the ultimate goal of a wilderness area is the re-attainment of an original or primeval character. Given sufficient time, proper direction and protection from human interference, nature will eventually transform a man-altered wilderness into a primeval environment.

In general, wilderness areas call for no development beyond a few not-too-well defined trails, hiking shelters, and access roads with parking spaces near their boundaries. They may be dedicated as nature sanctuaries and may form parts of national, State, county, or metropolitan park or forest systems. A limited number of artificial operations such as tree-cutting and planting, fire prevention and other protective measures may be necessary. Transmission lines, beacon towers, and roads of any sort should be prohibited.

Although it does not seem advisable to suggest any breakdown of the wilderness into subtypes there are phases or degrees of wilderness character which may be recognized.

First, the usual wilderness will consist of a tract in which the original forest cover has been cut over, thus disturbing the natural processes of plant and animal life. It fulfills the previously noted basic requirements of a wilderness but does not, to any appreciable extent, possess scenic character of extraordinary quality.

Secondly, there are throughout the country certain natural areas of surpassing beauty or of extraordinary scientific interest. Many of these areas have already been set aside as National or State parks, but many still remain open to the dangers of commercial exploitation and depreciation. These areas may be of sufficient caliber to command national interest, or may be outstanding only in the region in which they are located. Defacement of such tracts would be an irreplaceable loss; their great value lies in their being retained in a natural state. Certain of these are and will be approached by roads; others must be reached only by considerable physical effort on the part of an individual.

These superlatively scenic wildernesses should be subject to no alterations in the form of paths, guard rails or structures, which might perceptibly affect the natural appearance of the area. Distinguishable trails leading to points of special scenic interest are the only modification which may be permitted. In most cases the area will need a protective belt in which may be located access road, parking area, and structures which will form headquarters for approaching the tract itself.

Thirdly, there are occasional instances left in the United States where the advance of civilization has left untouched certain portions of the original primeval environment which once extended over the entire continent. They remain in the form of virgin forests on mountain slopes or in deep coves, deserts, dunes, and other similar areas which seemed unfriendly to civilization. Such areas have a two-fold significance: A scientific interest in original processes of nature unaltered by man, and a psychological value for the re-creating of man through contacts with absolutely untouched, primeval surroundings.

All existing original forest wilderness areas should be set aside as public conservation areas, and a suitable proportion of various other types should also be conserved. Unless properly protected, such priceless tracts are always in danger of destruction from ravages of fire, insects or diseases, and human exploitation or despoliation. Needless to say, they should receive absolutely no human alteration beyond protective measures. Modification means nullification.

2. *Monuments.*—Monuments are public conservation holdings established wholly or dominantly because of their significance from the point of view of history, natural science, or archeology. On such reservations, as in the case of wilderness areas, "even the simplest types of active recreation, if permitted at all,

are subordinated to the primary purpose for which such monuments are established."[1]

Examples of such types of monuments are:

(a) *Historical.*—George Washington's Birthplace, Colonial National Monument (Williamsburg, Yorktown, Jamestown), Nancy Hanks Lincoln Memorial (Indiana).

(b) *Natural Science.*—Grand Canyon, Jewel Cave (South Dakota), Muir Woods (California).

(c) *Archeological.*—Aztec Ruins (New Mexico), Navajo National Monument (Arizona), Mound City Group (Ohio).

National military parks, although named as such, rather than as national monuments, fall logically for classification purposes under the heading of historical monuments.

Certain areas have already been set aside as monuments which are really wilderness areas, as in the case of Katmai National Monument in Alaska (2,697,590 acres) and Mount Olympus in Washington (298,730 acres). It would seem desirable that such an area should be definitely designated as a national wilderness, leaving the term "monument" to be applied to those reservations which would not come under the wilderness classification.

II. *Travelways*

From the point of view of recreational significance, travelways are fourfold: Motorways, trailways, waterways, (each with adjacent wayside areas), and airways. In all these instances travel is the basis of recreational interest.

A. MOTORWAYS.—Motor travel for pleasure is now America's most popular form of outdoor recreation, if one may judge by the survey of leisure time activities of 5,000 people conducted by the National Recreation Association (1933). Yet the automobile has been regarded by its designers chiefly as a means of transportation from one point of interest to another. That little thought has been given to making pleasant the trip en route is evidenced both in the designing of cars and of the average highway. Successive models of cars are engineered with increasing emphasis on speed and power. The highway is too often designed with no thought given to pleasing grades and alinement, no zoning or other restriction of use of adjoining territory, no effort to provide easy stopping places along the way, or to preserve and point out features of interest and beauty.

Four types of nonurban motorways may be distinguished: Parkways, freeways, highways and byways.

[1] Report of the National Resources Board (1934): Recommendations for State and interstate systems of parks and related recreation areas.

A *parkway* is an elongated park with a road (single or divided) running through it. Normally, it has restricted traffic (pleasure traffic only) and administrative or physical control of access. A *freeway* is a motorway of varied or uniform width of right-of-way, with unrestricted traffic, but with physical control of access. A *highway* is a trafficway of more than local significance, having usually, but not necessarily, a uniform width of right-of-way, with unrestricted traffic and access. A *byway* resembles a highway in all but its purely local traffic significance. The relative recreational value of these four types is fairly obvious from the above definitions.

Much may be done, however, in the direction of making motorways of greater recreational interest, through increased consideration of scenic values in the original locating of roads, by the provision of scenic extensions of rights-of-way, and the creation of various types of wayside areas or waysides.

Until very recently little, if any, thought was given in locating a motorway to the relation of the road to adjacent scenic values, or to beauty of alinement and profile of the road itself. Now, however, the best practice in road building recognizes that the ideal way is not to slash a road through the countryside with long tangents, and heavy cuts and fills, then subsequently to attempt "beautification" with introduced plant materials. Rather it is to fit the motorway onto the topography as naturally as possible, to preserve native plant growth, and to locate the road so as to take advantage of varied views and other natural scenic values without irreparably damaging them.

Scenic extensions of the right-of-way may be defined as wedges or strips of varying widths in addition to a right-of-way of uniform width; such extensions to include, for protective purposes, existing woods, watercourses, meadows, or other types of scenery; or, for lack of such existing scenic features, to provide areas that may be given appropriate landscape treatment. Scenic extensions may apply not only to new motorways, but also to those already existing. Though there may be a suitable standard width of right-of-way, it is usually impossible for it to be sufficiently broad to include most of the features along the roadside that it would be desirable to protect, without also including a great deal of land which it is unnecessary to acquire for scenic protection. Inasmuch as this land is frequently agricultural, acquisition of it would not only materially increase the total cost, but would also remove such land from cultivation without reason. The suggested technique takes from the land-owner chiefly those lands for which he has least use, and the cost of acquisition is reduced accordingly. This method of securing scenic extensions of the right-of-way, supplemented by protective easements over non-scenic land would, in effect, be the visual equivalent of a very much greater right-of-way. A possible alternative is found in the practice of securing scenic easements rather than making outright purchases. In any case, roadside control should be resorted to in order to prevent such structures as billboards, shoddy wayside stands, and filling stations.

B. TRAILWAYS.—Trailways are systems of independent recreational trails, as contrasted with trails that occur only as features within regional areas. They may merely traverse country of exceptional scenic or historical interest without actually encountering any public reservations, but usually they will serve as connecting links between regional recreation areas. Their form may be lineal, as in the case of the Appalachian Trail, or that of a loop, as exemplified by the proposed demonstration trailways in New England, and in Cook County, Ill. They may be available to hikers, bicyclists, or horseback-riders.

Trailways and parkways are the only type of travel-way purely recreational in character. As compared with motorways, the pace of their use is slower and permits more leisurely contacts with nonurban environments. The very use of trailways involves physical recreation. Trails can approach with greater intimacy more varied types of terrain than is possible for motorways. In general, it might be said that trailways bear to motorways somewhat the same relationship as exists between wilderness and outing areas.

C. WATERWAYS.—Historically, waterways rank with trailways as primitive travel routes. Man early learned that water offered the easiest mode of travel, and soon developed the raft, canoe, and various types of boats. These forms have developed to the extent that various aspects of water traffic correspond, in navigation, to motorways and trailways, on land. As in the case of motorways, commercial and recreational forms of water traffic frequently exist concurrently.

A recreational waterway may be defined as the environment of recreational water travel. As such, the definition excludes limited water areas, of which localized recreational use is made. Usually, a waterway is linear in character but may become a loop in the case of large bodies of water which require at least several days to circumnavigate. A similar circuit may be achieved on river systems in some cases by means of portages or canals.

The nature of recreational use of various waterways will be governed in certain instances by the nature of the waterway itself. Small headwater streams are suited only to canoe travel and will naturally retain a primitive character. In the case of larger streams and lakes, however, protective regulation of some sort will have to be invoked. Zoning might serve to dedicate water courses to uses corresponding roughly to the four types of motorways. Zoning may in some cases be supplemented by purchase of tracts or easements along the water's edge either for scenic protection or for various water wayside areas. Where the waterway lies within a large public reservation, its use will be governed by the nature of the reservation.

D. AIRWAYS.—One would not ordinarily think of the air as a recreational medium. Of course it is of a different character from the other three types of travelways in that its scope is practically unrestricted, and there are no physiographic boundaries. But just as there is dual usage of motorways and waterways, there is also considerable flying for recreation, in addition to commercial use of airways. No one knows to what extent recreational air travel (along with other aspects of flying) may increase. If a safe, inexpensive helicopter plane should be made universally available by mass production, the whole fabric of our civilization might be changed, and locations of recreation areas would be materially affected.

At present, however, the chief factors involved in recreational flying are the provision of adequate airport facilities, and needed regulations to prevent construction of flat billboards or painted roof signs, intended to be viewed from the air, and advertising by skywriting.

E. WAYSIDES.—Waysides are stopping places along or closely adjacent to travelways (except airways) which are intended to increase the convenience and enjoyment of travel thereon. Four general types of wayside areas may be recognized but each type will be modified to meet specific requirements of the motorway, trailway, or waterway. These types are observation points, picnic grounds, overnight camps, and scenic spots. A discussion of these types as they pertain to motorways follows. Variations needed to make these types applicable to trailways and waterways will be obvious to the reader.

The *observation point* is a parking space near the highway, or such a space combined with pedestrian access to a nearby overlook, designed to facilitate the viewing of a panorama, exceptional view, or nearby object of interest (such as a scenic spot). The purpose of the observation point is to make enjoyment of scenic features more fully available to the motorist, as well as to interrupt the monotony of driving.

The purpose of *picnic grounds* is to meet the picnicking needs of the motoring public and at the same time to protect private property and scenic features from thoughtless depredation. Persons wishing to picnic seldom desire to trespass on private property or willfully to destroy natural beauty, but indiscriminate use of wayside property inevitably has such results. The provision of places under public ownership will largely eliminate trespass and misuse.

Overnight camps may vary from a simple area for tent or trailer camping to a cabin camp with extensive facilities including stores and shops, lodge, service stations, and wash-houses, etc.

A tenting or trailer area should be so located that a maximum of attractiveness and convenience is obtained. Its primarily utilitarian nature, however, should be borne in mind so that destruction or impairment of a natural feature of exceptional interest or beauty may not result.

The popularity of the wayside cabin camp is indicated by the large number of private establishments which have sprung up to meet the demand for them. Some of these private camps, particularly those in the West, are practically villages. Unfortunately, the standard of service is not uniformly high, and the structural and ground plan design usually leaves a great deal to be desired. A general distribution of overnight camps, publicly owned, and managed either by a public agency or by a private concessionaire under public supervision, would offer a high standard which would tend to be reflected in turn in private establishments.

The *scenic spot* is a roadside feature of considerable yet incidental interest—such as a waterfall, or exceptionally interesting rock formations—worth preserving, but not of sufficient importance to be a motoring objective in itself. Such a feature near a motorway is in imminent danger of depreciation or exploitation under private ownership. Therefore, it should be publicly acquired, and preserved intact—not given over to such active uses as picnicking and camping. These may be taken care of on adjacent property if the nature and location of the scenic feature and its surroundings attract a sufficient number of people to make it advisable.

Conclusion

There is much variation among the several agencies officially interested in recreation, in regard to the use of terms which apply to various kinds of nonurban recreational areas. It seems vital that these agencies adopt terms which can be applicable to all systems of recreational areas.

The method of classifying recreation areas previously outlined cuts directly across the prevalent classification of such areas which is based on jurisdiction: (national, State, county or municipal park, forest, parkway, etc.) It should be readily apparent, however, that there is no fundamental discord between the two methods. Both the terms "park" and "forest" have been rather loosely applied to public reservations set aside for conservation and recreation. Some authorities have used the term "park" to refer exclusively to reservations of a wilderness character, some to outing areas, and many have applied the term to both types without realizing or making a distinction between them. In popular usage the word "park" has also been interchanged with the word "forest."

Both words need clarification of meaning and subclassification of function if they are to be universally understood by both authorities and public. Reservations of a homogeneous character might well be specifically designated as outing areas, wildernesses, or monuments. Several types of recreation areas, however, may be included within a single large reservation. These will necessitate a careful definition of physical limits and of development policy. The tract as a whole may then be given the appropriate customary designation of national, State, county or municipal park or forest.

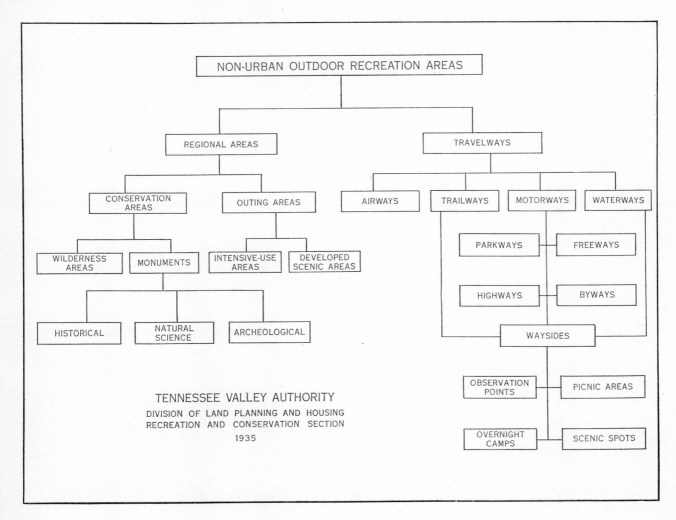

TENNESSEE VALLEY AUTHORITY
DIVISION OF LAND PLANNING AND HOUSING
RECREATION AND CONSERVATION SECTION
1935

217

Index

Date Due